THE LIBRARY
ST. MARY'S COLLEGE OF MARYLAND
ST. MARY'S CITY, MARYLAND 20686

D1596538

The Politics of Childhood

Also by the editors:

Jim Goddard:
CONTEMPORARY CHILD CARE POLICY AND PRACTICE (*Fawcett, B., Featherstone, B. and Goddard, J.*)

STATE CHILD CARE: Looking After Children? (*Hayden, C., Goddard, J., Gorin, S. and Van der Spek, N.*)

Adrian James:
CONSTRUCTING CHILDHOOD: Theory, Policy and Social Practice (*Allison James and Adrian James*)

HELPING FAMILIES AFTER DIVORCE: Assistance by order? (*with L. Sturgeon-Adams*)

THE CHILD PROTECTION HANDBOOK (2nd Edn) (*joint editor with K. Wilson*)

Allison James:
CONSTRUCTING CHILDHOOD: Theory, Policy and Social Practice (*Adrian James and Allison James*)

CONSTRUCTING AND RECONSTRUCTING CHILDHOOD (*with A. Prout*)

THEORISING CHILDHOOD (*with C. Jenks and A. Prout*)

RESEARCH WITH CHILDREN (*with Pia Christensen*)

The Politics of Childhood

International Perspectives, Contemporary Developments

Edited by

Jim Goddard
Dept. of Social Sciences & Humanities
University of Bradford, UK

Sally McNamee
Dept. of Comparative and Applied Social Sciences
University of Hull, UK

Adrian James
Dept. of Social Sciences & Humanities
University of Bradford, UK

Allison James
Dept. of Sociological Studies
University of Sheffield, UK

Editorial matter & selection © Jim Goddard, Sally McNamee, Adrian James & Allison James 2005
Chapter 1 © Allison James & Adrian James 2005
Chapter 13 © Sally McNamee, Adrian James and Allison James 2005
Chapter 15 © Jim Goddard 2005
Remaining chapters © Palgrave Macmillan 2005

All rights reserved. No reproduction, copy or transmission of this publication may be made without written permission.

No paragraph of this publication may be reproduced, copied or transmitted save with written permission or in accordance with the provisions of the Copyright, Designs and Patents Act 1988, or under the terms of any licence permitting limited copying issued by the Copyright Licensing Agency, 90 Tottenham Court Road, London W1T 4LP.

Any person who does any unauthorised act in relation to this publication may be liable to criminal prosecution and civil claims for damages.

The authors have asserted their rights to be identified as the authors of this work in accordance with the Copyright, Designs and Patents Act 1988.

First published 2005 by
PALGRAVE MACMILLAN
Houndmills, Basingstoke, Hampshire RG21 6XS and
175 Fifth Avenue, New York, N. Y. 10010
Companies and representatives throughout the world

PALGRAVE MACMILLAN is the global academic imprint of the Palgrave Macmillan division of St. Martin's Press, LLC and of Palgrave Macmillan Ltd. Macmillan® is a registered trademark in the United States, United Kingdom and other countries. Palgrave is a registered trademark in the European Union and other countries.

ISBN 1–4039–3551–3 hardback

This book is printed on paper suitable for recycling and made from fully managed and sustained forest sources.

A catalogue record for this book is available from the British Library.

Library of Congress Cataloging-in-Publication Data

The politics of childhood : international perspectives, contemporary
     developments / edited by Jim Goddard ... [et al.].
          p. cm.
     "Arises out of the third international conference held by the Centre for the Social Study of Childhood at the University of Hull in 2002"–Introd.
     Includes bibliographical references and index.
     ISBN 1–4039–3551–3 (cloth)
          1. Children–Social conditions–Congresses. 2. Children–Government policy–Congresses. 3. Children's rights–Congresses. 4. Child welfare–Congresses. 5. Education–Congresses. I. Goddard, Jim, 1963–

HQ767.82.P65 2005
305.23–dc22   2004051502

10   9   8   7   6   5   4   3   2   1
14   13   12   11   10   09   08   07   06   05

Printed and bound in Great Britain by
Antony Rowe Ltd, Chippenham and Eastbourne

Contents

Part Four: Children, Power and Decision-making

11 Placing Children on the Political Agenda: New Zealand's Agenda for Children
Maree Brown and Jaleh McCormack

12 The Representation of Children in the Media: Aspects of Agency and Literacy
Máire Messenger Davies & Nick Mosdell

List of Tables and Figures

Tables

Figures

Biographical Notes: Chapter Authors

Ann Blair

Following a career in the advice sector, Ann studied law as a mature student at the University of Leeds and as a postgraduate at the University of Sheffield. Ann has been lecturer in law at the University of Leeds since 1994. Ann's principal research interests lie in the field of education law. She has written on topics including the law of sex education, home-school agreements and Special Educational Needs and disability discrimination in schools. Ann was formerly chair of governors of a Leeds High School and is contributing editor of the education law journal.

Maribel Blasco

Maribel Blasco is Assistant Professor of Spanish American Studies at the Department of Intercultural Communication and Management (IKL), Copenhagen Business School. She has a PhD in International Development Studies from Roskilde University, Denmark, with a thesis on the link between school performance, poverty and family relations. She has published work on secondary schooling and rights and on the link between family relations, affectivity and secondary school performance among low-income groups in Mexico. She is co-editor of Intercultural Alternatives: Critical perspectives on intercultural encounters in theory and practice, CBS Press (forthcoming 2004).

Jim Block

Jim Block has taught political theory and American Studies at DePaul University for more than two decades. He is the author of one book, *A Nation of Agents: The American Path to a Modern Self and Society* (Belknap Press of Harvard University Press, 2002) and numerous articles, and his current book project is entitled *The Crucible of Consent: American Child Rearing and the Forging of a Modern Nation* (Harvard University Press, forthcoming). In addition to Jim's research interests in liberal theory and American national formation, and more specifically the role of socializing institutions in that process, he is undertaking research projects on the role of the American counterculture in the formation of a post-industrial political agenda.

Maree Brown

Maree Brown is a Principal Analyst in the Ministry of Social Development in New Zealand. She has an MA in European Studies from Washington University in St Louis, specialising in comparative public policy, and has worked in a range of policy areas in the New Zealand public service. Since the mid 1990s, she has worked primarily on child and family policy initiatives. These include the former National Government's proposed Code of Social and Family Responsibility and, most recently, the 'Working for Families' package of social assistance for families with dependent children. She was project manager for the Agenda for Children strategy between 2001 and 2003.

Vicki Coppock

Senior Lecturer in Social Work and Childhood Studies at Edge Hill College of Higher Education, Ormskirk, Lancashire. She is also an experienced mental health social worker. She has a research and publications record in the critical analysis of theory, policy, legislation and practice in the field of mental health, with a particular emphasis on asserting a positive rights agenda for children and young people in mental distress. She is co-author of *The Illusions of Post-Feminism* (1995) and *Critical Perspectives on Mental Health* (2000) and contributor to *'Childhood' in 'Crisis'?* (Scraton ed, 1997) and *The New Handbook of Children's Rights* (Franklin, 2002).

Jim Goddard

Lecturer in Social Policy at the University of Bradford. He has worked for a number of years in residential care with children and with pressure groups in the child care field. Policy with respect to looked-after-children and leaving care is one of his main research interests.

Wiebina Heesterman

A Dutch national, Wiebina Heesterman moved to the United Kingdom in 1966 in connection with her husband's work. Once her children had left school, she gained a BA librarianship and an MSc information technology. She then worked as information systems manager and information scientist at the School of Law of the University of Warwick. During the 1990s Wiebina acted as a consultant for human rights projects at Interights, and the Universities of Dar es Salaam and Zimbabwe. She has recently completed a part-time PhD law degree on the subject of child labour. Retired from her post at Warwick she has started compiling an electronic index to the Concluding Observations of the Committee on the Rights of the Child.

Tamara van der Hoek

Tamara van der Hoek is a PhD student within the Department of Sociology at Tilburg University in the Netherlands. Her doctoral thesis is on Child Poverty in the Netherlands and is especially focused on exploring poor children's personal experiences and coping strategies. Along with her former colleagues from the Erasmus University Rotterdam, she has written – by order of the Dutch Ministry of Health, Welfare and Sports – a preliminary report [in Dutch] on the extent and impact of poverty among children in the Netherlands (2001).

Adrian James

Professor of Social Work at the University of Sheffield. He has published widely in the field of socio-legal studies, concentrating in particular on issues concerning the welfare of children in the context of divorce and marital breakdown. More recently, he has worked collaboratively with Allison James, developing a new approach to the social study of childhood that has combined Allison James' pioneering work in this field with his own socio-legal and social policy perspective.

Allison James

Professor of Sociology at the University of Sheffield. She has worked in the sociology/anthropology of childhood since the late 1970s and has helped pioneer the theoretical and methodological approaches to research with children which are central to the new childhood studies. Her work focuses on children as social actors and her research has included work on children's language and culture in relation to theories of socialisation, children's attitudes towards sickness and bodily difference and children's experiences of everyday life at home and at school. Her current work explores aspects of law and social policy as it relates to children's experiences of governance and the social and cultural construction of models of 'the child' and of 'childhood'.

Sally McNamee

Research Fellow at the University of Hull, where she was Associate Director for the Centre for the Social Study of Childhood. Her main research interests are constructions of childhood, children and leisure and child welfare in the family justice system.

Jaleh McCormack

Currently employed by the Children's Rights Alliance for England, Jaleh supports young people's self-advocacy in national decision-making. Her chapter with Maree Brown draws on her previous work at the Ministry of Social Development in New Zealand. She was a member of the Child and Family Policy Team that was responsible for the development of the Agenda for Children strategy. Her interest in children's issues and their participation in policy and research developed through completion of a Masters degree at the University of Otago and employment as a researcher at the Children's Issues Centre in Dunedin, New Zealand.

Máire Messenger Davies

Professor of Media Studies, and Director of the Centre for Media Research, in the School of Media & Performing Arts, University of Ulster at Coleraine. She was formerly a Reader at the Cardiff School of Journalism, Media & Cultural Studies, where she and Nick Mosdell carried out the Broadcasting Standards Commission-funded research that is reported in their chapter. After a career as a journalist, she studied the psychology of television audiences for her PhD. She has written a number of books and articles on the relationship between children, young people and the media, including *Television is Good for Your Kids* (1989, 2nd edition 2002), published by Hilary Shipman, and *Dear BBC: Children, Television Storytelling and the Public Sphere* (2001), published by Cambridge University Press.

Nick Mosdell

Having completed a BSc and an MPhil in Applied Psychology at Cardiff University, Nick worked as a research assistant/associate on a variety of research projects in the field of experimental cognitive psychology. He then moved to the Cardiff School of Journalism, Media and Cultural studies to work on a number of research projects concerning children and the media and broadcast news in general. He is now a lecturer in research methods and continues research into representation on television and on relations between the military and the media.

Rebecca de Schweinitz

Independent scholar living in Portland, Oregon. She did her graduate training in U.S. history at the University of Virginia and has taught courses on children's history, the civil rights movement and U.S. women's history at Brigham Young University. She is currently revising her dissertation, '"If They Could Change the World": Children, Childhood, and African-American Civil Rights Politics', for publication and working on a study of images of blacks in American children's literature. She has previously published work on turn-of-the-century women's fiction for girls.

Julie Seymour

Senior Lecturer in Social Research and Head of Department for Comparative and Applied Social Sciences at the University of Hull in the United Kingdom. Her research interests are in the areas of resource allocation, gender and the household, disability and informal care and issues of methodology. She has published in the fields of domestic labour, disability and informal care and negotiating power in intimate relationships.

Nigel Thomas

Senior Lecturer in Childhood Studies at the University of Wales, Swansea. He was for many years a social work practitioner and manager, before becoming a lecturer in social work in 1992. He has been responsible for postgraduate teaching programmes both in social work and in childhood studies. Nigel's research interests are principally in child welfare, children's rights and participation. His publications include *Children, Family and the State* (Policy Press 2002), *An Introduction to Early Childhood Studies* (with Trisha Maynard, Sage 2004) and a forthcoming book on young people in care (for Palgrave).

Annabel Tremlett

Annabel Tremlett spent 2000–2002 in Hungary, where she carried out a year's Youth Action volunteer placement with Voluntary Services Overseas (VSO). She then undertook a nine-month schools project funded by Future Capital (European Commission) and the American Friends Service Committee Budapest (AFSC). Since then, she has completed an MRes in the Department for Education and Professional Studies at King's College, London. She is currently continuing her studies there towards an MPhil/PhD and in 2004–2005 she plans to undertake further research into the education system in Hungary.

Abbreviations

BBC	British Broadcasting Corporation (UK)
BSC	Broadcasting Standards Council (UK)
CAFCASS	Children and Family Courts Advisory and Support Service (UK)
CAMHS	Children & Adolescent Mental Health Services (UK)
CFR	Child and Family Reporter (UK)
CG	Children's Guardian (UK)
DoH	Department of Health (UK)
DfEE	Department for Education and Employment (UK)
DfES	Department for Education and Skills (UK)
DLSE	Department of Labor Standards Enforcement (California)
DSM	Diagnostic and Statistical Manual
EBP	Evidence-based Practice
EU	European Union
ICYD	Investing in Child and Youth Development (New Zealand)
ILO	International Labour Organisation
ITC	Independent Television Commission (UK)
LEA	Local Education Authority (UK)
MSD	Ministry of Social Development (New Zealand)
MYD	Ministry of Youth Development (New Zealand)
NHS	National Health Service (Netherlands and UK)
NAACP	National Association for the Advancement of Coloured People (USA)
OECD	Organisation for Economic Co-operation and Development
OFCOM	Office of Communications (UK)
OFSTED	Office for Standards in Education (UK)
QP	Quality Protects (UK)
RSK	Roma Press Centre (Hungary)
SCLC	Southern Christian Leadership Coalition (USA)
SEN	Special Educational Needs (UK)
SENDA	Special Educational Needs and Disability Act 2001 (UK)
SENDT	Special Educational Needs Disability Tribunal (UK)
SSD	Social Services Department (UK)
UNCRC	United Nations Convention on the Rights of the Child
UNICEF	United Nations International Children's Emergency Fund
VSO	Voluntary Service Overseas

Part One
Children in Theory and History

1
Introduction: The Politics of Childhood – An Overview

Allison James and Adrian James

This book arises out of the third international conference held by the Centre for the Social Study of Childhood at the University of Hull in 2002. This conference aimed to explore, from a multi-disciplinary perspective, the politics of childhood. Or, perhaps to be more accurate, through having this as its organising theme, the conference endeavoured to discover what a politics of childhood in the 21st century might look like – to identify some of the key issues, debates and matters of contemporary concern. This volume, therefore, is an attempt to set out some initial markers of current thinking in this sphere and to indicate areas for future research and theorising.

It is, of course, somewhat unusual to couple 'children' with 'politics'. Across the world, children are, for the most part, excluded from any active participation in the politics of nation states. Even within more local political arenas, their everyday engagement as social actors or participants may be limited and is often rather tokenistic. Cynical politicians, in the US and in many European societies for example, may harness the pulling power of children by citing the 'voices of children' and by encouraging their presence in order to garner support for particular policies. On the other hand, in other parts of the world, there are examples of the deliberate exploitation of children by governments, both legitimate and illegitimate, in the pursuance of political acts of all kinds – from warfare and guerrilla action to the assertion of religious principles. In these instances it becomes starkly clear that though, as minors, children may not have any political rights, as people they are not spared from the effects of political acts that adults perpetrate, whether this be in their interests or simply as bi-lateral 'damage' – for instances of benefit seem to occur far less often – of adult-centred agendas.

By focusing deliberately, then, on the links between 'politics' and 'childhood', this volume seeks to underscore the significance of 'childhood', as an important phase in its own right, in the life course – and not just in terms of it being the nurturing ground of adulthood in regard to children's cognitive and physical development. Rather, it is an attempt to locate the socially constructed character of childhood in a variety of political arenas, following the new tradition within childhood studies (James, Jenks and Prout 1998). It also attempts to reveal the extent to which what Jenks (1996) calls the futurity of childhood is becoming an increasingly overt feature of the political landscape within many societies. Whether this is in terms of local policies of social welfare, which directly address the needs of children, or more macro global economic forces that impact on the communities and neighborhoods in which children live, 'childhood', as we shall see, is not immune from the politics which these policies and movements represent.

In this sense, as this volume unfolds, we are more correctly describing a plurality of 'childhoods', for it is the very diversity of children's experiences in different social contexts which alerts us to the importance of the political dimension of childhood as a life-course phase. While all children have a childhood – in the sense that they are born and mature towards adulthood – the ways in which that period of life is lived out and the very many different experiences which it can embrace would seem to slash right through any sense of a universal or shared 'childhood'. Diversity rather than commonality would seem to be a key feature of childhood that is underlined by exploring its political dimensions – and this is not just highlighted by the differences between societies, but also by differences within societies and, indeed, within the neighborhoods in any one society. As the chapters in this volume attest to, 'childhood' is fractured by the major fissures of class, gender and ethnicity and by the relentless march of poverty on a global scale as much as by the domestic politics of the peculiarities of a child's family and/or household composition; and, over time, by changes in ways of thinking about children – about what they need, what they represent and what they will become.

For these reasons, it is perhaps all the more remarkable that it is onto this world stage that the United Nations Convention on the Rights of the Child (UNCRC) has made its entrance. There can be few more bold and intrinsically political acts in the late twentieth century than the introduction of a convention that seeks to promulgate a set of rights that embrace *all* children, wherever they may live, and there can surely be no more remarkable political phenomenon than the fact that such a convention has achieved virtually global support. The implications of this crucially important development in the politics of childhood are too wide and varied to be analysed consistently in the context of this volume and it might be argued that the UNCRC is aspirational rather than practical. Be that as it may, it is also undeniable that the UNCRC now provides a backcloth for many of the issues and developments considered in this volume and a yardstick against which national responses to those issues that are of fundamental importance to children and their childhoods are measured.

In this sense, the politics of childhood has a broad agenda and, in Part 1, we begin to map out its scope through exploring three rather different discourses of childhood and revealing the politicisation of 'childhood' that each endorses, albeit indirectly and unintentionally. At the outset, then, we are engaging with the politics of childhood with a decidedly small 'p' by examining the political context of its 'social construction' at three different historical moments. Two of these occur in the US and one in the UK, but taken together they represent examples of how 'change' can occur in thinking about childhood and the knock-on effect this has for children's lives. However, what these chapters also draw attention to is the specificity of these constructions to particular political contexts and historical moments, signifying the importance of the challenge currently being made by childhood studies to more universalistic conceptions of childhood.

In Chapter 1, Nigel Thomas explores the ways in which children's needs are conceptualised within welfare policies in the UK and considers the implications such conceptualisations embody for current ideas of childhood – in particular, for our beliefs and values about what kinds of needs children have and how, as adults, these can be operationalised through the implementation of particular policies and welfare agendas. Thomas takes as his main focus *The Framework for the Assessment of Children in Need and their Families* (2000), which attempts to set out some guidance for social work practice, together with the issues raised by the provision of services for young carers in the UK. Through detailed analysis of the concepts of children's needs embedded in the *Framework* and brought to light by some recently completed research into young carer's views of the services and assistance with which they are provided, Thomas concludes that contemporary discourses of childhood in the UK are effectively based on a deficit model. Children are understood to 'lack' or to be 'in want' of certain capacities, a perspective which, Thomas argues, leads to their disempowerment and political marginalisation.

In contrast, Chapter 2 sees Jim Block arguing, from a US perspective, for a discourse in which children are – in some ways – placed centre stage. Charting the political progress of the American republic in the 19th century, Block suggests that it was through fashioning 'childhood' as a life-course phase in which individual initiative was to be encouraged that America sought a solution to the lack of external controls which characterised the newly emergent republic. The demand for new forms of social order in modernity were met, he argues, by a focused concentration on the education and socialisation of the young. In this sense, then, children were to be 'empowered' as individuals – for they held the keys to the future – but yet, for the stability of the newly emergent society, they had also to be encouraged in various forms of self-restraint. However, while this paradoxical and conflictual role carved out for American youth served the US well in the 19th century, in the context of its newly democratic, liberal society, by the 21st century this role has become increasingly problematic. The contemporary politics of American childhood are, Block argues, characterised by a heady mixture of permissive reactionism and, unless new forms of selfhood and socialisation are found, this is likely to fail to provide the next generation of children with the cultural resources necessary for a post-modern society.

Chapter 3 develops further the political role of ' the child' in the creation of a nation's future, through Rebecca de Schweinitz's analysis of how ideas of childhood and children's rights became key discourses within the struggle for African-American civil rights. Focusing on an incident which occurred in the deep South in the 1930s – the alleged ravaging of two white women by nine black boys – de Schweinitz shows how public opinion was rallied, through sentiment, to defend the accused in the name of the 'child'. Their skin color and ethnicity became secondary to their status as children who, through no fault of their own, were recognised to be without a proper 'childhood'. Over time, this discourse of a childhood betrayed became a major political motif for the civil-rights movement as a whole, the experiences of nine little boys thereby being made to serve more universal, political ends.

Such, then, are some illustrations of the ways in which discourses of proper childhood and of what children need come to permeate social understandings and to underpin the social construction of childhood at particular historical moments, ideas which may be also seen to serve particular political ends via an insistence on the universalism of childhood. Indeed, despite the diversity of children's lives and everyday experiences, it is precisely this universal understanding of childhood which underpins the UNCRC, perhaps the most obvious context within which the politics of childhood have most recently been debated.

In Part 2 of this volume, therefore, we begin to explore in more detail the ways in which such universal ideas about children's rights unfold in particular local contexts. We do this by exploring an arena in which not only are children traditionally marginalised but one which has also become the focus of much politicised debate: children's participation in the labour force and in national economies. World-wide, the practical issues raised by children who work have led to heated debates not only focused around children's need for protection from exploitation but also about their rights to work and to participate in society as workers.

In Chapter 4, Weibina Heesterman introduces these ideas by addressing policy issues related to the rights of the child to protection from exploitation embedded both in international conventions and in the different approaches to child labour legislation in three affluent societies – the Netherlands, the UK and California in the USA. This is a useful departure from the traditional focus of much child labour research on third world or developing economies. Moreover, it provides illuminating contrasts and continuities with such studies. Describing the approach that each of these societies takes to child labour, Heesterman provides a comprehensive coverage of the content and main points of the legislation and argues that the definitions of child labour and child work they contain are important in mediating our understanding and approaches to the issue of children and work. Thus she concludes that, although ratifying children's rights conventions may not lead to any improvement of conditions for children and young people, the UNCRC does at least point towards a more equal future for them.

Chapter 5, by Tamara van der Hoek, develops this theme by looking, in detail, at the experiences of Dutch children who live in poverty in an otherwise affluent society. Such a focus, on the child's perspective on their own poverty, is not unique (e.g. Ridge, 2002), but it is rare. Most studies, both of adults and children but especially of the latter, objectify the poor. Here, then, we see an instance of the importance of not working with common definitions of childhood, and therefore assumptions about the similarities of children's experiences, even within the context of a single society. Through van der Hoek's account, we come to understand children's own perspectives on their family's poverty. Drawing on a recent study in the Netherlands, the chapter explores children's coping strategies and argues that earlier studies of child poverty have ignored such perspectives, preferring instead to assume that 'poverty' provides a sufficient description of their lives. What van der Hoek provides instead is a picture of children taking an active stance in relation to their family's poverty, employing a variety of coping strategies that enables us to see them as participants in their economic circumstances rather than simply its victims.

In Chapter 6, Julie Seymour extends this understanding of children as participants in the labour force by providing a very particular view of children's everyday social lives – those which unfold in family-run British pubs, hotels and boarding houses. This chapter discusses the emotional labour which children and young people engage in when living in the site of their parents' business. Emotional work and labour comes in many different kinds and contexts, from the domestic to the commercial, and even within the same context it is experienced in vastly different ways. Some fields of emotional work by children, such as that of young domestic carers within the family, have been explored by other authors (e.g. Becker *et al.*, 1998), but this form of work – of 'emotional labour', as Seymour characterises it, recognising its commercial context – has not received anything like as much attention. Once examined, it proves to be rich in lessons about the ambiguities and richness of emotional labour undertaken by children. The contribution of children to the family business is thus shown to be more complex than merely domestic labour and Seymour argues that children's contribution to their family business should not be seen as exploitative. Rather, she foregrounds children's active strategies to resist, or turn to their own advantage, the demands made on their time and the emotional labour that they are expected to contribute. In this way, children exercise agency in producing profitable, social or entertaining outcomes from their labour.

Such examples provide us with empirical illustrations at the local level, and from children's perspectives, with which to think rather carefully about the broad sweep of social and political policies as they touch the everyday lives of children. In this sense, nowhere are the politics of childhood more evident, or arguably of more crucial importance, than in the field of education. This is clearly apparent in Part 3 of the book, which brings together three chapters that focus on children at school in Mexico, in Hungary and in England and Wales. Whilst each chapter explores a different set of issues, each also draws out the centrality not only of the school, as an institution through which the cultural politics of childhood become a social reality, but also of schooling as one of the key mechanisms in the structuring of not only relationships between adults and children but also of the relationship between citizens and the state.

In Chapter 7, Maribel Blasco considers the impact on family relationships within a low-income urban neighborhood in Guadalajara, Mexico, of the extension of secondary education as a consequence of the Education Act 1993. Since the Act came into effect, secondary education has been not only compulsory but also the constitutional right of all Mexican children. At the same time, however, the Act has also made parents 'co-responsible', with the State, for ensuring that children attend school. By placing both enforcement of, and accountability for, the provision of secondary education in the hands of their families, the State has ensured that children's rights now have to be negotiated within the family. This is because children depend on the goodwill, capabilities and 'choices' of the adults in their lives – typically parents or other family members, who are responsible for them – in order to support them in exercising this right. In granting children the right to schooling, therefore, this crucial piece of legislation has also contributed to a reframing of the meanings of social rights, responsibilities and citizenship, concepts that are now refracted through and negotiated within families.

By way of contrast, in Chapter 8 Annabel Tremlett illustrates the close relationship between education policies and discriminatory social practices, which combine to disadvantage Roma children in Hungary. Although the chapter deals with the position of a specific minority group in a particular country, it also serves as a case study of the relationship between culture, politics and the education of children more widely. It has resonances for countries throughout the world, since it illustrates that education is the principal gateway to citizenship – the denial of which, as an intentional outcome of social policy or otherwise, also leads to the denial of citizenship. As Tremlett argues, however, the perceived 'failure' of Roma children as a result of such policies cannot be laid solely at the feet of the Hungarian government. It is, in fact, part of a wider process that illustrates how a society can be structured for a dominant majority – whether ethnic, cultural or social – and how a focus on 'failure' can stagnate debates about the education, and therefore the citizenship, of minority groups.

In the last chapter of this section, Ann Blair shifts the focus onto children in England and Wales where, by contrast with Mexico, they are seldom seen as holders of rights in an education context. She argues, however, that this formal position contrasts with an increasing acceptance of the view that the participation of children in decisions that affect them is an essential element of good educational practice. This apparent inconsistency between law and practice has been thrown into sharp relief by the recent introduction of citizenship education into the curriculum. This encourages children to learn about wider social participation and what it means to be a good citizen, but within a context – the school – in which they are denied any rights to participate. As Blair points out, children's lack of formal participation rights is highly significant in the field of education law, where parental rights have always prevailed; inevitably, once children's participation is invoked as a 'right', the question arises as to how far it is legitimate for the State to interfere with parental autonomy. However, the absence of any right to participate that is enshrined in legislation means that it is extremely difficult to assess how effective such informal practices are in ensuring that children are enabled to participate. Without such a right, the basic structure of relationships between adults, children and the State will remain unchanged, with the education system being constructed as a market in which parents, rather than children, are the consumers.

Part 4 of the book considers issues concerning children, power and decision-making in society more generally. Thus, in Chapter 10, Maree Brown and Jaleh McCormack focus on the background to, and implementation of, New Zealand's 'Agenda for Children'. This policy framework was published in June of 2002 by the New Zealand Ministry of Social Development and constitutes an overarching strategy for improving outcomes for children. It contains a number of guiding principles and action areas that are applicable across a range of government agencies. In tracing the origins of the Agenda, the chapter considers the influence of the children's rights movement and of new thinking about childhood from within the academic perspective of the 'sociology of childhood'. It also considers the consultation process that helped to produce the agenda, a process that resulted in responses from thousands of children. The policy approach of the Agenda focuses on such obvious matters as tackling childhood poverty, low educational achievement and various health problems. However, what is described as a 'whole child' perspective within the Agenda also produces a focus on involving children in decision-making and addressing their problems in the context of their wider family and social relationships. This makes the agenda interesting in itself, but also by comparison with strategies for children in other countries (the authors themselves cite related developments in the Republic of Ireland and the United Kingdom).

Chapter 11 outlines the results of a research project by Maire Messenger Davies and Nick Mosdell on the views of children and adults towards the use of children in the mass media; more specifically, the use of children on television. The project was part of a wider, policy-focussed initiative on the use of children in broadcasting. Whilst the research is located within traditional media studies concerns, it moves away from the more usual focus on children in this context – as passive victims of violent imagery or manipulative advertising – towards a more nuanced concern with their engagement, as an audience, with other children as actors and media participants. The research was commissioned by the UK's Broadcasting Standards Commission and stemmed from a concern with the use of children in documentaries, game shows and other forms of media entertainment. This part of the project sought the views of children and adults, living within families, on how children were presented on screen. This was done within the context of seeking to assess the effectiveness and appropriateness of existing guidelines on the use of children in broadcasting. Interviews, based on a focus-group approach, took place within families. This allowed the authors to comment on the dialogue between children and parents in such a context. Overall, the research allows for numerous insights into a rarely-studied world, that of the everyday engagement of families, and of children in particular, with the appearance and use of children on television.

A world that has been more closely studied is that of parents and children experiencing the throes of family breakdown, whether this is through the breakdown of the relationship between parents as a result of separation and divorce or through family breakdown as a result of parenting failures such as the neglect or abuse of children. In Chapter 12, Sally McNamee, Adrian James and Allison James report on the results of a two-year study that explored how child welfare professionals construct their understandings of childhood and the impact of these on their practice in family proceedings in England and Wales. Such proceedings take place under the provisions of the Children Act 1989, which appears to place considerable importance on the wishes and feelings of children in determining what is in their best interests. The findings of this project suggest, however, that focusing on the wishes and feelings of the child is not easy to achieve in practice because there are underlying issues about the structure of relationships between adults and children that make the recognition of children as competent social actors in such circumstances inherently problematic. Such issues are of fundamental importance in the context of the provisions of the UNCRC, since they raise the possibility that such structural considerations, which are a fundamental part of the cultural politics of childhood, might be problematic in other cultural and political contexts.

This is followed by Vicki Coppock's chapter, which assesses the involvement of children in mental health decision-making in light of the progress of children's rights discourses. Coppock also considers the influence of welfare reform processes and perspectives from the 'sociology of childhood' in altering perceptions of the role of children as patients in the mental health field. She argues that, in spite of such influences, managerialist agendas, medicalising discourses and positivistic methodologies provide strong limits to the involvement of children in mental health decision-making. She begins with a historical and policy overview before considering recent developments that appear to offer hope of progress but that are contradicted by legal decisions and professional practice. She concludes that the practices of mental health service delivery remain fundamentally adult-driven and that some features of contemporary mental health policy, such as the focus on evidence-based practice, have served to reinforce such an approach rather than challenge it.

In the final chapter, Jim Goddard seeks to bring together the work of our various authors in an assessment of some of the issues facing childhood studies. He does so in various ways. Firstly, the chapter considers what the other chapters have had to say on the main themes that shaped our structuring of the book, such as the power relations between parents, children and the state, the economic position of children and their education. The book then goes on to consider wider commonalities in the findings of the chapters. This assessment contributes to subsequent thoughts on possible future directions for childhood studies. In considering such future directions, the chapter examines some wider themes connected to some of the areas covered in this book. It particularly focuses on developments with an international component, both positive and negative.

References

Becker, S., Aldridge, J. and Dearden, C. (1998) *Young Carers and their Families.* Oxford: Blackwell.

James, A., Jenks, C. and Prout, A. (1998) *Theorising Childhood.* Cambridge: Polity Press.

Jenks, C. (1996) *Childhood.* London: Routledge.

Ridge, T. (2002) *Childhood poverty and social exclusion. From a child's perspective.* The Policy Press: Bristol.

2
Interpreting Children's Needs: Contested Assumptions in the Provision of Welfare

Nigel Thomas

Introduction

The aim of this chapter is to examine some of the different uses of concepts of 'children's needs' and their implications for professional practice with children. I begin by revisiting Martin Woodhead's critique of 'children's needs' (1990, 1997) and asking how it can help us understand the use of 'children's needs' in professional practice. Following this, I look at the use of the concept of 'children's needs' in the Children Act 1989 in England and Wales and then at two specific examples – (1) the *Framework for the Assessment of Children in Need and their Families*, and (2) services to 'young carers'. This is followed by considering some research into different conceptions of needs held by professionals and families, which leads to the suggestion that the concept of 'children's needs' may perhaps be reclaimed. To do so, it is necessary to look at the philosophical foundations of 'basic human needs', and then at how children and young people can contribute to defining their own needs. Finally, this brings us to consider the political marginalisation of children, the relationship between needs and rights discourses, and the alternatives to deficit models of needs and of childhood.

Deconstructing 'children's needs' – Woodhead revisited

This chapter takes as its starting point Woodhead's argument concerning the cultural construction of children's needs, based on his seminal 1990 paper and his 1997 postscript. Woodhead's point, as he emphasises in the postscript, was not to 'reject the evidence that there are some universal prerequisites for children's health, care and learning' but (1) to argue 'that apparently unproblematic, taken-for-granted certainty implied in statements about the "needs of children" does not stand up to close scrutiny' and (2) to look at 'the way this rhetorical device defines power relationships between experts and families, service providers and consumers, in ways that have little to do with the children themselves' (1997: 77).

The principal value of Woodhead's analysis was to show precisely how statements about children's needs function as rhetoric, by conflating fact and value in such a way as to exclude questioning. A statement of the type 'children need A' leaves us to assume the further logical steps '... in order to achieve B' and '... and B is desirable because ...' These steps are not made explicit and are therefore not subject to argument. The result is that the purported 'need' is constituted as an inherent part of children's nature, rather than as a means to a particular end which may be promoted by some groups and accorded less priority by others.[1]

The second valuable thing about Woodhead's paper was that it offered a typology of statements about need. He distinguishes: (a) '"need" as a description of children's psychological nature', evidenced by drives such as those for sustenance or closeness to people;[2] (b) '"need" as an inference from what is known about the pathological consequences of particular childhood experiences' such as institutionalisation; (c) '"need" as a judgment about which childhood experiences are most culturally adaptive'; and (d) '"need" as a prescription about which childhood experiences are most highly valued in society' (1990: 72). In effect, these categories form a continuum from the inherent to the externally imposed. It would be hard to argue that the need for food is not fundamental to children's nature (and, indeed, to adults' nature) and also hard to argue that the 'need' to study physics at school is anything but a cultural or ideological prescription.

The disentangling of internal and external becomes more difficult in relation to what is thought to be required for psychological health or 'optimal development', as Woodhead shows in his discussion of Bowlby's arguments. What constitutes psychological health is to some extent a social construct; to what extent this is so is arguably a question that can be determined at least in part by psychological and physiological evidence. For instance, psychological outcomes that are associated with apathy, loss of appetite, disease or mortality are 'bad' in some sense that transcends culture. On the other hand, there is evidence that such symptoms may themselves appear differentially in different cultures. These issues clearly deserve further exploration, but that is not my purpose here.

Prioritising 'children's needs' – the Children Act 1989

My main purpose in this chapter is to explore how Woodhead's analysis, in particular his demonstration that statements about 'children's needs' are rhetorical and his typology of such statements, can help us to understand what goes on when health and welfare agencies make assessments of children's needs. I want to explore the idea that the uncritical combination of different notions of children's needs tends to create an illusion of comprehensiveness or holistic-ness, but that behind this lies a selectiveness about which 'needs' are considered to merit intervention and support and which ones are not.

As Woodhead points out, in some respects conceptualising childhood in terms of 'needs' can be seen as 'a progressive and enlightened framework for working with children. It gives priority to protecting and promoting their psychological welfare, where adult priorities have centred more on children's economic utility, their duties and obligations, rather than their needs' (1990: 60). In England and Wales, the Children Act 1989 is often taken as an example *par excellence* of this reconceptualisation – although in UK law there are prior examples, most notably in the Children Act 1948.

The Children Act 1989 is also a good example of the bundling together of what Woodhead would identify as different kinds of 'needs' statements. Section 1(3), in outlining the factors to which courts should have regard in considering a child's welfare, refers to 'his physical, emotional and educational needs'. Section 17 identifies a category of 'children in need' who are eligible for local authority services: a child is *in need* 'if he is unlikely to achieve or maintain ... a reasonable standard of health or development, without the provision of services' and *development* is defined as 'physical, intellectual, emotional, social or behavioural development'. The same definition of development is used in section 31, which sets out the grounds on which a care or supervision order may be made.[3]

The Act therefore takes for granted a concept of 'children's needs' that embraces not only basic physical needs and presumed needs for healthy psychological development – Woodhead's categories (a) and (b) – but also educational 'needs', which are more likely to relate to what is thought to be culturally or politically desirable for children to achieve – Woodhead's categories (c) and (d). Secondly, it adopts a concept of 'children's needs' that seems to be closely linked with the idea of *development*. The smooth elisions from 'welfare' to 'needs' to 'development' that are made at more than one point in the Act suggest that its underlying assumption is one of children as *becoming* rather than as *being* (Jenks, 1982), with perhaps an element of 'child as project' (Hallden, 1991). Third, some attempt has been made to recognise that different children have different developmental trajectories, with the injunction to compare with 'what could reasonably be expected of a similar child'. Finally, and crucially, the model of needs on which assessment and service provision is to be based is a *deficit model*, where normal children in normal situations are assumed not to need services, and where the point of services is to bring a minority of children nearer to the norm.

These, then, are the 'needs' which social workers and others are expected to take into account and to assess when they are considering whether to assist children and families or whether to remove children from their families. How is this all-embracing conception of 'children's needs' – which, as we have seen, mixes up physiology and psychology, culture and ideology, fact and value – 'operationalised' in practice? Clearly this will depend on a number of factors, including the beliefs and values of individual practitioners, the organisational cultures in which they operate, the guidance issued by government, and the interaction between these. Let us look at two examples of how this works. One is the use of the *Framework for the Assessment of Children in Need and their Families*. The other is the issue of provision of services to 'young carers'.

Contextualising 'children's needs' – the *Framework for the Assessment of Children in Need and their Families*

The Framework for the Assessment of Children in Need and their Families (Department of Health *et al.*, 2000; National Assembly for Wales, 2000) is part of a series of attempts to guide and structure social work practice with children and families that has been made by the British government in the years since the Children Act 1989 was implemented in 1991. Initially, the references in government guidance to 'children's needs' were frequent but not very specific. The original 1991 guidance on arrangements for the placement of children said, for example, that 'both the immediate and long-term needs of the child should be considered and provided for' (DoH, 1991a: 2), and referred specifically to needs for health care, education and family contact and to the child's 'race, culture, religion and linguistic background'. This is hardly comprehensive in its range, and there is no systematic guidance on how these needs should be assessed, although it is clear that children and parents are expected to be consulted. A distinction is sometimes made between 'needs' that children may have simply by being children, or by being children of a particular type, and *unmet* needs – needs that have necessitated the provision of a service or that have arisen from it. The guidance *Patterns & Outcomes in Child Placement*, issued at the same time (DoH, 1991b), described 'needs' in terms of problems; and the earlier 'Orange Book' on comprehensive assessment in child protection (DoH, 1988) spoke of 'problems' rather than of 'needs'. The *Looking After Children* materials, developed in the wake of the Children Act to encourage better assessment and planning for children in care or accommodation, focused much more directly on needs and made a more serious attempt than hitherto at comprehensiveness. The *Assessment Framework* follows in this tendency, with a discourse characterised by a would-be-holistic concept of 'children's needs'.

The *Looking After Children* system, designed as a tool both for research and for practice, conceptualised children's developmental needs in terms of seven 'dimensions': health, education, behavioural and emotional development, identity, family and social relationships, social presentation, and self care (Parker, *et al.*, 1991; Ward, 1995; Jackson and Kilroe, 1996). A detailed analysis, in terms of Woodhead's typology, would show how each of these seven 'dimensions' of developmental needs includes a mixture of type (a), type (b), type (c) and type (d) 'needs'; indeed, the *Looking After Children* conceptualisation has been criticised as being culturally and politically loaded (Knight and Caveney, 1998; Garrett, 1999a and 1999b; see also Jackson, 1998). The *Framework for the Assessment of Children in Need and their Families* adopts the same system of classification, but attempts to locate this in a wider context by setting out three 'domains' in which assessment should operate – the child's developmental needs, parenting capacity, and wider family and environmental factors.

However, the apparent comprehensiveness of the concept of needs underlying the *Framework* begins to break down in the process of being operationalised. The first stage comes with the guidance that accompanies the *Framework*. The package *A Child's World*, widely used in the training of child welfare professionals in how to work with the *Framework*, is rich in material on how to assess the child's developmental needs and the capacity of parents to meet those needs (see Horwath, 2000). It is much weaker on the third domain, wider family and environmental factors. Although represented diagrammatically as the base of the triangle, and presumably intended to be fundamental to the whole conceptual framework, this domain is largely missing from the training package; apparently because at the time the pack was commissioned the plan was for a two-domain approach, and the third side of the triangle was only added at a relatively late stage. This is significant in itself.

The second stage in operationalisation is when child welfare agencies begin to implement the *Framework* locally, clarifying objectives and setting up systems to achieve them, briefing and training staff and providing resources. The third stage is when individual practitioners and teams put the work into practice. An evaluation of the early stages of implementation of the *Framework* in Wales (Thomas and Cleaver, 2002) found a tendency for agencies to concentrate on administrative procedures such as the completion of the forms and records introduced with the *Framework*, and on achieving the time targets for completion set by the government, rather than on the thinking underlying the *Framework* itself. There was also some evidence that practitioners found it much easier to collect information under the various headings provided than to analyse and evaluate it or to use the results to set objectives and make plans.[4] It was not possible to say from this particular study whether, in practice, some dimensions of need received more attention than others, but experience and related research both suggest that the focus is likely to be quite selective. Penn and Gough (2002), for example, found that practitioners in health, education and social welfare tended to focus strongly on certain 'needs' rather than others, especially those related to emotional support and to the quality of interaction between parents and children. Indeed, part of the purpose of *Looking After Children* was to strengthen the focus in social work practice on the educational 'needs' of children in care, which research had shown attracted a low priority in comparison to more immediate concerns over placement and family contact (see Jackson, 2001). It remains to be seen whether such selectivity will continue with the use of the *Framework for the Assessment of Children in Need and their Families* and its successor, the 'Integrated Children's System', or whether a more broadly-based approach to the identification of need will result.

Contesting 'children's needs' – the issue of 'young carers'

Another area in which the discourse of 'children's needs' has been the site of some fundamental dispute is that of 'young carers', a topic that has generated considerable controversy since this group was first identified by Aldridge and Becker (1993). It has been argued both that the concept of 'young carers' distracts attention from the inadequacy of current community care services and legitimates the abuse of children and, conversely, that respect for children demands that we take seriously their wishes to be involved in looking after parents or other family members (Keith and Morris, 1995; Morris, 1995, 1997; Olsen, 1996; Aldridge and Becker, 1996).

Although estimates of numbers vary widely because of difficulties both in definition and in identification, it is nonetheless clear that there are many children and young people who take some responsibility for the care of family members who are ill or disabled, and that some of them are the sole or main carers for people with high dependency needs. A picture commonly conjured up by the phrase 'young carer' is of a child heroically tending a parent with severe physical disabilities, leading some disabled parents to react with anger to this definition and the way in which it is used to objectify them and to deny their ability to be parents. In contrast, a significant proportion of young carers are living with parents who have episodes of acute mental illness or severe drug and alcohol problems, and whose ability to be effective parents may be severely compromised.[5]

Responses to this situation by child welfare agencies vary widely and are widely thought to be generally inadequate. However, my focus here is not on the adequacy or inadequacy of the response, but on some of the thinking about 'children's needs' that appears to underlie it. Clearly, there are conflicting views and assumptions about the nature of childhood and what constitutes a proper childhood. These have been discussed elsewhere (Olsen, 2000). There is also an ambiguity about the nature of parenting, or caring, that emerges in discourses about 'role reversal' or children 'parenting their parents'. When researchers refer to 'false maturity', a 'dysfunctional relationship between carer and care receiver', and a 'transfer of role' that 'could affect a child's natural development' (Frank, 1995: 20–1), there are embedded assumptions about what is *normal* and *natural* that we might wish to question.

For service agencies, a pressing issue is whether to locate their response to 'young carers' in a context of adult disability services or of services to children and families. In the UK, there are quite different legal and policy discourses involved – disability legislation provides for carers to have support and to be able to ask for an assessment of their needs alongside those of the cared-for person, whilst child care legislation is explicitly focused on children's developmental needs. In our study of the perspectives of 'young carers' in Wales, young people we spoke to expressed anger and dismay at the failure of professionals to treat them as responsible people (Thomas, Stainton *et al.*, 2003). From talking to young carers about their experiences, it was clear that their needs for emotional support and for ordinary social contact and recreational activity were of great importance to many of them. However, neither of these appeared to be needs that state agencies were good at identifying or meeting, although they were often met effectively by 'young carers' groups.

Within the Children Act 1989, as we have seen, a *deficit model* of need is both implicit and explicit. One effect of responding to the situation of a young carer by assessing whether s/he is a 'child in need', as defined in section 17 of the Act, is that the caring responsibility may only be recognised by being problematised – as something that prevents the child from achieving a 'reasonable standard of health or development'. The most extreme example of this, discovered in a parallel study of Welsh agencies' responses to 'young carers', was a local authority whose policy was to assess young carers under section 47 of the Children Act, on the basis that it was suspected that they were suffering significant harm and that, if appropriate, a child protection case conference would then be held (Seddon *et al.*, 2001).

Many of the children we interviewed were clear, however, that they wanted to carry on taking some responsibility for caring and they saw it as an important part of their family life. At the same time, they had *needs* for support with their caring role, needs which were not being met (Thomas, Stainton *et al.*, 2003). However, the system seemed to be unable to overcome the dichotomy between responding to these needs for support, as they would with an adult carer, and responding to 'children's needs', as defined by the Children Act. Whatever talk there is about responding to children's needs holistically, it seems, therefore, difficult in practice to avoid being selective about which 'needs' actually count.

Reconstructing 'children's needs' – thoughts on a way forward

The research by Penn and Gough (2002), mentioned earlier in this chapter, is a study of definitions of family support used by different agencies in one local authority area. This found a high degree of selectivity in what counted as a need requiring intervention or assistance, whether for children or for families. Using a modified version of

Trivette's typology of user needs (Trivette *et al.*, 1997), which is useful because it defines needs very widely and attempts to do so from a service user's perspective, they found a marked gap between what were seen as social or health services and wider community services, the latter being largely invisible to the processes of assessment and intervention (even though the local authority in this instance had highly developed and accessible leisure services, for example). There was also a blindness to much knowledge of the ways in which drug and alcohol impinged on the lives of families in the community, or of the effects of poverty on them. Intervention was largely concerned with emotional support and with the quality of interaction between children and parents. Discussions with service users, on the other hand, suggested that such users had a much wider view of what counted as a need requiring support (and one that made much more frequent reference to money).

As Penn and Gough (2002: 30) put it: (i) 'families have basic needs for resources which are not being met'; (ii) there are public and private sector services 'that are explicitly for personal growth, enjoyment and recreational purposes', but although many people 'measure the quality of their lives in terms of [these latter] opportunities', social work and voluntary agencies promoting family support tend to ignore them. In this sense, the definitions of need being used in practice seem to exclude 'needs' in Woodhead's categories (c) and (d) and only partially include 'needs' in category (a).[6]

The British way is, however, not the only way of delivering family support. Baistow and Wilford (2000) contrast the provision of services in the UK and in Germany. In the UK, children are defined as 'in need' or 'at risk', while in German legislation the accent is apparently on 'perceived need' and 'entitlement to help'. Children and young people also have more independent rights to seek help in Germany. The effect is that families' own definitions of what counts as a need or what counts as support carry greater weight. Similarly, in recent publications (e.g. Ward and Rose, 2002) there has been more interest in developing an 'ecological' (Bronfenbrenner, 1979) approach to child welfare services that takes real account of the effect of community and society on children's lives, rather than focusing narrowly on family interactions. Jack and Jordan (1999) have explored the usefulness of concepts of 'social capital' in understanding these issues. However, in the UK, these considerations have only just begun to impinge on actual practice in child welfare work, as we have seen.

We have here a seeming paradox. On the one hand, Woodhead's critique suggests that one problem with the use of 'needs' in child welfare is that the concept bundles together several quite different ideas. On the other hand, I am implicitly criticising child welfare policy and practice for failing to consider children's needs broadly enough and suggesting that by doing so they are failing children and their families. In his original paper, Woodhead suggested that it might be better 'to abandon this problematic way of construing childhood altogether' (1990: 73), although he has since made clear that this was a rhetorical point rather than a serious proposal. I, too, would argue that the concept is a useful one, provided that it is regularly unpacked into its constituent parts (what Bourdieu might call 'epistemological vigilance').[7] In particular, there is value in a concept that does attempt to embrace different kinds and levels of need, from needs related to physical survival and basic mental health to needs for access to culture and leisure.[8] Such a global concept may, however, contain traps for the ideologically unwary. It also presents a challenge to those concerned with supporting children and families to take account of the full range of things we all need for a good life, rather than focusing on deficits in narrowly defined areas.

Clarifying human needs – the philosophical foundation

Before exploring further how this might work, it is necessary to look in more depth at the philosophical foundation for concepts of basic human needs; of which, children's needs are a category. Doyal and Gough (1991), for example, make a convincing case for objective and universal concepts of human needs. They demonstrate the impossibility, or at least the inconsistency, of wholly relativistic accounts of need. Whether they are based on neo-classical or neo-liberal, on Marxist, feminist or phenomenological premises, all these accounts are seen to depend, at some point, on a conception of human needs that transcends culture and politics.

Like Woodhead, Doyal and Gough point out the embedded logic of needs statements, following Brian Barry's formulation that 'all need statements conform to the relational structure "A needs X in order to Y" (Barry, 1965: section 5A)' (Doyal and Gough, 1991: 39). By introducing 'avoid serious harm' as the Y function, they make it possible to distinguish *basic needs* from those 'needs' that are really 'wants'.

Doyal and Gough also conceptually separate needs from drives, on the grounds that the two do not always coincide. On the other hand, they recognise that the connection is an important one, grounding our humanity in physicality rather than in abstract reason. However, our humanity is also grounded in sociality and Doyal and Gough make effective use of the concept of 'life-chances'. On the other hand, as they explore attempts to ground needs simply in terms of 'life-plans', they run into the objection that individuals may have life-plans which others would not want to see fulfilled (an obvious example being Hitler). They therefore adopt a definition of needs based on the ability to participate in social life, a definition which can remain valid for any individual in any society.[9]

On this basis, they argue that the basic human needs are those for *health* and *autonomy*. Autonomy, they suggest, is based on: (1) understanding, in particular language and cognitive skills; (2) mental health, which translates as capacity, rationality and confidence; and (3) opportunities, or freedom of action.

To this conception of human needs, according to Doyal and Gough, both rights and obligations can be attached. It is reasonable to say that individuals have rights to the basic requisites for participation in human social life, and that those in a position to make this possible have an obligation to do so. They also make a case, on the basis of mutual self-interest and interdependence, for these rights and obligations being not to *minimal* but to *optimal* satisfaction of these basic needs: 'That we might debate what this level practically entails and how it should be given effect does nothing to detract from the moral imperative of collectively helping others to reach the high levels of need-satisfaction which we already know can be achieved' (Doyal and Gough, 1991: 107).

Doyal and Gough's concern is with universal needs, although they also have something to say about 'special' needs and make a powerful argument for the recognition of different needs within a common humanity:

> In concentrating on the needs which all members of our species have in common the discussion thus far has been genderless, raceless, classless, ageless, cultureless. We are, of course, not denying that there is a sense in which particular groups have specific needs. Obvious examples are women, groups subject to racial oppression and people with disabilities. Members of each group are commonly subject to *additional* threats to their health and autonomy ... As a result they require *additional and specific satisfiers* and procedures to address and correct them. The fact that this is the case, however, does not entail that the basic needs of members of such groups are any different from those of all other persons.
>
> (Doyal and Gough, 1991: 74)

This connects with the second main theme of this book, which is the extent to which the concepts of childhood embedded in policy tend to *universalise* children's experiences and fail to *differentiate* between them in local settings. However, Doyal and Gough do not consider issues around the assessment of individual needs, which is a primary concern of social work and health services and to which we will return shortly.

Children defining their needs

This issue of objectivity is one worth exploring a little further. The argument that there is an objective definition of basic human needs, which is to some degree independent of self-perception, is well made by Doyal and Gough. However, objectivity in this sense does not necessarily imply externality; in other words, it does not imply that our needs have to be defined by others. There is no reason, in principle, why others should be assumed to be more expert on our needs than we are. However, this is an assumption to which recipients of health and social care services – and, indeed, education services – are often subject; and it is an assumption to which children are normally subject. Ryburn (1991) has pointed out, for example, that many care planning meetings proceed as if the participants believed (a) that social workers must know better than clients what is in the clients' interests and (b) that adults must know better than children what is in the children's interests. Once stated in these terms, such assumptions are hard to sustain; but they usually remain unstated. As Cohen (1980: 11) puts it, 'a child's ignorance of his or her own self-interest does not improve the adult's knowledge of that child's best interest'. In fact, there is some evidence that children may be better and more consistent judges of what is important in their lives than are adults (see particularly the study by Yamamoto *et al.*, 1987). Waksler (1991), Butler and Williamson (1994) and Mason and Falloon (2001) have all, in different ways, shown how children's perceptions of what count as harmful events or situations may be very different from adults' perceptions. There is, as always, a tension between children's right to define their own needs and interests, and adult responsibility to care for and protect them. I have argued elsewhere that one important response to this is an emphasis on *dialogue* (Thomas, 2002). Roche (1995) and Schofield and Thoburn (1996) have made similar arguments.

The tension is, in part, around temporality or perspectives of time. Children are thought to take a shorter perspective and to be more present– rather than future-oriented. If true, the underlying assumption is that this is a defect, and that adults are, of course, correct to take a longer view. But is a child necessarily wrong to say 'I understand your concern for my safety or long-term welfare, but I am frankly more interested in being happy now' – especially as for many children the future is quite uncertain? As Robert Mnookin put it, 'how is happiness at one age to be compared with happiness at another?' (Mnookin and Szwed, 1983: 10; for a graphic illustration of this dilemma see Thomas, 2002: 186.)

Some of these issues are, by their nature, always going to be hard to resolve. It is clear that adults' responsibilities for children's welfare cannot be set aside, and it is clear that to some extent the definition of children's needs – both in general and in particular – calls for expertise. At the same time, it is surely essential to also make space for children to define their own needs. So how far can children's self-definition be taken and what would it mean in practice for children to define their own needs?

The practice of defining needs can be seen as having several different components. One component is saying what basic needs are, for people in general, or for groups of people. Another is specifying how those needs ought to be met, for groups of people or for individuals. Another is prioritising different needs, again for groups of people or for individuals. In all these activities, there is potential space for children, individually and collectively, to contribute to defining their own needs. Once children are accepted as experts on their own lives, then the possibilities begin to open up – for groups of children to make demands and advise on what will improve their lives (in other words, to operate as an *interest group*), and for individual children – especially those who have been defined as 'children in need' – to contribute to the assessment of their own individual, even 'special', needs and to prioritising those needs.[10] Looking back to Woodhead's typology of children's needs, this may be particularly relevant for needs in categories (c) and (d), where there are most likely to be different views of what is most important. It remains to be seen whether practice using the *Framework for the Assessment of Children in Need and their Families*, which certainly talks about engaging with children and finding out what they think, or with its successors, can rise to the challenge of putting children's perspectives in the foreground.

Marginalisation, children's rights and children's needs

Discourses of children's needs can have the effect of rendering children politically *marginal*. However, it is my contention that a needs discourse does not necessarily do that and also that replacing it with a rights discourse does not in itself overcome the problem. In both cases, it is the precise character of the discourse and how it is used that counts. A needs discourse that has space within it for children and young people, individually and collectively, to define their own needs can potentially be used to combat marginalisation – as can a rights discourse that allows children to state and define their own rights.

Rights and needs are not necessarily competing concepts, nor do they inhabit mutually exclusive discourses. It is perfectly possible, as Doyal and Gough have shown, to talk about people (a) having funda- mental needs and (b) having the right to have those needs met. The United Nations Convention on the Rights of the Child does not talk about children's needs – except, significantly, in Article 23, where there is a reference to 'the special needs of a disabled child' (paragraph 3). However, it is arguable that much of the content of that Convention could as well be expressed in terms of needs as of rights. It is a matter of the words we use, and those may be supremely important – but it is not necessarily an either/or choice.

Talking in terms of rights does not in itself automatically create the space for self-definition. Others may presume to tell us what our rights are, just as they may tell us what our needs are. Flekkoy and Kaufman (1997) have drawn attention to the absence of children's involvement in drawing up the UN Convention, which at the time (the 1980s) went largely unquestioned. It is arguable, perhaps, that 'rights talk' invites self-definition more readily than does the discourse of needs; but the link is largely a contingent one. It depends, crucially, on the kind of rights discourse that is adopted. Above all, it depends on taking seri- ously the right of children to participate in decisions as a fundamental, if not the fundamental, right (see Farson, 1974).[11]

If children's marginalisation from discourse about their needs and rights is, as is argued elsewhere in this volume, a political issue, per- haps political scientists can help us to understand it. Carole Pateman (1970), for example, has shown how participation underpins real democracy, and demonstrates the value of participation in political and industrial settings in giving a sense of efficacy and in political socialisation, as well as in helping to produce better decisions. The implications of this for adult-child relations are clear. As I have argued elsewhere (Thomas, 2002), Bachrach and Baratz's (1970) concept of 'nondecision-making' is relevant to an understanding of how children are invisibly excluded from contributing to the determination of what may be crucial questions for their lives.

Conclusion – escaping the deficit model

There is an ambiguity at the heart of terms like 'need' and 'want'. 'Need' can be something which we *have to have*, which we *want*, or which we *lack*. 'Want' also has an old-fashioned or dialect sense of *need* or *lack* as well as its modern colloquial sense, which is closer to *desire*. Needing, wanting and lacking are all, therefore, tied in some way to the idea of a gap, a space to be filled, or a deficit to be made up. As we saw in relation to the Children Act, professional concepts of 'needs' are often deficit models, with the focus not so much on what we all need to grow and be fulfilled as on what particular individuals or groups lack in comparison to others. There are good reasons for this – there is a lot of deprivation out there – but there are also problems if people are seen simply in these terms, especially if the defining of what they lack is done by others at a social or professional distance.

When these deficit models of needs interact with a deficit model of childhood – because childhood in itself is frequently understood in terms of lack, of incapacity, of immaturity – then the combination is a powerful one, and one that demands to be turned around if we are to have an empowering social practice. Moss, Dillon and Statham (2000) have talked of the 'child in need' and 'the rich child', using the example of child care services in Reggio Emilia, where a conception of the child as resourceful rather than needy is fundamental to the way in which services are planned. In a later contribution, Moss and Petrie (2002) call for a redefinition of children's services as 'children's spaces', seen less as systems for meeting predefined or targeted needs than as *places* where children can *be* and *do*.

There are, therefore, several steps that have to be taken if the concept of 'children's needs' is to be successfully rehabilitated:

1) to unpick the embedded logic of statements about children's needs and clarify what underlying assumptions are being used;
2) to take seriously a holistic approach to children's needs, and not use it to mask a hidden selectivity about which needs really count;
3) to engage children and young people in the process of defining and prioritising their own needs – both collectively and individually;
4) to recognise that *universal* human needs take *particular* forms in particular contexts;
5) to connect *needs* discourse with *rights* discourse and, in particular, with the child's right to participate;

6) finally, to begin to move on from 'needs' – or to put 'needs' in their proper place – by focusing more on children's strengths and resourcefulness.

Notes

1. An exception which Woodhead notes is in the United Nations Declaration of the Rights of the Child, which states 'The child, for the full and harmonious development of his personality, *needs* love and understanding.' This still, of course, leaves open the question of what counts as the 'full and harmonious development of his personality' and who is qualified to decide this.
2. 'Drives', of course, are not identical with objective needs, a point also made by Doyal and Gough (1991), whose arguments I consider in more detail later.
3. The main ground is that the child is suffering, or likely to suffer, *significant harm* as a result of care 'not being what is would be reasonable to expect a parent to give'; *harm* includes 'the impairment of health or development'; *development* is defined as 'physical, intellectual, emotional, social or behavioural development'; and *significance* is to be assessed by comparing the child's health or development 'with that which could reasonably be expected of a similar child' (Children Act 1989, section 31).
4. Questionnaires completed by social workers showed that overall they valued the initial and core assessment records as tools for practice, and those completed by managers showed that they thought the introduction of the Framework and the records had improved understanding of the needs of individual children and awareness of gaps in service provision. Interviews with parents involved in core assessments seem to show that families valued the relative clarity and transparency of the assessment process, even in cases where the contact with social services was not, in itself, welcome (Thomas and Cleaver, 2002).
5. It is worth noting that an important feature of the *Assessment Framework* is that it draws heavily on research into the effects of parental mental illness, drug and alcohol abuse and domestic violence on the ability of parents to meet their children's 'developmental needs' (Cleaver, Unell and Aldgate, 2000).
6. On the other hand, welfare agencies and courts, in practice, do have a history of confusing basic needs with cultural prescriptions – a recent extreme example being a court in the US which ordered a woman to stop breastfeeding her eight-year-old son.
7. See Webb *et al.* 2002: 83–4.
8. However, many presumed 'needs' may be dependent on cultural values; the need for a culture cannot itself be one of them.
9. 'An individual is "in need" for the purposes of social policy to the extent that he [*sic*] lacks the resources to participate as a full member of society in its way of life' (Harris, 1987 cited in Doyal and Gough, 1991: 52).
10. This may mean getting away from the idea of a 'hierarchy of needs' (Maslow, 1943). (The use of the word 'hierarchy' in this context is interesting, with its roots in the idea of a society ruled by priests.) Doyal and

Gough (1991: 36) point out that Maslow's 'strict temporal sequencing' of his different levels of need is 'simply false'.

11. 'The acceptance of the child's right to self-determination is fundamental to all the rights to which children are entitled' (Farson, 1974: 27). Farson goes so far as to suggest that protecting children and protecting their rights may be mutually incompatible; I would not concur with this.

References

Aldridge, J. and Becker, S. (1993) *Children Who Care: Inside the World of Young Carers*, Loughborough University: Young Carers Research Group.

Aldridge, J. and Becker, S. (1996) 'Disability rights and the denial of young carers: the danger of zero-sum arguments', *Critical Social Policy* 16, 55–76.

Bachrach, P. and Baratz, M. (1970) *Power and Poverty: Theory and Practice*, New York: Oxford University Press.

Baistow, K. and Wilford, G. (2000) 'Helping parents, protecting children: ideas from Germany', *Children and Society* 14 (5), 343–54.

Barry, B. (1965) *Political Argument*, Basingstoke: Macmillan.

Bronfenbrenner, U. (1979) *The Ecology of Human Development: experiments by nature and design*, Cambridge, Mass.: Harvard University Press.

Butler, I. and Williamson, H. (1994) *Children Speak: Children, Trauma and Social Work*, Harlow: Longman.

Cleaver, H., Unell, I. and Aldgate, J. (1999) *Children's Needs – Parenting Capacity*, London: Stationery Office.

Department of Health (1988) *Protecting Children: a guide to comprehensive assessment for social workers*, London: HMSO.

Department of Health (1991a) *The Children Act 1989 Guidance and Regulations Volume 3: Family Placements*, London: HMSO.

Department of Health (1991b) *Patterns and Outcomes in Child Placement: messages from current research and their implications*, London: HMSO.

Department of Health, Department of Education and Employment and Home Office (2000) *Framework for the Assessment of Children in Need and their Families*, London: Stationery Office.

Doyal, L. and Gough, I. (1991) *A Theory of Human Need*, Basingstoke: Macmillan.

Farson, R. (1974) *Birthrights*, Collier Macmillan.

Flekkoy, M. and Kaufman, N. (1997) *The Participation Rights of the Child: rights and responsibilities in family and society*, London: Jessica Kingsley.

Frank, J. (1995) *Couldn't Care More – a Study of Young Carers and their Needs*, London: The Children's Society.

Garrett, P. M. (1999a) 'Questioning the new orthodoxy: the *Looking After Children* system and its discourse on parenting', *Practice* 11, 53–64.

Garrett, P. M. (1999b) 'Mapping child-care social work in the final years of the twentieth century: a critical response to the "looking after children" system', *British Journal of Social Work* 29(1), 27–47.

Hallden, G. (1991) 'The child as project and the child as being: parents' ideas as frames of reference', *Children and Society* 5 (4): 334–46.

Harris, D. (1987) *Justifying State Welfare*, Oxford: Blackwell.

Horwath, J. (ed.) (2000) *The Child's World: Assessing Children in Need*, London: Jessica Kingsley.

Jack, G. and Jordan, B. (1999) 'Social capital and child welfare', *Children and Society* 13 (4), 242–56.

Jackson, S. (1998) 'Looking after children: a new approach or just an exercise in form-filling? A response to Knight and Caveney', *British Journal of Social Work* 28 (1), 45–56.

Jackson, S. (ed.) (2001) *Nobody ever told us school mattered : raising the educational attainments of children in public care*, London: British Agencies for Adoption and Fostering.

Jackson, S. and Kilroe, S. (eds) (1996) *Looking After Children: Good Parenting, Good Outcomes: Reader*, London: HMSO.

Jenks, C. (1982) 'Introduction: constituting the child' in Jenks, C. (ed.) *The Sociology of Childhood: Essential Readings*, London: Batsford.

Keith, L. and Morris, J. (1995) 'Easy targets: a disability rights perspective on the 'children as carers' debate', *Critical Social Policy* 44/45, 36–57.

Knight, T. and Caveney, S. (1998) 'Assessment and Action Records: will they promote good parenting?', *British Journal of Social Work* 28 (1), 29–43.

Maslow, A. (1943) 'A theory of human motivation', *Psychological Review* 50, 370–396.

Mason, J. and Falloon, J. (2001) 'Some Sydney children define abuse: implications for agency in childhood' in Alanen, L. and Mayall, B. (eds) *Conceptualizing child-adult relations*, London: Routledge/Falmer.

Mnookin, R. and Szwed, E. (1983) 'The 'best interests' syndrome and the allocation of power in child care' in Geach, H. and Szwed, E. (eds) *Providing Civil Justice for Children*, Edward Arnold.

Morris, J. (1995) 'Easy targets: a disability rights perspective on the 'young carers' debate' in *Young Carers: Something to Think About* (Papers presented at four SSI workshops May–July 1995), London: Department of Health.

Morris, J. (1997) 'A response to Aldridge and Becker – disability rights and the denial of young carers: the dangers of zero-sum arguments', *Critical Social Policy* 17, 133–135.

Moss, P. and Petrie, P. (2002) *From Children's Services to Children's Spaces*, London: Routledge Falmer.

Moss, P., Dillon, J. and Statham, J. (2000) 'The "child in need" and "the rich child": discourses, constructions and practice', *Critical Social Policy* 20 (2), 233–254.

National Assembly for Wales (2000) *Framework for the Assessment of Children in Need and their Families*, Cardiff: Stationery Office.

Olsen, R. (1996) 'Young carers: challenging the facts and politics of research into children and caring', *Disability and Society* 11 (1), 41–54.

Olsen, R. (2000) 'Families under the microscope: parallels between the young carers debate of the 1990s and the transformation of childhood in the late nineteenth century', *Children and Society* 14 (5), 384–394.

Parker, R., Ward, H., Jackson, S., Aldgate, J. and Wedge, P. (eds) (1991) *Looking After Children: assessing outcomes in child care*, London: HMSO.

Pateman, C. (1970), *Participation and Democratic Theory*. Cambridge: Cambridge University Press.

Penn, H. and Gough, D. (2002) 'The price of a loaf of bread: some conceptions of family support', *Children and Society* 16 (1), 17–32.

Roche, J. (1995) 'Children's rights: in the name of the child', *Journal of Social Welfare and Family Law* 17 (3), 281–300.

Ryburn, M. (1991) 'The myth of assessment', *Adoption and Fostering* 15 (1), 20–27.

Schofield, G. and Thoburn, J. (1996) *Child Protection: the voice of the child in decision making*, London: IPPR.

Seddon, D., Jones, K., Hill, J. and Robinson, C. (2001) 'A Study of Young Carers in Wales', report for Wales Office of Research and Development for Health and Social Care, University of Wales Bangor.

Thomas, N. (2002) *Children, Family and the State: Decision-making and Child Participation*, Bristol: Policy Press.

Thomas, N. and Cleaver, H. (2002) '*Framework for the Assessment of Children in Need and their Families*: Study of Implementation in Wales', Report to Wales Office of Research and Development for Health and Social Care (SCC00/1/001), University of Wales, Swansea.

Thomas, N., Stainton, T., Jackson, S., Cheung, W. Y., Doubtfire, S. and Webb, A. (2003) '"Your friends don't understand" – invisibility and unmet need in the lives of "young carers"', *Child and Family Social Work* 8 (1).

Trivette, C., Dunst, C. and Deal, A. (1997) 'A resource based approach to early intervention', in Thurman, S., Cornwall, J. and Gottwald, S. (eds) *Contexts of Early Intervention: systems and settings*, Baltimore: Paul H. Brooks.

Waksler, F. C. (1991) 'The hard times of childhood and children's strategies for dealing with them' in Waksler, F. C. (ed.) *Studying the Social Worlds of Children: sociological readings*, London: Falmer.

Ward, H. (ed.) (1995) *Looking After Children: research into practice*, London: HMSO.

Ward, H. and Rose, W. (eds) (2002) *Approaches to Needs Assessment in Children's Services*, London: Jessica Kingsley.

Webb, J., Schirato, T. and Danaher, G. (2002) *Understanding Bourdieu*, London: Sage.

Woodhead, M. (1990) 'Psychology and the cultural construction of children's needs' in James, A. and Prout, A. (eds) *Constructing and Reconstructing Childhood: contemporary issues in the sociological study of childhood*, Basingstoke: Falmer Press.

Woodhead, M. (1997) 'Psychology and the cultural construction of children's needs' in James, A. and Prout, A. (eds) *Constructing and Reconstructing Childhood: contemporary issues in the sociological study of childhood* (2nd edition), Basingstoke: Falmer Press.

3
The Politics of Modern Childhood: American Socialisation and the Crisis of Individualism

Jim Block

Introduction

This chapter traces the rise of a distinctively modern child-rearing practice in the United States,[1] and it is important to identify, at the outset,
the historically unprecedented features of the American case, arising
from its unique time and place in Western modernisation. This will
enable us to consider its implications for the wider politics of childhood and for processes of modernisation more generally. Given the
on-going globalisation of the world economy, the chapter suggests that
forms of social attenuation and fluidity are being precipitated which
recall the nineteenth century American experience. At the same
time, the globalisation of culture beams ubiquitous presentations of
American youth culture to the world. This process, a fast-forwarding of
the evolution of American socialisation from its nineteenth century
origins to its 'logical' conclusion in a distinct world of youth, in effect
defines the contemporary role of childhood for many who lack an
alternative scenario of child-rearing in the modernising process. This
threatens, therefore, to make this more local 'crisis of socialization' a
worldwide phenomenon (Barrett and McIntosh, 1991).

As we explore the emergence of a more child-centered socialisation
in the first half of the nineteenth century, it is also necessary to specify
carefully its ultimate implications for the democratisation of contemporary societies. There are, as Anthony Giddens (1998) has argued,
some inevitable repercussions of the breakdown of traditional paternal
and parental authority, involving enhanced roles for not only women
but also the young. And this new child-rearing, as we shall see,
redefined children as major participants in cultural replication in a way

previously unimagined, setting in motion a logic of empowerment whose heightened consequences we now experience. At the same time, we must be cautious about attributing this 'turning the world upside down' to modernisation itself without noting the constitutive role of a distinctive American cultural frame.

Moreover, this increasing focus on the young had as its goal, even in the US, not the liberation of individual potentialities but, instead, the drafting of the young to actively participate in the internalisation and subsequent enactment of public norms. That this radically reconfigured their role in the socialisation process, by opening up the way to more enhanced forms of empowerment, is undeniable. However, subsequent efforts to rethink childhood must not confuse recent outcomes with the historic process itself; nor must they overlook the lingering constraints of that process on youth today. Only by coming to terms with the particularities of the American case, what it achieved and failed to achieve in shaping a modern child-rearing, will it be possible to re-imagine the place of the young in post-modernity as part of a wider consideration of the political role of children and youth.

The turn to child-rearing in the New Republic

The origin of the United States in one of the two great late eighteenth century revolutions established it as a society whose populace turned from mere components into members of society who were to determine their own paths and places within the larger social structure. Generally understood as the 'rise of the social realm' in the nineteenth century (Barrett & McIntosh, 1991 ; Donzelot, 1979), these members were now to be appealed to, by institutional elites, on the basis of shared values, traditions and aims rather than through the presumption of their ratification of hierarchical decision-making. This shift, involving the decline of explicit external controls on adult social practice, was accomplished in part by turning to the socialising roles of the family and the educational system as crucial mechanisms of social control (Deleuze & Guattari, 1983; Donzelot, 1979) that prepare the young for life in modern society.

This process, which has affected all European societies undergoing modernisation, has, however, to be sharply distinguished in the American case in two ways: contextually and culturally. Where public institutions within Europe retained much of their historically accumulated power in shaping visible social norms, structures of opportunity, and communal vigilance, an unprecedented situation faced Americans in the early republic: an absence of mechanisms effecting social integration. This was an absence of not only all external constraints but also of functioning institutional structures to generate informal pressures that would ensure adult adaptation to, and compliance with, social integration. Under the unique American conditions – and, from the perspective of social formation, disadvantages – of vast geographic and social mobility, the collapse of imperial political structures and social hierarchies after the War of Independence, and the emergence of weak, decentralised internal institutions that were incapable of effective internal governance, there were simply no controls on adult conduct available. Thus, the quintessentially modern story of the late adolescent who leaves home to find fame and fortune – in Europe, an account of the exceptional youth – becomes in the US the emblematic account. Given its prototypical form by two best-sellers of the late eighteenth and early nineteenth centuries, *Robinson Crusoe* and Ben Franklin's *Autobiography,* the adolescent flight from home and social order into unstructured space – either rural wilderness or urban jungle – is the ubiquitous subject of early republican fiction (Block, 2002: 332–354).

With the bold call of the Declaration of Independence, newly proclaimed Americans were offered the transformative cultural vision of a free society of free individuals. This cultural triumph of liberty, while more extreme than anything previous, was itself the culmination of two centuries of a religious individualism without parallel in Europe. As discussed elsewhere (Block, 2002), radical Anglo-American dissenting Protestantism, which had shaped the later phases of the English Reformation and precipitated the English Revolution, became, through emigration, the dominant form of popular culture in the colonies by the period of the American Revolution. Rooted in an uncompromising commitment to a personal relation to divine authority, its proponents agitated repeatedly for the dissolution of traditional institutional hierarchies and the reconstitution of all institutions on a modern popular – that is, voluntary – basis. With the voluntary participation of members finally inscribed in the culture, through Jefferson's commanding rhetoric, as the source of all institutional legitimacy, the modern era was born. This would, of necessity, entail the fundamental reshaping of all institutional realms including – not least – the family. This process would consume the entire nineteenth century in the formation of American nationhood.

After the revolution, dreams of individualism were further fanned, in the early part of the nineteenth century, by the spreading rhetoric of economic individualism, religious equality and social self-reliance. Obtaining adult commitment to social order became, therefore, ever more tenuous, leaving fears of institutional dissolution and social fragmentation a permanent feature of public consciousness and popular culture throughout American history. The emphasis in the emerging model of adulthood on capacities for individual judgment and self-determination, critical to success in the new society, only magnified the dangers to collective stability.

Americans encountered, therefore, the crisis of establishing a modern social order without parallel until our own time. As a result, they were immediately thrust into what would become the overriding political problem of modernity: how to create political order in a voluntarist society. That is, how could stability for the new nation be established upon the unprecedented foundation of an individualistic and self-regarding citizenry? The classic liberal account of the free society focuses on individual consent to the social contract. The plausibility of this account, however, is challenged by the disorder and anxieties of the early republic; the new society was a vast institutional vacuum with no common agenda amidst a diversity of backgrounds and beliefs.

Forging a coherent national identity with core values and cohesive identities from this self-reliant citizenry could never be achieved, therefore, by convincing citizens of the rationality of unquestioning obedience to socially mandated norms. As a result, logical doctrine – failing to resolve the tension between voluntarism and order – gave way to an emphasis on character formation. The objective was not to effect a coherent theory of obligation that citizens would confirm, but instead to inculcate the virtues that would facilitate an adaptive integration to the new order. In this novel situation, the resolution was forged within that part of the population most susceptible and amenable to such character shaping such that, as in modern voluntarist societies generally, the establishment of social order came to rest, to an unprecedented degree, upon the institutional socialisation of the young.

Faced with post-revolutionary chaos, citizens newly released to their own devices quickly realised its dangers. Given the lack of adequate control over adult behaviour, what they quickly recognised was the unique accessibility of the young as the focus for enforcing accommodative conduct. Only in the family and educational system was the shaping of character legitimate; that is, consistent with the revolutionary discourse of freedom. Socialisation and child-rearing were understood to remain realms of ascriptive authority, as in traditional societies, and thus represented formal exceptions to the contractual voluntarism of liberal institutions. This meant, in turn, that the young were not regarded as full citizens but were instead subject to the will of their elders and, in any case, were, by their very biological dependence, unable to effectively resist adult pressures and demands. As historian George B. Forgie has noted, 'in a society that valued progress and equality, and in which authority of any kind, no matter how mild, was on the defensive, the family was the one archaic, hierarchical institution compatible with modernity and with democracy' (1979: 16). By default, the task of social continuity fell to the family and educational system.

The project of Republican socialisation

Effective socialisation of the young would in turn make adult voluntarism – and the national premise of freedom itself – possible. A society of adults who regarded themselves as free (with the attendant problems of social control) and were, moreover, provided a wide latitude for self-initiating activity, would only be sustainable if adult choices were prepared through a prior training in the limits and constraints intrinsic to liberal selfhood. That is, before adolescents and young adults moved permanently beyond the purview of their parents and communities, they would have to be instilled with an enduring acceptance of collective values, incentives, activities and limits. Building in, from the earliest ages, structural boundaries defined as the embodiment and realisation of the 'free individual' and 'free society' was thus the prerequisite to adult release.

Thus, unlike other societies that rely on lifelong external controls and explicit institutional demands, in the US, institutions shaping childhood have always carried the primary burden of holding the Republic together. For example, when social cohesion was threatened in the period after the 1960s by the emergence of counterculture and post-material values, the ensuing turmoil was quickly labeled as the 'family' and 'socialisation' crises of our time. In this scenario, the socialising institutions were not performing their indispensable preparatory and consolidating role and society, as a whole, was suddenly perceived to be in danger. Yet minister Joseph Lathrop of Massachusetts, 'anxious for my country,' had already warned the nation in a public sermon in 1787 – the year the Federal Constitution was drafted – that 'liberty' was threatened by its 'children and youths'. Their 'thoughtless levity, wanton mirth and wild dissipation,' being 'slaves to their own lusts and to the evil manners of the world, indiffer-

ent to the 'gospel' and the danger of 'civil commotions and dis-
turbances', raised the continuing specter of 'civil war' (Lathrop, 1991).
Moses Mather, even earlier, in 1775, indissolubly linked the future
stability of a 'free government' premised on 'natural rights' to the
determination to 'instruct and impress' on 'young and tender minds'
of the 'rising generation' the 'principles of virtue and the rudiments of
government' (Mather, 1991). Thus, the management of new expressions of voluntarism, such as those evident among today's youth,
rather than being a dire problem capable of immediate resolution, have
instead been 'defining tasks' that the US has set for itself.

Thus, we see from the 1820s national campaigns reaching down to
the 'family values' crisis of our own day, a family and educational
system that can enlist – otherwise unreachable – adults in establishing
domains of normative regulation and behavioural discipline. The hope
was that containing and directing the young early would deflect the
dangers presented by a voluntarist and loosely regulated society. To
many of the early writers on child-rearing, this seemed, at first glance,
no more difficult than continuing the rigorous, authority-centered
demands and expectations of traditional socialisation and education.
But this earlier model was increasingly discovered to be inappropriate
for the American context. John Locke, the great liberal theorist of
voluntarist adult society, whose *Second Treatise* was so influential
on American political thought, had, in another seminal work, *Some
Thoughts Concerning Education*, already identified the challenge that
liberal institutions posed for the socialisation process by perspicuously
identifying the central role that the early shaping of the young would
play in a society that gradually released its adults from significant
restraints.

Locke had also recognised that the very responsibilities demanded of
adults in a liberal society – to direct their own lives and choose for
themselves the many aspects of their livelihood, religion, domicile,
marriage partner and so forth – placed a new and profound strain on
the training of the young. Forming a citizenry capable of sustaining a
dynamic modern society required new and somewhat contradictory
human capacities. In short, the very youth who needed to be shaped
with internalised constraints and social commitments would be the
adults needing to negotiate a voluntarist, weakly regulated, individualistic society, able to act independently in the absence of external cues.
This dilemma, which would in time produce a structurally empowered
yet conflicted role for the young in American history, appeared at first
to be an unresolvable paradox: needing to produce citizens who

believed in their own independence, Americans demanded of child-rearing that it create an adaptive character which enabled the individual to regard itself as both under constraint *and yet* fully free.

For this reason, alongside obedience to discipline and restraint, the young also had to be educated in the new powers of self-reliance, individual initiative and self-confidence, powers necessary to utilise the unprecedented options within their fluid new economy and society. Their preparation demanded, therefore, internalised modes of regulation that enabled them to be both self reliant **and** institutionally deferential, capable of great initiative and independence **yet** subject to rigorous self-regulation and collective norms once they left their families and communities of origin.

Traditional socialisation, reasoned Locke, in which 'the *Mind* be curbed, and *humbled* too much in Children' and 'their *Spirits* be abased and *broken* much, by too strict a hand over them,' produced only '*dejected Minds*, timorous and tame, and *low Spirits.*' A '*Slavish Discipline* makes a *Slavish Temper,*' that of an individual who will 'very seldom attain to any thing,' having been relieved of 'all their Vigor and Industry' (1968: 148 & 150). Even as children and youth, then, individuals could not simply be externally forced into subordination. This would only produce citizens with dependent and passive characters, citizens as in the old world who were unable to take advantage of the unique conditions and demands of modern life. To 'make Able and Great Men' was a 'great Art,' for one had to 'avoid the Danger' of slavishness and yet tame the 'unguided Nature' without which the young would become simply cauldrons of 'Power and Dominion' (1968: 148 & 207). The great task, then, was 'how to keep up a Child's Spirit, easy, active and free; and yet, at the same time, to restrain him from many things he has a mind to ... he, I say, that knows how to reconcile these seeming Contradictions, has, in my Opinion, got the true Secret of Education' (1968: 148).

Winning the child's will

This conundrum, confronted at the outset of the republic, precipitated the solution which would ground the transition to modern society. Beginning in the 1820s, a vast literature burst upon American culture intent upon defining the kind of socialisation required for republican selfhood. Child-rearing manuals, advice and self-help books for youth and young adults, educational programs and didactic fiction were all intended to guide the community in shaping its new members. A broad spectrum of theologians, ministers and religiously committed writers, including Horace Bushnell, Catherine Beecher and Lydia Maria Child, undertook the reframing of the American character in light of the new realities of republican society. From their foundation in Anglo-American Protestantism, they drew values to redefine the prerogatives and responsibilities of parenthood, the powers and limits of childhood and the mechanisms for insuring the transmission of values that would prepare the young for a dynamic popular society.

In their understanding, freedom and obligation could only be reconciled within individuals raised to equate personal liberation with the project of responsible self-regulation. If children could be persuaded that the free society was only secure if it received the institutional commitment of each citizen, whose very freedom depended in turn on monitoring and sustaining this personal responsibility, they would grow up prepared to manage the self-limitation of their own deviance in accordance with the common good. The burden of adult self-constraint and self-containment was, henceforth, to be undertaken by the very subject of discipline – the requirement to manage one's 'freedom' within given limits.

This dependence of free citizenship on self-monitoring and self-channeling toward social accommodation was, in the view of its proponents, unavoidable. Adult independence meant that the ultimate responsibility for the regulation of conduct had to be necessarily and unavoidably transferred from the socialising institutions to the individual. In the absence of any other consistent and effective locus of lifelong control, individuals themselves alone possessed the continuing availability and capacity to regulate and monitor their own behaviour. At the same time, by establishing freedom as the obligation to manage one's activity within given social limits, rather than simply stifling the dangerous individualism released by the new dispensation of liberty, this solution turned them toward collective utility. This process of voluntary self-restraint is one reason (among many) why liberal citizens never know if they are free or caged – magically, they are both.

The task of ensuring voluntarist ideals, then, was to gain the child's uncoerced commitment to its own developing self-regulation through a radically restructured socialisation process in the family and education system. In other words, the strategy was to **win the child's will** to the task of its own disciplined maturation. Was such a project, assuming it was anything more than a manipulation of the child's sense of reality, even possible? How could socialisation be structured to produce an early ordered regimen of conduct and goals that was at the same time a call to later independent activity? Could the novel life-cycle shift of responsibility and power to the youth be effected, in the absence of any models or precedents and within a social condition relentlessly undermining traditional domestic and civil controls?

The breakthrough to this unprecedented challenge came early, born of both necessity and desperation. The diffuse group of cultural activists comprising the initial campaign drew upon the older dissenting Protestant ideal of individualism. In this tradition, unlike liberalism, individualism was framed in terms of a voluntary personal commitment both to the collective and to the use of personal talents on its behalf. The challenge – to strengthen the child's willing integration in the society while enabling it to regard itself as on the path toward a free citizenship – was to be met, they suggested, by radically reconstituting the parent-child relation. Toward this end, they developed elaborate new parenting strategies rooted in the *new bond,* a reconceptualisation of domestic authority that would, in time, refigure the modern psyche.

At the center was a new affectively based socialisation. This would elicit compliance by means of loving adult commitment, gentle guidance, positive reinforcement and increasing trust, enabling socialising adults to gain, by expectations of reciprocation, the child's own trust and the gradual conflation of its individual will with collective ends. Through the use of love and gentleness, praise and nurturance, they banked on getting the child to pursue designated conduct. By means of this affective engagement, supported by the use of psychological pressures employed explicitly 'for the child's own good,' parents would be able to generate obedience as a willed fulfillment of obligations on one's own, without the experience of submission. Positive incentives and rewards for appropriate maturation would also be employed throughout this process to lead the young toward their own commitment to pursue a voluntary path of active integration within the dynamic institutions of the new society.

The underlying goal of the process was to effect internalisation: the establishment of the regime of obligation within, boundaries and limits co-extensive with – and thus indistinguishable from – the child's affective life itself, such that following one's impulses was synonymous with having one's moral values '*within* you that will move and guide you' (Todd, 1850: 34). The 'object should be not merely to make the child obey externally, but internally' with the 'conviction that he consults his true interest in doing so' (Goodrich, 1839: 26). These writers understood the transformative impact of affective connection in generating 'the silken thread, by which the plant is drawn toward its prop' (Sigourney, 1838: 36). By 'keep[ing] the heart so susceptible' to 'their attachment,' the necessary 'restraint' at the center of child-rearing will henceforth be 'invisible' (Muzzey, 1858: 100 & 151; Child, 1831: 26).

Controls could be internalised in consonance with the subject's own will, as strength-based virtues, systematically and sympathetically offered to prepare and anchor the emerging capacity for self-governance. The aim was to identify and elaborate subject-affirming strategies that would enable the emerging individual to build its internal controls: engaging the child's affects by fusing pleasure and virtuous conduct; promoting a positive self-image by teaching the child through example; encouraging judgment by patient reasoning with the child; nurturing decision-making by providing choices in a trial-and-error process; facilitating and recognising distinctions by individualising each child and growth by individualising life stages; providing opportunities for replication of behaviour to facilitate consistency. Together these would produce a system of internal regulation, variously defined as reason, conscience and habit, and those virtues of self-control, self-government, self-discipline, self-containment, self-reliance, self-scrutiny and self-channeling whose very linguistic structure announced a new moral order.

The crucible of the modern citizen

The magnitude and difficulty of this shift in relations between adults and children amounted to a cultural transformation of domestic and internal priorities. The traditional authoritarian role had utilised coercion and fear – the only regime citizens raised under earlier conditions understood. This was cast aside as dysfunctional, seen only as provoking youths into rebellion and flight. Under conditions of eventual self-governance, adult socialisers now had to learn how to gradually transfer the initial responsibility for discipline to the child. Unquestioned parental authority, only to be exercised early to facilitate the internalisation of incentives and boundaries, was therefore supposed to contract as the child became increasingly capable of appropriately controlling its own functioning. The role of socialiser was thus recast as 'tutor for liberty,' as a model of positive identification who elicited proper behaviour through support for the child's emerging internal mastery.

Just as parenthood was being redefined, childhood itself was being differently constituted in the new society. With adults struggling to cope with their own needs, children were often left to make their own adjustments. Being 'less bound by prescriptive memories, more adaptable, more vigorous,' they were often at an 'advantage' in grasping the new social context. This subtle but powerful shift in generational relations meant that the young and 'not their parents became the effective guides to a new world, and they thereby gained a strange, anomalous authority difficult to accommodate within the ancient structure of family life' (Bailyn, 1960: 34 & 22–23). Weakened generational hierarchy and authority was compounded by the early movement of adolescents and young adults beyond religious establishment, class parameters and local vigilance.

In order to effect this preparation for adult release, for the first time, the young had to be made active participants in their own socialisation, addressed directly on the details of their role and its central project of self-regulation. As they matured, they had to be instructed how to expect and to exercise greater power and to develop the responsibility to manage it. The young were to be encouraged to levels of individual expression and responsibility never before permitted to their age groups, and were offered incentives to encourage the use of these new capacities toward socially mandated activities and goals. Ever greater mastery of early powers of self-directed activity was to be rewarded by increased levels of power and expression, until the maturing individual demonstrated the capacity for a life of self-regulated initiative.

The full development of these virtues would allow the young person to surmount the critical point in liberal socialisation, *the crisis of adolescence*. Adolescence in this new developmental model became – long before it was explicitly recognised and theorised by G. S. Hall and others at the turn of the twentieth century – a decisive period in the modern life-cycle. Adult independence mandated the necessary and unavoidable transfer of responsibility for self-containment and self-obligation from intermittent others to the demanding and inescapable self. Though prepared for this shift by the new liberal childhood, this transfer became the defining feature of liberal adolescence and young adulthood by the 1830s. But because of this demand, the transitional life stages of late childhood, adolescence and young adulthood were rent, from the outset, by unprecedented generational conflict. They also became, as evident in contemporary society, the point of structural resistance, the clearest time during which the individual – increasingly mature enough for independence but as yet unintegrated into society – could refuse responsibility for a life of liberal self-containment and self-accommodation.

The surmounting of this developmental hurdle by adolescents became the crucial marker, not only psychologically but also politically. Once the young had taken responsibility for self-direction and self-containment, the project of citizen formation was complete. Though Locke had not specifically foreseen the tensions endemic to adolescence, given his experience of a routinised English society with mandated adult roles, he had nonetheless realised the unparalleled importance to society of building a smooth transition to adult individualism. He proposed that child-rearing be structured around an early unquestioned internalisation that would gradually give way to the child's growing willingness to own, and take responsibility for, its own activity. The 'secret of Education,' then, was not to simply establish a midpoint between tight control and sympathetic nurturing, but to weave them together in a developmental sequence that would enable them both to maintain a central place in the child's psychological economy.

Thus he advocated the necessity of utilising 'Fear and Awe' from the earliest days of the child's life. This would give parents unquestioned and unchallenged 'Power over their Minds' during the period they were least able to resist, so that they 'perfectly comply with the Will of their Parents.' The careful delineation of appropriate conduct would ensure, as an *'early* Practice', the replacement in the child's mind of what is 'thought fit' by society for mere 'Desires' of their own (Locke, 1968: 146, 145 & 143). But equally crucial was that very early the 'Rigour of Government' be 'gently relaxed,' their 'Love and Friendship' gradually increased, and the child 'trusted to himself and his own Conduct,' so that a 'good, a virtuous, and able Man' may be 'made so within.' And in order to ensure a smooth transition, Locke counselled that the harshest 'Compliance' of 'their Will' occur 'before Children have Memories, to retain the Beginnings of it.' That would make early authority seem 'natural to them' rather than arbitrarily imposed and, as a result, the strongest childhood memories would be of an ever-growing friendship with parents and other socialisers – a virtual overcoming of natural inequities – in the course of their maturation (Locke, 1968: 146 & 147).

This veil obscuring the reality of child compliance spread over American child-rearing, not because of the influence of Locke's arguments but because the same shifts in socialisation that Locke had addressed in his work were effected in the new society. The likelihood that, after the revolution, a mobile and individualistic youth would achieve eventual self-governance and eventual equality with elders made an affection-based socialisation necessary, if not inevitable. Rather than insist on explicit and self-conscious deference to their authority, parents quite willingly wrapped their demands and expectations in appropriate incentives of more complex roles and rewards within a step-by-step process toward self-governance. This allowed the young to focus on their own challenges and responsibilities on the path toward achievement and developmental maturation. The young, for their part, were not inclined to challenge the emerging structure of generational accommodation, by re-examining their past to quibble about parental pressures and channeling. Their focus was forward, upon their dramatically expanding options for initiative and advancement and upon abating the anxieties attending their success in an individualistic and competitive society.

In this way, a system of voluntary compliance was established in which individuals believed themselves no longer bound by social constraints but by limits of their own making. The central achievement of socialisation was the possession of 'character', now construed as the independent ability to function within the norms of the new social arenas. This moral system provided support for both personal initiative and the new common authorities of the adult liberal world. Raised with a 'self-regulating' character, attuned within to collective morality, the young were now equipped to leave their families and communities of origin. This novel 'agency model' of self and society was an individual able to balance the self-reliance and initiative necessary in an open society with the deference required for social integration. The agent was constituted to operate with great self-confidence and discretion, but always within the collective ends and authorised means set forth by the new society.[2]

So prepared, the new citizens went forth in orderly fashion to shape the dynamic society of the early Republic, turning the fearsome liberal 'state of (desocialised) nature' into a self-regulating society of self-socialising republican citizens. With the increasingly widespread and effective functioning of this socialisation and education process, the myth emerged that the 'character' of adult citizens resulting from it was the product, not of established institutional process or design, but rather a natural realisation of selfhood in a free society. By the post Civil War period, with vast new opportunities and incentives emerging in industrial society, with the new families and schools largely in place, the icon of a 'self-made' individual achieved cultural dominance. This was symbolised by the ubiquitous Horatio Alger myth, a popular literary genre of the era featuring youth, often orphans, who raise themselves to be successful economic actors and responsible citizens. That is to say, individuals were now presumed – and institutionally expected – to move inexorably, and as if without socialisation, toward the cues and rewards of liberal society.

This myth, of course, was that of American individualism, the consequence of the unconditioned will constituting a character that pursued its own wishes, moderated principally by personal reason and conscience. This enabled the new model of citizenship, the basis for later nineteenth and twentieth century American selfhood, to establish itself as the normal and even 'natural' model of individual development and human desire. By shaping a citizenry that embodied this character type, American society achieved an enviable integration, unleashing untold popular energies while overcoming pervasive doubts about the stability of post-traditional individualism. Socialisation receded as incidental to the self-shaping of the 'autonomous' citizen. In this idyllic conclusion lay both the power and capacity for mystification of American socialisation.

The American model today

Although the implications of this American construction of childhood for other modernising societies can only be briefly alluded to here, it is certain that economic globalisation and migration have ruptured the links with their traditional way of life and its institutional authorities for young people from all social classes. Individuals are moving pell-mell in pursuit of education, opportunity and even survival in patterns that are reminiscent of the early American experience. Despite strong efforts to retain the values and traditions of origin, the price of integration in the new order is, typically, adaptation to modern norms and procedures. This process of global relocation, moreover, is accompanied by the drumbeat of American youth culture – its music, movies and styles with their flaunting of novelty and release and disregard for generational hierarchy and constraint.

The impact on the socialisation of the young, as traditional family and educational structures are left behind, is profoundly disruptive. It creates what Giddens (1998) calls a problematic 'proliferation of family forms', including divorce, single parenthood, non-marriage and alternative family structures. While sanguine about such developments, he holds out the hope that, amidst the turmoil of a less rigidly structured child-rearing, will emerge a new 'story to tell about the family today,' how it is 'becoming democratized, in ways which track processes of public democracy (1998: 92–3).

The evidence from the American case, however, suggests a more complex picture, one in which families and children caught in these global shifts may lack the cultural resources to manage a successful transition. The demands of adjustment imposed on parents and children in the early American republic were, to be sure, as cataclysmic. However, they were cushioned by long prior exposure to a culture of increasing individualism and the on-going evolution of a voluntarist family structure. The premise that individuals will adapt creatively and productively to the challenges thrust upon them by the most recent wave of modernisation is, unfortunately, not borne out by the European experience of neo-traditional, i.e. politically fundamentalist, mass movements during the last century. In many societies today, not only are the economic forces radiating unmanageable shock waves on basic patterns of domestic life but even the forces of contemporary culture represent a systematic and unwanted imposition of alien values. American popular culture is widely regarded in the traditional world as threatening to existing cultural patterns.

Even American youth, with their liberalised socialisation experience, face challenges of unprecedented magnitude. The recurrent discussions of family breakdown, the struggles of young women and men for identity, the dangerously desocialised behaviour of peer group culture, present a picture of endemic instability within American socialisation practice. The very demands of voluntarism and individualism that transformed the American socialisation process have only sharpened its structural conflicts over time. With the ever-expanding demands of modern complex social organisation, youth have been constantly outstripping their elders with their quicker adaptation to urban and industrial society. The family and the schools have, in turn, been forced to keep pace, to catch up with the innovative demands of the young and to shape them for a world they understand, if anything, less well than the young themselves. The lesson that they have gathered from the earlier project – to win the child's will – have been employed repeatedly as the only convincing tool, given the voluntarist dynamic of liberal society.

While effective in inducing the child's commitment in the short run, this solution has been a double-edged sword. It has required continual accommodation within the family and schools to evolving child interests and wishes in order to retain the child's trust and engagement. It has also required continual innovation to prepare the child for modern options and functionality in the wider society. It has created a child-centered socialisation, and ultimately society, which affords only integration instead of real power. This structural resolution, the permissive family of the last fifty years, thus retains the synthesis of voluntarism and accommodation only in a severely compromised form – as socially-induced compliance on the one hand, spiritless commitment on the other. By retaining all the power, and refusing to promote the restructuring of mutual rights and responsibilities, parents in the permissive family watched their own power wane without helping anything to take its place.

The contradictions inherent in the permissive family and educational system and the increasing failure of socialising institutions to resolve them led to the attack on these institutions in the 1960s, to their temporary collapse and to the pervasive sense of irresolution that exists in America today. As a rising culture of reaction tries to shore up traditional socialising arrangements, with efforts of the religious and cultural right to restore authority in families and schools and strong cultural and behavioural controls over the young, those who hoped to transform the permissive family into a truly democratic one remain stymied by the complexity of the project and the absence of public support for innovation. Children and parents today are floundering amidst sharply conflicting demands and expectations, aspirations and fears, represented by this culture war of the last several decades. This confusion, on the part of adults, has led to the undermining of their credibility and de facto empowerment of the young, but not to the mobilisation of the legacy of democratic practice and individualism to shape a viable post-modern child rearing. Informal innovations are evolving at every level of socialisation, but the popular fear of revisiting earlier decades of empowered youth has obscured their visibility and policy implications.

Conclusion

It is difficult to forsee how the delicate integration of democratising socialisation processes, requiring great internal strengths and cultural supports, will arise, either in the US or elsewhere, given the profound stresses now being felt, without significant attention and social resources applied specifically to assisting families in transition (Barrett and McIntosh, 1991: 131–159). Outside of the efforts of individual therapeutic clinicians and sporadic youth empowerment initiatives, societies in the post-modern world have barely begun the educative work in schools and communities of preparing parents, teachers and children with more participatory and mutual, even rights-oriented, approaches to decision making and priority setting. It is foolish to believe that these adjustments will occur without forethought and planning.

Both in the US and elsewhere, the specter of globalisation offers a convenient escape hatch, enabling prophets of doom to claim that its shifts are too unstable to comprehend and too complex to manage. The price of such neglect, of course, is a worldwide dislocation of the young from environments promoting stability and growth. In the face of these challenges, the politics of childhood has become more important than ever. We must consider whether traditional child-rearing can or should be reconstituted. If the unprecedented features of post-industrial child-hood – a greater access to education, resources and culture – and the tra-jectory of the family have altered the structures of primary authority beyond recovery, new forms of selfhood and socialisation must be con-structively implemented and carefully nurtured. Whatever the direction chosen, the preparation of the young for post-modernity will be only as effective as the institutions the adult world provides for them. A con-temporary politics of childhood and, indeed, post-industrial politics as a whole, will only regain relevance by addressing these concerns which, perhaps more than any other, affect the future of modern society.

Notes

1. This chapter draws on a forthcoming book, *The Crucible of Consent: American Child-Rearing and the Forging of a Modern Nation,* to be published by Harvard University Press.
2. For a full discussion of the emergence of the agency paradigm and its histor-ical development in American culture, see Block 2002.

References

Bailyn, B. (1960) *Education in the Forming of American Society,* New York: Vintage.

Barrett, M. and McIntosh, M. (1991) *The Anti-social Family,* 2nd edn, London: Verso.

Block, J. (2002) *A Nation of Agents: The American Path to a Modern Self and Society,* Cambridge, Massachusetts: Harvard University Press.

Child, L. (1831) *The Mother's Book,* Boston: Carter and Hendee.

Deleuze, G. and Guattari, F. (1983) *Anti-Oedipus,* New York: Viking.

Donzelot, J. (1986) *The Policing of Families,* London: Hutchinson.

Forgie, G. (1979) *Patricide in the House Divided: A Psychological Interpretation of Lincoln and His Age,* New York: Norton.

Giddens, A. (1998) *The Third Way: The Renewal of Social Democracy,* Cambridge: Polity Press.

Goodrich, S. (1839) *Fireside Education,* London: William Smith.

Lathrop, J. (1991) 'A Sermon on a Day Appointed for Publick Thanksgiving,' in: Sandoz, E. (ed.), *Political Sermons of the American Founding Era: 1730–1805,* Indianapolis: Liberty Fund.

Locke, J. (1968) 'Some Thoughts Concerning Education,' in: Axtell, J (ed.), *The Educational Writings of John Locke,* Cambridge: Cambridge University Press.

Mather, M. (1991) 'America's Appeal to the Impartial World,' in: Sandoz, E. (ed.), *Political Sermons of the American Founding Era: 1730–1805,* Indianapolis: Liberty Fund.

Muzzey, A. (1858) *The Fireside: An Aid to Parents,* Boston: Crosby, Nichols, and Company.

Sigourney, L. (1838) *Letters to Mothers,* Hartford: Hudson and Skinner.

Todd, J. (1850) *The Young Man. Hints Addressed to the Young Men of the United States,* Northampton: Hopkins, Bridgman & Co.

4
The 'Shame of America': African-American Civil Rights and the Politics of Childhood

Rebecca de Schweinitz

Introduction

African Americans, from former slaves like Frederick Douglass and Harriet Jacobs to twentieth-century activists like W. E. B. Du Bois and Martin Luther King, Jr., commonly used ideas about childhood to explain the meaning of America's struggle for racial equality (Douglass, 1845; Du Bois, 1903; Jacobs, 1861). But unlike participants in that struggle, historians have not recognised the centrality of ideas about childhood to the civil rights movement. The recent explosion of interest in the history of childhood, however, has encouraged scholars to explore changing notions of childhood and the lived experiences of children in the past, and to connect the history of childhood to larger historiographical subjects and debates. This chapter suggests that ideas about childhood and children's rights in the post-WWII era significantly influenced the political culture of the United States and were central to the struggle for African-American civil rights and to public perceptions of that struggle. During this period, the politics of childhood encouraged America to protect its future and to prove its political fitness, and even legitimacy, by extending to *all* American children the rights of childhood.

Lost childhood in the 1930s

In the spring of 1931, word spread around the South that the black 'Brutes' responsible for ravaging two white women on a train near Scottsboro, Alabama had been convicted of their unspeakable crimes and sentenced to death in the electric chair. In the minds of white southerners, justice was finally to be done. After all, the *Chattanooga News* (1931) reported, the difference was like 'night and day' between 'the nine men who perpetrated those frightful deeds, and [a] normal, kind-hearted man who guards his little family and toils through the day, going home to loved ones at night with a song in his heart.' The difference between the way in which the white South and those defending the accused presented the Scottsboro case was also like night and day. While prosecutors and the white southern press described the nine defendants as men, savage and sexual, unquestionably capable, and so probably guilty of heinous crimes against southern woman-hood, defenders highlighted what came to be perhaps the most com-pelling aspect of the case. The nine accused were not men at all, but boys, children – the youngest only thirteen at the time, the oldest not yet twenty. These were not *men* capable of frightful deeds, or even men with families to guard, although the depression had forced them to seek work. These were *boys*, with mothers who worried when they did not return home and cried until they could not cry any more when they found out the Alabama penal system held their sons. As William Pickens, a field secretary for the National Association for the Advance-ment of Coloured People (NAACP) wrote in an editorial: 'newspapers ... refer to these colored children as negroes, saying nothing about their being mere children and leaving the impression on the ignorant public that they are men. That is part of their scheme to get them murdered without waking up public sympathy' (Pickens, 1931).

As Pickens and other defenders of the nine knew, black men, regard-less of their innocence, had little hope of eliciting public sympathy and less hope of finding justice. But black *children*, at least if they could be thought of as *children* first, might bring public pressure to bear on a southern court system dedicated to racial prejudice. White northerners, they knew, shared many of the South's racial beliefs, but beginning in the late eighteenth century they had become increas-ingly invested in sentimental definitions of childhood. Childhood, as defined by the white middle class, had become a sacred state, pro-tected by legal codes and cultural ideals (Zelizer, 1985; Grossberg, 1988). And so, the story of the Scottsboro 'boys,' as they quickly came to be known, was told and retold over the course of the next decade (as the case dragged on) in the black press, labour newspapers, reli-gious periodicals, national and international media, and even in some moderate southern papers as a story, not of crimes against white wo-manhood, as the white South insisted, but as a story of crimes against childhood.[1]

In this version, hailed as the '*real* story of Scottsboro,' each of the defendants were like 'puny' Eugene Williams, who did not 'look a day over his thirteen and a half years' and who grew up, the oldest of six children, in a leaky two-room hut on a muddy ally. The ninety cents his mother made taking in washing and ironing each week bought little food, so Eugene decided he would have a better chance of helping his family if he took to the rails. He might find a job down the line. At least there would be one less mouth to feed at home. Eugene and the other boys were admittedly 'poor and ignorant,' and most of them probably would never amount to much, but they were good boys, trying to do right by their families under the most deplorable of circumstances (Scottsboro Defense Committee, 1936).[2]

Just one year earlier, at the White House Conference on Child Health and Protection, President Hoover had supported the creation of a 'Children's Charter' which recognised 'the rights of the child as the first rights of citizenship' and pledged the US government's protection over specific points related to 'the health and welfare of children ... regardless of race, or color, or situation, wherever [they] may live under the ... American flag' (White House Document, 1930). But if the nine Scottsboro boys had a 'right' to a proper childhood, it was a right that had gone unrealised. In fact, as defenders noted, instead of finding state protection during their innocent and vulnerable years, the Scottsboro boys found themselves living in utter poverty and suffering from the very ills that America was supposed to guard its young against. Moreover, the state, which should have been taking care of them, had turned against them. Police harassed them, the courts lynched them, and jailers beat them. 'Nine negro children grow[ing] to young manhood in jail' – these boys, defenders argued, represented the 'shame of America' (Scottsboro Defense, 1936).

One reporter's description of the scene in Alabama in July of 1931 exemplified the ways in which defenders elicited public opinion in favour of the boys by calling on sentimental notions of childhood:

Down in Kilby prison tonight there sit in death row eight negro boys ... the youngest a slender stripling of fourteen. Unless the Alabama Supreme Court intervenes this mere child, who looks as though at any minute he might fling himself on his mother's breast and cry over a lost top or broken toy, will march with his seven fellows to the electric chair which sits grimly awaiting his hundred pounds of flesh just beyond the green door fifty feet from his cell ... the image of forlorn youth (Letter from Birmingham, 1931).[3]

Calling public attention to images of lost childhood had worked before, in other political contexts. Lewis Hine's photographs had shamed America into restricting industrial child labour and raising compulsory school attendance requirements. Images of stunted childhood had led to measures such as city ordinances on milk pasteurisation and congressional support for state-sponsored infant and maternal health clinics. Such images had led the US government to create the Children's Bureau, to hold deci-annual White House Conferences on children's issues and to establish the Children's Charter. It was also images of childhood betrayed – children who were forced to grow up because their families were torn apart, because of hard physical labour, cruel punishments, or the loss of sexual innocence – that had made Harriet Beecher Stowe's *Uncle's Tom's Cabin* such a powerful polemic against slavery. And it was precisely such images, captured by Dorthea Lange and other New Deal photographers, which were beginning to solidify political action on behalf of migrant families during the Depression.

But it was, after all, 1931, and while defenders of the boys did marshal public opinion to their cause and eventually free some of the boys (the younger ones first), black childhood, especially in the South, was not sacred in the way in which white middle-class childhood and all white womanhood was. For some, in fact, the idea of a separate state of childhood for blacks that needed protecting seemed impossible, since, according to racist philosophies, blacks, regardless of their age, lived in a perpetual state of childhood. As W. E. B. Du Bois (1935: 725–6) put it, 'they cannot conceive Negroes as men.'[4] It was sadly ironic that, in fact, black men could only attain the status of men when they seemed to threaten white womanhood and that, under such conditions, real black boys were denied their true status as children.

Over the course of the next twenty years, however, America would decide that the rights of childhood did indeed extend to black children and that the federal government should act to protect those rights. By the mid-1950s, linking the rights of childhood to civil rights became a powerful and effective way of eliciting public and political action. Many scholars have noted the ways in which World War II and the Cold War contributed to growing expectations on the part of African Americans for civil rights and to a general climate which required the US government to at least curb racism's most blatant manifestations. Those same events also stimulated increasing concern for America's children and gave child advocates new, compelling ways of arguing for greater protections for all children. As it turned out, extending the rights of childhood to all of America's children also meant extending civil rights to all Americans, as the two causes became, for a time, inextricably linked.

National security and the rights of childhood

During and after WWII, a number of questions arose. How can we safeguard our own country from Hitler-like despots? How can we keep democracy secure here and insure its triumph on the world stage? Also, how can we avoid the horrors of war in the future and live in peace? The answers to these questions all centered around children and involved extending the rights of childhood to all of the nation's young. It seemed that the Children's Bureau's assertion that 'the kind of vision we have in regard to children will largely determine the future of the world' might be true (Oettinger, 1958: 128).

To answer disturbing questions about the future of the country and the world, child welfare advisors, educators, and scholars increasingly turned to research on personality development. New studies linked prejudice to certain personality types, types which also tended to demonstrate ego weakness, fear, irrationality, emotionalism, irresponsibility, extreme egocentrism, uncreativeness, an inability to deal with anxiety, compulsive behaviours, and a tendency to follow authoritarian figures – not qualities which make ideal citizens (Arter, 1959; Bettelheim and Janoitz, 1946). Researchers described the prejudiced child as the 'disturbed child': 'fearful, insecure, maladjusted, unhappy; unconsciously seeking a scapegoat on whom to project his distressed feelings' (Alpenfels, 1948: 5). 'Subject to feelings of superiority', such children, scholars affirmed, would 'easily become victims of personality arrests' and were 'no safer than members of the minority group in situations where prejudice and discrimination are involved' (Kilpatrick, 1949: 564). Moreover, since prejudiced people were much more likely to turn to fascist-like rulers than were healthy, 'tolerant', people, racism threatened the survival of the nation itself.

Other studies during this time highlighted the emotional damage that segregation and discrimination fostered in black children. In their famous Doll Study, for instance, Kenneth B. and Mamie P. Clark found that the majority of African-American children they tested showed a marked preference for white dolls over 'colored' dolls

(Clark, 1952). Another oft-quoted study of black children similarly found that:

> Among kindergarten, first, and second grade [negro] children, there is much evidence of negative self-feelings and personal conflict concerning group belonging. Many children experience serious ego-threats as a result of group prejudices. Negro children reveal most vividly and often, the feelings of insecurity resulting from anticipated rejection or insult from white children (Radke, Trager and Davis, 1949: 442)

Such findings, child advocates warned, represented a serious 'harvest of neglect' (Lane, 1946: 273). If children, as new social science research testified, needed to be 'infused with a proper and wholesome self-esteem', then it was obvious that black children were hardly being given a 'fair chance to achieve a healthy personality.' In fact, child-experts argued, the daily toll of racism meant that black children in America suffered from an excessive number of personality defects. Greater care, studies warned, was needed in developing their personalities, otherwise they might, in frustration, turn to crime, moral cynicism and other anti-democratic ways (Caliver, 1943: 236–7; 1950; Clark, 1953: 113–7).

But while the current state of race relations did not bode well for the future well-being of the nation or its citizens, the good news, researchers reported, was that 'race prejudice is not instinctive' (Alpenfels, 1948: 4). There was a time, advocates asserted, before children were 'corrupted, by what Shelley calls "the world's slow stain" '(Ferguson,1951: 4). In fact, they said, '[I]f only children were brought up wisely, they could be happier ... able to live more successfully with one another ... [and] relatively free of ... intolerance' (Bettelheim and Janoitz, 1950: 290).

Luckily, there were already child-centered institutions in place perfectly fitted for the task – schools. Since its founding, America had regarded schools as the institution responsible for inculcating desirable qualities in its future citizens (see Block, this volume). By the 1940s, schools were considered not just the most 'important or potentially powerful agency in promoting assimilation,' but also 'in substituting reason for prejudice, knowledge for misunderstanding (Davie, 1939: 454–5),' encouraging 'critical social action ... techniques for co-operative living' (Burrell, 1948: 450) and in helping to extend the rights of childhood to all of America's children. 'Better public education, for both races,' advocates argued, would be the means by which the 'disease' of prejudice was 'conquered, economic opportunity created ... and tolerance built up' (Chambers, 1939: 467). As one white southerner and future editor of two prominent North Carolina newspapers told his classmates in his 1940s high school valedictory address, 'Our schools can do more than any other influence to break down the wall of prejudice. If schools have a world-wide mission, it is to clear up the idea that some are born superior to others in human rights' (Gaillard, 1988: 23).

Schools, advocates asserted, could re-make America as they met the emotional and mental health needs of all children and fought against prejudice – a task that seemed vital to the personality development of individual children and hence to the security of democracy. But World War II had revealed that an alarming number of Americans had grown up without even basic literacy skills, which made them unfit for military service and kept them from fully contributing to the American way of life. Child advocates and politicians alike cited military rejection statistics as alarming evidence of the kind of gross inequalities in American education that made the country vulnerable to its enemies. 'Negroes represented eleven percent of the first million draftees,' they quoted, 'but represented sixty percent of those rejected on account of functional illiteracy' (Caliver, 1943: 236). Such figures, both during World War II and as America's Cold War against communism developed, brought sustained attention to the cries of child advocates and education experts who called for measures to address the educational inequalities so evident in rural and Negro schools. America might not want to increase spending on education, but 'the lack of national wealth and strength' and 'the expense of the ignorance, inefficiency, and unsocial conduct which results when educational provision' was not made, seemed even greater costs (Caliver, 1940: 320). After all, warned experts, even 'the dullest mind' could not be neglected 'in one part of the country without penalties to the entire nation' (Meyer, 1946: 14). As the US Commissioner of Education explained the situation: 'We live in epic times. We are participants in a dramatic clash between two opposing sets of ideas' and epic times, he insisted, demanded that America sustain a 'high general level of education throughout the country,' improve the 'physical and mental health' of all its children, and develop its 'full potential manpower resources' (Studebaker, 1948: 2).

Child advocates also argued that inequalities in education not only wasted America's most precious resources, they actually turned those resources *against* America. Scholars asserted that low literacy rates among blacks 'cost us much in maladjustment, in crime, poverty, social conflicts, and disorganization'(Roucek, 1939: 499) and that the war 'made clear the connections between inadequate schools and juvenile delinquency' (Lundburg, 1943: 9). Experts looked at schools as potential 'bulwarks against delinquency,' but only if there were enough adequately equipped schools with qualified teachers (Children's Bureau, 1943: 7). America had the choice, they warned, to either improve educational opportunities for rural and minority children, which would add material and cultural wealth to the nation, or to continue producing 'unhappy, unproductive, and maladjusted' individuals who were likely to become delinquent or worse (Wexler, 1948).[5] Delinquency, poor relief, crime and other 'unsocial phenomena' were the costs of America's unequal schools (Brameld, 1940: 44). Children denied educational opportunities in the most democratic nation on earth, experts suggested, might even turn against democracy. In any case, it was a choice, the Children's Bureau said, 'between education and catastrophe' (Buck, 1943: 197).

Some experts also argued that severe educational inequalities weakened America internationally. Leaders argued that 'as long as our house is in disorder our actions will speak so loudly that others cannot hear what we say' (Frost, 1947: 4) and numerous studies comparing schools throughout the nation revealed much disorder or, as child advocates put it, 'uncovered conditions unworthy of a democracy' (Lenroot, 1940: 3–4). In fact, some observers suggested that the 'conditions in the poor south – or in places such as Harlem' were more 'tragic' than those which surrounded refugee children in World War II Europe (Universal Declaration of Human Rights, 1949: 141). The state of rural and black schools, they insisted, stood out as a 'blight on our national life,' (Schwellenbach, 1946: 136) revealing to the world that democracy, in the richest nation of the world had much 'unfinished business' (Eliot, 1952: 21).[6]

Evidence of racism directed toward American children also elicited intense international criticism because of a burgeoning world-wide sense that childhood was a sacred state that needed to be protected – a state that racial discrimination obviously violated. America's own efforts to extend the rights of childhood to all children reflected a larger trend that took place in much of the world. For example, not only had the 1948 United Nations Universal Declaration of Human Rights insisted that 'everyone is entitled to all the rights and freedoms set forth in this declaration, without distinction of any kind, such as race,' but Article 25 had also put the weight of the United Nations behind the idea that 'motherhood and childhood are entitled to special care and assistance.' It was bad enough that many Americans were 'not fully incorporated into [the American] democratic way of life', but it was an even greater offense to international values that many Americans did not enjoy the 'birthright of every child' (Lenroot, 1941: 3–4).

Schools and American democracy

In *Cold War Civil Rights: Race and the Image of American Democracy,* Mary Dudziak (2000) explores the ways that national security concerns intersected with the push for civil rights for African-Americans. America's concern for its image abroad, she argues, is what inspired civil rights reforms. Dudziak also notes that school segregation especially hurt America's image and was 'singled out for hostile foreign comment in the United Nations and elsewhere' (2000: 101). She does not, however, explain why it was public school segregation that provoked such strong international reactions. Nor does she explain why the Supreme Court choose to dismantle segregation with a case involving school children when, as she notes, there were a number of other cases that the Court could have chosen to rule on. But as the Scottsboro case revealed in the 1930s, and as other images that received widespread play in the international press in the 1950s and 60s would continue to reveal, images of children suffering from American racism generated intense criticism from outside as well as inside the country. If racial discrimination was an obvious defect of American democracy, then racial discrimination against children seemed an even more perverse affront to American ideals. Equality of opportunity became a rallying cry not just for civil rights activists but for a myriad of political and child welfare experts who saw it as 'the cornerstone of democracy' and the key to its survival (Lundberg, 1943: 8–9).

For education to be the cornerstone of democracy, however, schools not only had to give all children equal opportunities, they also had to *be* an 'experience in democratic living.' As the US commissioner of education counseled, 'education will not move democracy forward by merely teaching courses of study.' Instead, the school must become 'a place where democracy is practiced' (Studebaker, 1940: 35).[7] Educational experts noted that 'in the past the effort to develop good citizenship was largely restricted to learning the structure and history of democratic organisations while actual democratic behaviour was practically ignored with little or no attention paid to the spirit of the democratic person-to-person relationship.' But now, they asserted, every school 'must become a laboratory and nursery for citizenship,' teaching not only what democracy is, but also 'to love it, and to live it' (Douglas, 1937: 18).

But if it was only through the 'experience of democratic living' that children could be 'freed from ignorance, prejudice, suspicion and fear ... [and] educated for justice, liberty, and peace,' then it was unlikely that America's children would learn their lessons (UNESCO, 1946: 9). A 1949 checklist for determining '*How democratic is your school*' encouraged students to ask themselves questions such as, 'Are members of minority groups in your classes accepted by other students without condescension or aloofness?'(US Office of Education, 1949).[8] If such was the measure of a democratic school then Southern schools for whites only or Northern schools in racially segregated neighbourhoods were obviously not laboratories for good citizenship. And it hardly seemed possible that dilapidated schools composed entirely of black students would inspire those children to understand and appreciate the virtues of American democracy. As scholars increasingly pointed out, children asked to recite the pledge of allegiance and salute the flag in racially segregated schools, whether black or white, had every reason to distrust authority and 'rebel against society and against its hypocritical morals' (Blanshard, 1942: 122).

But of course, if prejudice, stereotypes, and the lack of personal relationships between different people were responsible for the problems of the world then, as Children's Bureau Chief Katharine Lenroot explained, children were the 'key with which to unlock the paradox of history.' For if the nation could 'reshape the life of one generation' then it 'could reshape the world' (1948: 3). Children held all the keys – they were the ones to change the world. If only their worlds were changed, so that *every* child enjoyed the rights of childhood.

The Brown decision and the rights of childhood

It was in this context that the United States Supreme Court made its historic decision in *Brown v. Board of Education*. Legal scholar Robert Mnookin (1985) has suggested that it was no accident that the decision which effectively dismantled America's colour line was a children's case. The Court, indeed, had ruled in other segregation cases before. But this case was more compelling than any pertaining to black adults. While the nation was willing to sit by and watch black men and women suffer under the segregationist practices and violence of Jim Crow, it was less willing to accept that children encountered the same discrimination and hostility. The cases involved in the *Brown* decision meant not just extending *civil rights* to African-Americans, but extending the *rights of childhood* to all children. The decision specifically upheld the right of children to the 'opportunity of an education ... on equal terms' and a right to a healthy mental development, making it sound very much like the Children's Charter (1954). While it would take another decade for Congress to address equal employment and voting rights for blacks, the court was willing to grant black Americans in the mid-1950s 'the first right of citizenship in a democracy ... to grow throughout childhood in good ... emotional and social health and security.' Ideas about childhood and public discussions linking the rights of children to a stronger democracy and world peace, as well as widespread beliefs, backed by current research, that children could effect significant social change, had made it difficult not to make what was deemed 'a morally right decision' in the *Brown* case (*Life,* 1955: 29).[9]

But, as observers on both sides of the fence at the time noted, getting rid of segregation was not just a matter of changing laws. Hearts, too, had to change. But that was exactly why America's children had been given the responsibility. And all the best research indicated that children were more than capable of the task. Parents, however, stuck in their obviously maladjusted personalities, resisted, with the very noble intention, not surprisingly, of saving their children. So civil rights activists had to continue to fight, themselves often turning to sentimental ideas about children, like they had in the Scottsboro case, to try and turn America's hearts.

One of the best examples of this was during the 1963 March on Washington. There, in his most famous oration, the Reverend Dr. Martin Luther King, Jr. spoke to Americans not as a minister, a civil rights activist, or even as an African-American man who had suffered from the many manifestations of racial prejudice and hatred. Instead, he spoke as a parent, explaining, in terms that every American father and mother could understand, the meaning of the civil rights movement. 'I have a dream that my four little children will one day live in a nation where they will not be judged by the color of their skin but by the content of their character... . Now is the time to open the doors of opportunity to all of God's children.'[10] Whether white Americans agreed with or even understood his desires for a new social, economic and political order, they could, at least, understand his dream that his children would have a better life. Identifying himself as a parent and calling on widespread beilefs about childhood made King's politics accessible to everyday Americans.[11] As scholars have noted, 'King's dream had no real nay-sayers' (Kirp, 1982: 25). After all, even if some whites did not like the idea of *black* equality, no one in 1960s America could argue against the sacredness of childhood.

Penned a few months before the March, King's famous 'Letter From Birmingham Jail,' explained the struggle for racial equality in similar, child-centered terms. He wrote:

> there comes a time when the cup of endurance runs over... . when you suddenly find your tongue twisted and your speech stammering as you seek to explain to your six-year-old daughter why she can't go to the public amusement park that has just been advertised on television, and see tears welling up in her eyes when she is told that Funtown is closed to colored children, and see ominous clouds of inferiority beginning to form in her little mental sky, and see her beginning to distort her personality by developing an unconscious bitterness toward white people; when you have to concoct an answer for a five-year-old who is asking: 'Daddy, why do white people treat colored people so mean?' (April 16, 1963)

Given the reasons behind the 1954 Supreme Court ruling and the country's post-war domestic-centered political orientation, equating the movement with a black father's dream for his children, with the ability of children themselves to dream, made the struggle for black equality understandable, even compelling, to the American public, black and white. Scholars have noted that King and the Southern Christian Leadership Coalition 'skillfully attuned its methods and its message to the idealism of the black church ... SCLC worked with the grain of southern black history and culture' (Fairclough, 1987: 404). King, and other civil rights leaders and organisations, however, also 'worked with the grain' of *American* culture, drawing on the *nation's* most important ideals and myths to argue for black equality, most notably, the nation's ideals and myths about childhood.

The March on Washington had actually been conceived of as a children's march from Alabama to the nation's capital. Following the Birmingham campaign, James Bevel, considered perhaps the best movement strategist, had proposed that they take school children, eager to be a part of the movement, on a longer march. Bevel knew that because of sentimental ideas about childhood the country would pay close attention if it involved young people. 'The nation would be enthralled' (Halberstam, 1998: 442).

Although the March was eventually (at least officially) restricted to those age fourteen and older, Bevel was right about what caught the nation's attention. A few months earlier, the SCLC had asked that Bevel and Andrew Young come to Birmingham to help recruit college students to participate in demonstrations. But hundreds of high school, junior high, and even elementary school age children enthusiastically joined the cause as well (Branch, 1988: 750–3). With their participation, the Birmingham campaign confirmed that it was children, and evidence of the ways that racism perverted ideal childhood, which pushed the public to the side of civil rights activists. Few people, black or white, paid attention to the campaign before school children began marching on May 2nd and leaders had little hope of realising any of their demands. But after the children joined in and police chief Bull Connor released his racist fury on them, Birmingham's black adult community and people across the country responded, including Kennedy's administration and members of Congress. The administration immediately sent Burke Marshall, the head of the justice department's civil rights division, to assess the situation. Congressional leaders compared Connor to Nazi storm troopers and called his assaults on school children a 'national disgrace' (Fairclough, 1987: 137) and 'the cries for equality in Birmingham' led President John F. Kennedy to voice his support for strong civil rights legislation. In a television and radio address he insisted:

> We face ... a moral crisis as a country and as a people ... It is time to act ... We cannot say to ten percent of the population that ... your children can't have the chance to develop whatever talents they have; that the only way that they are going to get their rights is to go into the streets and demonstrate.... . I am asking for your help in making it easier for us to move ahead and to provide the kind of equality of treatment which we would want ourselves; to give a chance for every child to be educated to the limits of his talents (June 11, 1963).

Kennedy was not the only one motivated to act boldly. Both blacks and whites who had previously stayed away from the movement experienced such a strong emotional response to the images of children under attack in Birmingham that they began to support the protests. As James Bevel said: 'It was time to defend the kids' (Hampton, 1990: 134).[12]

King explained that nonviolent protest 'dramatized the essential meaning of the conflict and in magnified strokes made clear who was the evildoer and who was the victim.' (Fairclough, 1987: 229). But it was really only when children became the victims that the meaning of the conflict came through. It was one thing for politicians and the public to see images of black adults being beaten and taken to jail, and quite another for them to see dogs and fire hoses unleashed on children. Attorney General Robert Kennedy had tried to convince civil rights leaders not to use children, arguing: 'an injured, maimed, or dead child is a price that none of us can afford to pay' (Fairclough, 1987: 126). But that was exactly the point. Not just adults, but countless black children had already been injured, maimed, and killed in the name of white supremacy. 'The disease of racism [was] already shaping the lives of these children and limiting their place' (Halberstam, 1998: 438).[13] Children, according to twentieth century definitions, could only be helpless victims and they deserved protection. By linking the cause of racial equality to the plight of children, by revealing that the 'invisible man' was sometimes a child, civil rights leaders touched America's conscious in a manner that would not let it turn away (Ellison, 1952). After Birmingham, Americans understood the price of prejudice. Especially when, a few months later, six black children were killed as a result of the bombing of a black church.

Interpreting the struggle for Civil Rights

The tactics that worked so well in the Birmingham campaign would be repeated and leaders would cite the images of children under attack from the Birmingham and Selma campaigns as key in helping to create the pressure to pass the Civil Rights Acts of 1964 and 1965. Throughout the history of the movement, it seemed to be images of children suffering under the pangs of Jim Crow that captured the attention of the nation and ultimately won widespread support for civil rights. At a 1944 NAACP Youth Council Conference workshop, leaders told attendees: 'The public is a tough nut to crack ... . Generally the public is apathetic ... Your job is to make them sympathetic' (Current, 1944). Use words, symbols, and ideas to attack others, they advised. Simplify, 'driving your program home, and identifying your fight as justifiable' (Lee, 1944). In the years after World War II, and especially after the Brown decision, nothing seemed to crack the public, to justify the struggle for civil rights, as much as proving that the social science researchers who testified before the Supreme Court were right; segregation hurt children. Pictures of Emmett

Till's mutilated body, neatly dressed black school children being attacked by white adults, police dogs, and fire hoses disturbed an America that was not yet unequivocally committed to the idea of *African-American* equality. Northern whites, who otherwise considered civil rights organisations too radical, were shocked by photos of Dorothy Counts, the Little Rock Nine and headlines of schools being bombed. Such images made clear that American racism had 'no restraining influence of decency', that it threatened not just the civil and political rights of blacks, it threatened childhood (Williams, 1987: 52).[14]

But if linking the plight of African-Americans to ideas about childhood garnered sympathy and support for civil rights it also, however, shaped and limited that support. Historians of women and gender have shown the limits of basing pleas for social, political, and economic change on women's special qualities and gender distinctions (Scott, 1986). Basing pleas for change on notions of childhood have proven just as limiting, for childhood, like gender, signifies relationships of power. White America was willing to come to the aid of black children – or at least to protect the ideal of childhood. But as the controversies surrounding busing and affirmative action revealed, only if it did not affect white children too much. When integration struggles moved north and westward and it became clear that achieving racial equality would require more than an abstract belief in democratic principles and the rights of childhood, even white liberals began sounding very much like southern segregationists. As one white New York City parent complained about busing:

> Of course I understand that Negro and Puerto Rican parents want a decent education for their children, just as I do for mine... . we must be prepared to live with them as equals and even to make sacrifices to that end. Just so long as we are not expected to sacrifice children! (Stern, 1964: 2–3)

The country was also less willing to systematically address the concerns of black adults. Black children were guaranteed the rights of childhood; schools were desegregated (at least officially), and Head Start programs funded, but many of the African-American communities' other concerns were never seriously addressed. Moreover, the nation experienced a massive white backlash in the late sixties as soon as blacks moved away from linking their cause to children's rights, began focusing on labour and housing issues, Vietnam, and Black Power, and abandoned child-like resistance strategies. Linking ideas about childhood to the plight of African-Americans had required the state, in its role as parent, to protect blacks. But decidedly un-childlike blacks, intent on realising economic independence and equal property rights – long the American determinants of manhood – neither required or deserved the state to act, however timidly, as a guardian to the African-American community. Positive interpretations of the struggle for racial equality depended on ideas about childhood.

Conclusion

Ideas about and images of children have been used to elicit support for a wide variety of social and political causes in twentieth-century America and throughout the world. This exploration of the connections between ideas about childhood and the struggle for African-American civil rights shows the centrality of ideas about childhood to the history of the civil rights movement and that how we think about children can, and does, influence important socio-political issues. It also suggests, however, the limits of basing pleas for social and political change on ideas about childhood – limits that more recent political activists have also discovered. In the 1990s, for instance, images of young Elian Gonzalez and the murdered teenagers at Colorado's Columbine High School were used to raise questions about restrictive US immigration policies and lax gun control laws. But in neither case could images of children or appeals to ideas about childhood effect fundamental political change on those issues.

Since images of children and ideas about childhood have so commonly been used to elicit support for civil rights, but since racial equality remains elusive, it is, perhaps, not surprising that, today, books like Ken Light's *Delta Time* (1995), Jonathan Kozol's *Amazing Grace* (1996) and Alex Kotlowitz's, *There Are No Children Here* (1992) demonstrate the problems of American minorities by showing that the lives of many children in both the rural South and America's cities still bear no resemblance to the childhood we idealise. Indeed, today's minority children may not face lynch mobs or dogs and fire hoses, and they are more likely to receive a fair legal trial, but many remain victims of poverty and race. Just like those nine boys in 1931.

Notes
1. On the Scottsboro Boys case see Goodman (1995) While he explores different perspectives of the case Goodman does not examine the case in terms of historically grounded ideas about childhood.

2. See also *The Nation* June 3, 31. This article can be found in the NAACP Papers part 6 (reel 8).
3. A newsclip of this letter dated May 4, 31 can be found in the NAACP Papers part 6 reel 2.
4. Du Bois was specifically referring to historians of Reconstruction, but his comment can certainly be applied more broadly.
5. See also Caliver (1940); Meyer (1946).
6. Mary L. Dudziak (2000) argues that America's concern for its image abroad is what inspired civil rights reforms. Dudziak also notes that school segregation especially hurt America's image, and was 'singled out for hostile foreign comment in the United Nations and elsewhere (101).'
7. On these points see also Studebaker 1942; Phillipson 1953; Children's Bureau, 1946.
8. This particular checklist was reprinted in *School Life* vol. 31 no. 9, p. 2.
9. On the use of social science research in the *Brown* ruling see also Jackson (2001) and Patterson (2001). Jackson suggests that one reason scholars have not noted the centrality of social science research on race prejudice and children to the 1954 *Brown* ruling is because of later criticisms of that research – criticisms which, as his book shows, failed to take into account the context that research was conducted and produced in as well as what that research was trying to communicate. My study helps provide more of the context surrounding the *Brown* decision and the social science research that helped form it. Kenneth Clark and others whom Jackson talks about were just a *few* of the many different kinds of 'experts' and public officials involved in *public* discussions about children, prejudice, education, and civil rights in the 1940s and 50s. Moreover, the kinds of arguments that social scientists made to the Supreme Court also appeared in a variety of cultural forms, including parent's magazines, fiction, biography, African-American periodicals, and children's literature. Patterson points out that of the five cases covered in the *Brown* ruling, the Topeka case took 'top billing' because the psychological child-centred arguments that the Legal Defense Fund attorney's relied on in that particular case 'resonated' with the presiding judge in Kansas, and with the Supreme Court. I would add that they likely resonated with the American public as well.
10. There were, of course, speakers other than King at the March on Washington, and King himself had more to say about the Movement than that he had a dream for children. It seems striking, however, that almost immediately (at least in the national media and in popular memory) the March became connected with ideas about childhood. Charles Payne (1995), among other historians, decries the 'Big Event' telling of the Civil Rights Movement and the ways the media distorted the movement. It seems, however, that rather than dismissing the way the story of the movement was told in the press and remembered by every-day Americans we need to look more closely at how and why the story was told in the way that it was, and what that telling meant for the movement, other than perhaps 'distorting it.' On this and other points discussed in this chapter see the larger study from which this paper is taken (de Schweinitz, 2004).

11. This was especially true, since, as Elaine Tyler May (1988) explains, both fathers and mothers in post-WWII America were encouraged to focus their energy, attention, and ambitions on their children.
12. David Garrow (1980) explores how images of violence in the Birmingham and Selma campaigns captured support for the Movement. It was, however, not just images of violence that moved the public and their political representatives, but rather, and I believe significantly, images of violence against children, that, time and again, were chosen to convey the meaning of civil rights events and issues. Arthur Waskow (1975) argues that the photograph of a Birmingham police dog leaping at the throat of a black school boy turned 'the 1960s generation of "new Negroes" ... into a major social force. Intense pressure upon president John F. Kennedy to initiate federal action began to be applied the moment that photo appeared ... . financial and political support for all civil rights organizations multiplied at once.' After the Birmingham campaign, the movement 'meant not only an abstract demand for social change but the concrete and immediate protection of their children (page 234).'
13. Halberstam also looks at the debate among civil rights leaders on using children in the Birmingham campaign (see pages 438–440).
14. Williams is quoting Roy Wilkins. On this point see also Whitfield (1988) 46; Sitkoff (1981) 28.

References

Alpenfels, E. J.(1948) 'The Price of Prejudice', *National Parent Teacher* 5.
Arter, R. M. (1959) 'The Effects of Prejudice on Children', *Children* 6, no. 5.
Blanshard, P. (1942) 'Negro Delinquency in New York,' *Journal of Educational Sociology* (Oct.)
Brameld, T. (1940) 'Educational Costs,' in R. M. MacIver, (ed.), *Discrimination and National Welfare*. New York: Institute for Religious and Social Studies.
Brown *et al. v.* Board of Education of Topeka *et al.*, 347 US 483.
Bettelheim, B. and Morris J. (1946) 'Social Change and the Dynamics of Prejudice' in E. Hartley (ed.) *Problems in Prejudice,* New York: King's Crown Press.
Bettelheim, Bruno and Morris Janoitz, (eds) (1950) 1964. *Social Change and Prejudice*. New York: The Free Press of Glencoe.
Branch, T. (1988) *Parting the Waters: America in the King years, 1954–1963*. New York: Simon and Schuster.
Buck, P. S. (1943) 'Save the Children For What?' *Journal of Educational Sociology* (Dec.).
Burrell, A. P. (1948) 'American Education, The Contribution To The Dignity and Worth of the Individual,' *Journal of Education Sociology* (March).
Caliver, A. (1940) 'Secondary Schools for Negroes', *School Life*. 25 no. 10.
Caliver, A. (1943) 'The Negro Child in the World Chaos', *Journal of Educational Sociology* (Dec.).
Chambers, M. M. (1939) 'Culture Conflicts and the Welfare of Youth', *Journal of Educational Sociology* (April).
Children's Bureau (1946) *Conclusion Resolutions on Behalf of the Youth of the World*, Publication 315. Washington D.C.: U.S. Department of Labor.

Children's Bureau. (1943) *Controlling Juvenile Delinquency: A Community Program*. Publication 301. Washington D.C.: United States Government Printing Office.

Clark, K. B. (1953) 'Race Prejudice and Children', *The Child*. 17 no. 7.

Clark, K. B. and Mamie, P. (1958) 'Racial Identification and Preference in Negro Children', in E. E. Maccoby, T. M. Newcomb, and E. L. Hartley, (eds), *Readings in Social Psychology*, 3rd edition Henry Holt and Company: New York.

Current, G. (1944) 'ABC's of Mass Pressure: A Simple Bulletin of Techniques to Use in Mass Pressure', in: *Report of 1944 Youth Conference*, NAACP Papers Part 19 Series B Group II Box E-6 (Reel 5).

de Schweinitz, R. (2004) '"If They Could Change the World:" Children, Childhood, and African-American Civil Rights Politics' (Ph.D. diss., University of Virginia).

Davie, M. R. (1939) 'Minorities: A Challenge to American Democracy,' *Journal of Educational Sociology* (April).

Douglas, H. R. (1937) 'Secondary Education for Youth in Modern America,' *A Report to the American Youth Commission of the American Council on Education*. Washington D.C.: American Council on Education.

Douglass, F. (1970) *My Bondage and My Freedom*. Chicago: Johnson Publishing Company Inc. (First published 1845).

Du Bois, W. E. B. (1935) *Black Reconstruction; An Essay Toward A History of the Part Which Black Folk Played in the Attempt to Reconstruct Democracy in America*. Reprint Services.

Du Bois, W. E. B. (1965) *The Souls of Black Folks*, in *Three Negro Classics*. New York: HarperCollins Publishers (First published 1903).

Dudziak, M. L. (2000) *Cold War Civil Rights: Race and the Image of American Democracy*. Princeton: University Press.

Eliot, M. (1952) 'Furthering Individual Well-being Through Social Welfare,' *The Child*. 17 no. 2.

Ellison, R. (1952) *The Invisible Man*. New York: Random House.

Fairclough, A. (1987) *To Redeem the Soul of America: The Southern Christian Leadership Conference and Martin Luther King, Jr*. Athens: University of Georgia Press.

Felix, R. H. (1949) 'The Teacher's Role in Mental Health Defense', *School Life* 31 no. 4.

Ferguson, C. W. (1951) 'Public Spirited Youth', *National Parent Teacher* (Feb.).

Gaillard, F. (1988) *The Dream Long Deferred*. Chapel Hill: University of North Carolina Press.

Garrow, D. (1980) *Protest at Selma: Martin Luther King, Jr. and the Voting Rights Act of 1965*. New Haven: Yale University Press.

Goodman, J. (1995) *Stories of Scottsboro*. New York: Vintage Books.

Grossberg, M. (1988) *Governing the Hearth: Law and Family in Nineteenth-Century America*. Chapel Hill: University of North Carolina Press.

Halberstam, D. (1998) *The Children*. New York: Random House.

Hampton, H., Fayer, A. and Flynn, S. (eds) (1990) *Voices of Freedom: An Oral History of the Civil Rights Movement from the 1950s through the 1980s*. New York: Bantam Books.

Jacobs, H. (1987) *Incidents in the Life of a Slave Girl, Written by Herself*, Jean Fagan Yellin (ed.) Cambridge, Mass: Harvard University Press. (First published 1861).

Jackson, Jr., J. P. (2001) *Social Scientists for Social Justice: Making the Case Against Segregation*. New York: New York University Press.

Kennedy, J. F. June 11, 1963. 'The Negro and the American Promise.' *Congressional Record*, 88 Cong., 1 Sess., 10965–10966.

Kilpatrick, W. H., Stone, W. J. and Cole, S. G. (1949) 'A Frame of Reference for Intercultural Education', *Journal of Educational Sociology* (May).

Kirp, D. L. (1982) *Just Schools: The Idea of Racial Equality in American Education*. Berkeley: University of California Press.

Kotlowitz, A. (1992) *There Are No Children Here: The Story of Two Boys Growing Up in the Other America*. New York: Anchor Books.

Kozel, J. (1996) *Amazing Grace: Lives of Children and the Conscience of a Nation*. New York: Harper Perennial.

Lane, H. A. (1946) 'An Education-Centered Community Can Care for Children', *Journal of Educational Sociology* (Jan.).

Lee, A. (1944) 'Use of Propaganda,' in *Report of 1944 Youth Conference*, NAACP Papers Part 19 Series B Group II Box E-6 (Reel 5).

Lenroot, K. (1948) 'Children in a Free Society', *The Child*. 13 no. 1.

Lenroot, K. (1941) *A Democracy's Responsibility to its Children*, Pennsylvania State Conference of Social Work (Reading, Pennsylvania, Feb. 20).

Light, K. (1995) *Delta Time: Mississippi Photographs*. Washington D.C.: Smithsonian Institution Press.

Lundburg, E. O. (1943) 'Security For Children in Post-War Years: Objectives of State and Community Action,' *The Child*. 8 (July).

May, E. Tyler (1988) *Homeward Bound: American Families in the Cold War Era*. New York: Basic Books.

Meyer, Mrs. Eugene (1946) 'New Values in Education', *School Life* (Feb.).

Mid-Century White House Conference on Children and Youth (1950) *A Fair Chance for a Healthy Personality*. Washington D.C.: Conference publication.

Mnookin, R. (1985) *In The Interest of Children: Advocacy Law Reform and Public Policy*. San Francisco: W. H. Freeman and Co.

'A Morally Right Decision: An Arkansas School Board Does Some Searching and Negro Children Enter Desegregated Classes,' *Life* 39 no. 4 (July 25, 1955).

Oettinger, K. B. (1958) 'Current Concern of the Children's Bureau', *Children* 5 no. 4

Phillipson, E. (1953) 'Follow up of 1950 White House Conference Enters a New Stage: National Committee hands Torch To Other Groups', *The Child*. 17 no. 8.

Pickens, W. (1931) Editorial. *New York Herald Tribune*, April 15.

Patterson, J. T. (2001) *Brown v. Board of Education: A Civil Rights Milestone and Its Troubled Legacy*. New York: Oxford University Press.

Payne, C. (1995) *I've Got the Light of Freedom: The Organizing Tradition and the Mississippi Freedom Struggle*. Berkeley: University of California Press.

Radke, T. and Davis, M. (1949) 'Social Perceptions and Attitudes of Children', *Genetic Psychology Monographs*.

Rayburn, S. (1945) 'That Civilization May Survive', *School Life* (Oct.).

Roucek, J. S. (1939) 'Future Steps in Cultural Pluralism', *Journal of Educational Sociology* (April).

Scottsboro Defense Committee (1936) *Scottsboro; The Shame of America: The True Story and the true Meaning of this Famous Case.* New York: The Scottsboro Defense Committee.

Scottsboro Defense Committee (1936) *The Real Story of Scottsboro.* New York: Scottsboro Defense Committee.

Schwellenbach, L. N. (1946) 'Put Children First', *The Child.* 10 no. 9.

Scott, J. (1986) 'Gender: A Useful Category of Historical Analysis,' *American Historical Review.* 91 no. 5: 1053–1975.

Sitkoff, H. (1983) *The Struggle for Black Equality, 1954–1992.* New York: Hill & Wang.

Spock, B. (1951) 'Development of Healthy Personalities', *School Life.* 33 no. 6.

Stern, P. (1964) 'What Price Integration?' *Congress of Racial Equality Papers A*: I: 87 (Reel 3).

Studebaker, J. W. (1948) 'Communism's Challenge to American Education', *School Life* 30 no. 5.

Studebaker, J. W. (1942) 'The Education of Free men in American Democracy', *School Life* 27 no. 1.

'UNESCO,' *School Life.* 29 no. 1.

U.S. Office of Education (1949) *How Democratic is Your School? Checklists on Democratic Practices for Secondary Schools.* Washington D.C.: U.S. Govt. Printing Office.

Waskow, A. I. (1975) *From Race Riot to Sit-In, 1919 and the 1960s: A Study in the Connections Between Conflict and Violence.* Glouster, Mass.: Peter Smith.

Wexler, I. L. (1948) 'An Adventure in Neighborhood Councils. Located in CF 102, 49–52, 8–6–0, Box 434, Children's Bureau Papers, National Archives II, College Park, Maryland.

Whitfield, S. J. (1988) *A Death in the Delta: The Story of Emmett Till.* New York: The Free Press.

Williams, J. (1987) *Eyes on the Prize: America's Civil Rights Years, 1954–1965.* New York: Viking Press.

Zelizer, V. A. (1985) *Pricing the Priceless Child: The Changing Social Value of Children.* Princeton: Princeton University Press.

Part Two
Children, Money and Work

5
Child Labour and Children's Rights: Policy Issues in Three Affluent Societies

Wiebina Heesterman

Introduction

The previous two decades saw important changes in attitudes and approaches towards children and young people. Whereas in the past children tended to be treated as little more than appendages of their parents, the adoption of the *United Nations Convention on the Rights of the Child (UNCRC)* constructs young people as subjects of rights rather than mere objects to be protected. There are indications that the *UNCRC* is beginning to have an impact, in particular where a culture of rights is already in existence (Woll, 2000).

This chapter addresses policy issues related to the right of the child to protection from exploitation. It discusses the treatment of this right in International Conventions, followed by a comparison of different approaches to child labour legislation in three affluent[1] societies, where one may assume that child policies are not being determined by expediency or financial constraints. These are two European Union countries, Britain and the Netherlands, both States Parties to the *UNCRC*, the International Labour Organisation (ILO) *Minimum Age* and *Worst Forms of Child Labour Conventions* and California, a member State of the United States, which tends to leave human rights Conventions unratified after signing.[2]

In the West, the right to freedom from economic exploitation has long been considered uncontroversial. We have become used to a curious dichotomy where work performed by children is either a matter of exploitation that has to be curbed by forbidding them to work altogether, or a commendable educational activity that needs to be kept in check by hours legislation. Neither perspective asks why

labour standards, developed to protect adult employees from exploitation, such as 'safe and healthy working conditions' (Art. 7(b),
International Covenant on Economic, Social and Cultural Rights), should
not be applicable to young workers.

The literature on child labour

The literature relating to work by children and young people is wide-
ranging, and takes many different forms: child labour has been the
subject of International Conventions, government reports and academic papers. Until the 1980s, the interest in the work of children was
mainly historical (Cunningham, 1991; Trattner, 1970; Zelizer, 1985), as
the economic exploitation of children in Western Europe and the USA
was regarded as having been eliminated. The publicity surrounding the
events organised in connection with the Year of the Child (1979)
clearly showed that this belief was held in error: child labour occurred
on a much larger scale than expected, despite the ubiquitous enactment of legislation intended to curb the practice.[3] Before the late
1970s, few publications were concerned with present-day child work,
and then only in the affluent part of the world; for instance, a report
on the economic activities of school children in Britain (Davies, 1972).

   A spate of publications on the economic activities of children was set
in motion with studies commissioned by the Anti-Slavery Society and
the ILO, focusing on the exploitation of children in the Third World
(Challis and Elliman, 1979; Mendelievich, 1979). Despite their emphasis on developing countries, both contained sections relating to
child labour in industrial nations. Particular concerns have been raised
over the phenomenon of 'street children' working for survival in a
variety of trades, such as shoe shining, rag picking and hawking
(International Labour Office, 2002: para 85). It is often assumed that
these children spend the night anywhere, subsisting without the protection of their families, and are therefore exposed to police and other
abuses and maltreatment (Glauser, 1997: 147). Work with 'street children' shows, however, that this is a one-dimensional view: many of
these children return home to sleep after work, whilst others do so
every few days or during the winter months (Glauser, 1997: 147).
Many also contribute to the family economy.

   It is less well known that the 'street children' problem has its coun-
terpart in the developed world, occasioned by family breakdown,
failure of the asylum system, and, in Eastern Europe, the collapse of
the communist regime (International Labour Office, 2002: para 86).

Many of these homeless young people are in their teens. To give an example, out of 117 homeless people found in a Dutch town of some 160,000 inhabitants, eighteen were aged between twelve and eighteen (Tweede Kamer der Staten-Generaal, 2000–2001: 33). Few have contacts with home and family. Apart from the inadequate provision of substitute accommodation, these young people have little choice other than to engage in irregular and semi-illegal activities such as prostitution, a means of survival for children in many parts of the world (Fyfe, 1989: 117; Woodhead, 1999: 31).

Lately, doubts have been cast on the consensus that children in irregular activities should in all circumstances be regarded as victims to be protected through relocation from the labour market to the schoolroom, as earlier advocated (Fyfe, 1989; Alston, 1989; ILO, 1996). It has been argued that the Western ideal of a carefree childhood of play and schooling does not suit all contexts (Boyden, 1997). Instead, children deserve to be regarded as social actors with the competence to make the best of difficult circumstances, possibly by combining work and schooling (Woodhead, 1999: 29)

During the 1980s, research on child work in the affluent part of the world tended to concentrate on the advantages and/or detriments of the work of young people, such as the social and educational implications of teenage work (Greenberger and Steinberg, 1986). In the early 1990s, increases in violations of child labour legislation gave rise to a number of surveys on the extent and nature of child work, for instance in the UK (Hobbs, Lavalette *et al.*, 1992; Pond, Searle *et al.*, 1991) and the USA (General Accounting Office, 1991). Around the same time, preparations began for a complete overhaul of Dutch labour legislation in order to include two chapters concerned with children and young people. Research commissioned by the Ministry of Social Affairs and Labour Opportunities made use of interviews with children as well as with professionals working with young people (Neve and Renooy, 1989), a methodology taking account of the perspectives of young people which has become the norm for child research in the 1990s (see, e.g. Pettit, 1998). The fact that the employment of children is a common feature of life in many affluent countries has been confirmed by reports from Germany (Deutsche Bundestag, 2000) and Denmark (Frederiksen, 1999).

Approaches of Children's Rights Conventions

Two important International Conventions concerned with work by children and young people are the 1973 ILO *Minimum Age*

Convention and the 1999 ILO *Worst Forms of Child Labour Convention*.
Both Conventions place work by children and young people firmly in
the sphere of protection by means of exclusion from the workplace. In
consequence, the adoption of legislation specifically aimed at children
serves to accentuate the division between rights considered appropriate
for adults and those regarded acceptable for children. Other agreements, such as the 1973 ILO Minimum Age Recommendation and the
EU Council Directive 94/33/EC on the Protection of Young People at
Work, although also cast in the protective mould, provide for entitlements as well as regulation of hours and conditions of employment.
These take the form of minimum wages[4] and/or adequate rest periods.
Article 32 of the UNCRC, which is concerned with economic exploitation, is couched in language similar to the *Minimum Age Convention*.
However, the Committee on the Rights of the Child has indicated that
all provisions, including the right to protection from exploitation,
need to be interpreted in the light of four articles of over-arching
importance. These are Articles 2, 'Non-discrimination,' 3, 'The Best
Interest of the Child,' 6, 'The right to Life, Survival and Development'
and 12, 'Respect for the Views of the Child' (Committee on the Rights
of the Child, 1991: paras 13–14).

Implementation of youth policy and labour standards in the societies under comparison

Conventions concerned with children and young people, such as the
UNCRC and the ILO Conventions, aim at world-wide standard setting,
obligating States Parties both to incorporate their provisions in
national legislation and to take their enforcement seriously. To that
end, ratifying States undertake to submit periodic reports to the respective committees created to oversee the progress of States Parties
towards implementation of the provisions.

Unlike the UK and the Netherlands, the USA is not bound to observe
these guidelines because of its failure to ratify. According to a comparison of US domestic legislation with the *UNCRC* (Cohen and
Davidson, 1990), ratification of the Convention would advance the
cause of children. The chapter on economic exploitation was an exception, claiming that ratification would not make any difference to issues
of economic exploitation, as US federal child labour legislation already
met the standards of Art. 32 of the *UNCRC* (Boskey, 1990: 314). This
view ignores the fact that the Federal legislation lacks provisions for
child work in the entertainment industry, agriculture and newspaper

delivery, whilst glossing over the abuses in agriculture (Human Rights Watch, 2000) and the extent of sexual exploitation of juveniles (Weisberg, 1985).

So far, the USA has ratified the 1999 ILO *Convention on the Worst Forms of Child Labour* and two Optional Protocols to the *UNCRC*, on 'the Involvement of Children in Armed Conflicts', and 'the Sale of Children, Child Prostitution and Child Pornography', without becoming a party to the *UNCRC* itself. As these Protocols have been conceived as irrelevant to the US domestic situation,[5] the US does not appear to be subject to any children's rights Conventions that have a bearing on legal provisions concerning the work of children and young people. However, reports on the implementation of the requirements of the Optional Protocols need to take account of the general principles of the UNCRC, in the same way as the reports to the Convention itself (United Nations Commission for Human Rights, 2002).

The diagram below charts the relationship between a commitment to the rights of children, in particular to protection from economic and sexual exploitation, as translated into the national legislation of the societies being compared and the implementation of this right – ultimately a question of adequate funding.

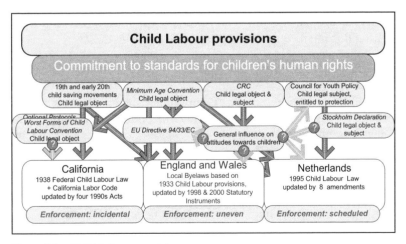

Figure 5.1   Child Labour provisions

One can see from this diagram that the two European States, on the other hand, are committed to the implementation of EU legislation, such as Directive 94/33/EC, as well as to International Conventions. Like other EU member states, they are also subject to standard setting by international agreements, such as the 1961 *European Social Charter* and *Recommendation 1286, a European Strategy for Children*, that emphasises the importance of taking account of the rights, interests and needs of children. Whilst the UK did not ratify the *Minimum Age Convention* until 2000, and opted out of part of *Directive 94/33/EC* until 1998, children's issues were promised a higher profile in the Green Paper published in September 2003. The emphasis is on care for younger children rather than issues relating to adolescents. It recognises, however, that young people may be involved in prostitution and/or become homeless and in need of independent accommodation. (Great Britain, Treasury, 2003: paras 2.44, 2.46). The Green Paper also sets out proposals for the establishment of an independent Commissioner for Children and Young People, stating that real improvements are possible only with the involvement of young people themselves (Great Britain, Treasury, 2003: para 5.1). In addition, it advocates the creation of a new offence of 'commercial sexual exploitation of a child,' no longer constructing victims as offenders. Although the proposed measures are in line with the recommendations of the Committee on the Rights of the Child (2002) and the Stockholm *Declaration* and *Agenda for Action* of the 1996 World Congress against Commercial Sexual Exploitation of Children, neither document is mentioned in the Green Paper.

Assumptions and expectations

The subject of child labour is dominated by expressions which depend on associative meanings. The term 'child labour' conjures up images of physical hard work and exploitation, characterised by 'activities, which impair the health and development of children', described as a 'subset of child work' (Fyfe, 1989: 19). In consequence, child labour is seen as a denial of childhood, robbing a child of the carefree existence which, in the West, tends to be regarded as his/her birthright. The view that children should be protected and shielded from any unpleasantness constructs them, at the same time, as helpless and as different from adults (Jenks, 1996: 120, 123). Both International Conventions and domestic legislation aiming at the regulation of child labour start from the premise that children are likely to be subject to 'harm' when venturing into the adult world of work. However, a distinction made in certain developing societies between the expressions 'child labour' and 'child work' illustrates the rule that meaning depends on context. Instead of distinguishing between the exploitative and the neutral, the expressions differentiate between the money-generating 'labour' which is the prerogative of males and takes place in the public sphere and the invisible, unpaid and little regarded 'work' of girls in the privacy of the home (Khair, 2000: 122).

Because of the perceived pejorative sense of the expression 'child labour' in the West, a more acceptable term is 'child employment', as in recent publications on the work of children in the UK (Lavalette, 1994). Unlike 'child labour', 'child employment' is regarded as an activity that helps young people to grow into responsible adults. However, any work in which children engage is considered subordinate to education, sometimes called the 'real work' of young people, an occupation which benefits society as well as each child. This has been expressed by Congressman Lantos in the USA as follows: 'the most important job for our young people, who represent the future of our nation, is to get an education' (1992: 67), whilst Qvortrup argues that schoolwork ought to be regarded as 'part of the diachronic division of labour' (2001: 100). The fact that schooling is a duty towards society, as well as a right of children, additionally finds expression in the *UNCRC*: that education be directed, amongst other things, to development 'of respect for human rights', 'the national values of the country in which the child is living' and 'responsible life in a free society' (Art. 29(1)(b-d)).

The word 'child' itself is open to a myriad of interpretations, in the West being invariably linked to 'age' in national legislation as well as in recent child rights Instruments (*UNCRC*, Art. 1, and its optional protocols; EU *Directive 94/33/EC*). Whilst children in developed countries are regarded as dependent until well into their teens, in many others they are expected to assume responsibilities from an early age (Boyden, 1997: 203). Here, for example, one could think of the predicament of children of AIDS-stricken families in the Third World, caring for younger siblings. However, even in the affluent North teenagers may find themselves compelled to take on the adult role of caring for parents with physical or mental health problems (Aldridge and Becker, 1993). Regarding these children as objects of pity, however, to be relieved of their burden rather than consulted concerning their priorities and supported in their task, deprives them of the satisfaction of being treated as responsible people (see also Thomas, this volume).

The nature of child work

Both in poor and rich countries, exploitative practices involving young people coexist with regulated occupations which seldom involve any contractual obligations.[6] Children perform a multitude of tasks under the guise of 'giving a hand,' such as housework and helping on family farms; activities seldom regarded as 'work,' however time-consuming and onerous they may be (Morrow, 1996; see also Seymour, this volume). In addition, it is unclear whether activities in which a child is exceptionally successful, over and above the achievements of the average adult, such as in the creation of web-sites ('Internet boy, 12, lands dream job', *Metro*, p. 3, June 5, 2000), should be regarded as child labour. Whilst so-called leisure pursuits, such as competitive sports and beauty contests, may be exploitative (Donnelly, 1997: 389–406), activities located in the work domain may be more akin to recreation (Beckhoven, 1991b: iv, 55–56). In consequence, it is often impossible to draw a firm line between educational, recreational and work activities.

Most definitions of child work are unsatisfactory. 'Paid work performed by children' ignores many activities that may prove too demanding or unsuitable for young people, such as (unpaid) work by young people under eighteen 'likely to jeopardise the health, safety or morals of young persons' (*Minimum Age Convention*, Art. 3(1)). Perhaps the most useful definition, covering more unconventional types of child work than any of the others, is one proposed by Save the Children (1998: 62): 'paid work or work that is not paid, but for which an adult would get paid.' However, it excludes light domestic work, such as 'helping around the home.' Whilst parents may expect a certain measure of such 'helping,' housework can all too easily become a burden, depending on the duration and nature of the activities.

Although it is often assumed that the cause of child labour is a matter of poverty in the developing world and of conspicuous consumption in the West, this is too generalised and too facile an inference. There are many different reasons why children work: a wish for greater independence, boredom, the belief that schooling does not benefit students anyway, the urge to learn something new, curiosity,[7] and also poverty; in the West, especially among immigrant and refugee populations. Although the Netherlands scores, with 7.7 percent, poverty much lower in the Innocenti Research's table of relative child poverty than the UK and USA (19.8 per cent and 22.4 per cent respectively) (UNICEF Innocenti Research Centre, 2000: 6), pressure caused by family hardship may affect Dutch children as well (see van der Hoek, this volume).

Rights and legislation

When translating a specific human right into domestic law, the standard approach is to test compliance with legal provisions through the courts. However, very little case law is available on child labour issues, prosecution of violating employers being an exception.[8] I now turn, therefore, to an evaluation of the implementation of the legislation in the three States by an examination of the following four aspects: i) rationale for the legislation, ii) content of the legislation, iii) enforcement mechanisms, and iv) evaluation and justification of the enforcement procedures.

i) Rationale

Although the ILO Minimum Age Recommendation enjoins national governments to give high priority to 'planning for and meeting the needs of children and youth in national development policies' (Art. 1), regulation of the work of children and young people is often treated as of little consequence.[9] It has at times been formulated in response to unacceptable situations, as in California.[10] However, a summary of California's child labour laws by the Division of Labor Standards Enforcement puts it as follows: '[they] are designed to help young people acquire work experience and income, while safeguarding their scholastic advancement and physical well-being' (State of California, 1998: Foreword). Similar arguments, 'to ensure that where children are employed they are given appropriate protection, that their safety and welfare are not damaged in the process and that their education does not suffer' have been used in Britain (*Employment of Children Bill – Research Paper 98/18*).

Although both the UK and the Netherlands need to comply with International Conventions and agreements, such as the ILO *Minimum Age Convention*, the *UNCRC* and EU *Directive 94/33/EC*, the results are very different. Britain amended its existing child labour legislation by passing a number of Statutory Instruments and the *Health and Safety (Young Persons) Regulations* 1997, after the end of the opt-out from *Directive 94/33/EC* and the ratification of the *Minimum Age Convention*. In consequence, the regulation of child employment consists of a patchwork of statutes and local bye-laws – in contrast with the Dutch approach, which resulted in a completely new 1995 *Working Times Act*.

The Dutch child labour provisions are largely based on guidance from the Council for Youth Policy. According to the Council, the Act was to be guided by the need of young people for participation in society in order to stimulate their growth towards autonomy by equal treatment to all employees, whether below or above the age of eighteen (Raad voor het Jeugdbeleid, 1990: 3). An overall ban on child labour for thirteen and fourteen-year-olds would still be needed, because of a tendency of children to overestimate their strength and to experiment, whilst lacking experience. Provision of rest periods was considered essential, as young people need more rest and sleep than adults, being at a time of life of major physical and mental change (Raad voor het Jeugdbeleid, 1990: 3, 10–12). In consequence, young employees enjoy standards similar to those of adult workers, such as protection from sexual intimidation, the right to social security, paid holidays, workplace tuition and minimum wages. Time spent at school is counted as 'working time' for sixteen to eighteen year olds (*Working Times Act*, s. 4.2, Arts. 4:4.–1.). This approach also implies that employed youth are required to pay social security contributions. Thirteen and fourteen-year-olds are still exempt, having initially been omitted from minimum wage settlements. However, a decision by the Hague Civil Court charged the Dutch Government to establish a minimum wage for the thirteen to fourteen age-group, in a case brought by the Federation of Dutch Trade Unions (*AF1787*, 11 Dec. 2002, Civil Court, s'Gravenhage [2002]).

ii) Content

All three jurisdictions specify a minimum age for entry into labour, linked to the end of compulsory education; namely, sixteen in the UK, sixteen with an element of part-compulsory education in the Netherlands and eighteen in California. However, Californian young people may leave school with a certificate of proficiency after their sixteenth birthday (Labor Code 1286), suggesting non-enforcement of the statutory age. In conformity with the ILO, *Minimum Age Convention* the UK and the Netherlands allow children under sixteen to engage in two hours of work after school, whilst such after-school work can legally take up to three hours in California. There is a difference between permissions relating to specific types of work for the youngest employees between the three jurisdictions. According to *CYPA* 18(2), children under fourteen may not be employed in England and Wales, unless in light work permitted by local bye-laws. In the Netherlands, a special exception is made for children from twelve upward who are working as part of an alternative form of sanction. Otherwise, thirteen and fourteen-year-olds are treated the same. They may be employed in specific types of light work of non-industrial nature, such as baby-sitting, car washing, serving in restaurants (under supervision), or picking fruit and vegetables, provided that on schooldays this work takes place in their own neighbourhood. Newspaper delivery and meal preparation in restaurants are excluded, as being too tiring and dangerous for young people under fifteen. In California, on the other hand, children younger than thirteen may legally be engaged in the physically demanding activity of hand-harvesting crops for up to eight hours a day, baby-sitting and door-to-door selling of sweets for charitable purposes. In addition, fifteen-year-olds are permitted to engage in restaurant work, apart from cooking and baking, 'except at soda fountains [...] and cafeteria serving counters' (29 CFR § 570.34, regulation 5).

Other differences concern rest periods, which in the UK and the Netherlands conform to the standards laid down in *Directive 94/33/EC*; namely, twelve hours of night-rest and half an hour rest every four hours of work. In addition, at least a third of the vacation is to be kept free for other pursuits. In contrast, California child labour legislation only provides for rest periods during the working day for children employed in the entertainment industry, apart from half an hour for mealtimes after five hours of work. However, adult employees are entitled to ten minutes rest after every four hours of work (Labor Code 551–552). There are no provisions to keep part of the vacation free from work and the period reserved for night-rest may be as short as four and a half hours for sixteen and seventeen-year-olds (State of California, 2000: 61). However, the Californian Labor Code provides, like the Dutch legislation, for a minimum wage for young workers as recommended in the ILO *Minimum Age Recommendation*, whilst minimum wage regulations do not apply to young people under eighteen in the UK.[11]

iii) Publicity and enforcement

In the UK, enforcement of child labour provisions lies with different LEA Education Welfare Services, resulting in uneven provision of personnel and resources.[12] There is no countrywide overview of tasks, as the responsibility lies with the separate local authorities. In contrast, both California and the Netherlands have mounted guides to child labour laws on the Internet, whilst the task of enforcement of the legislation is part of the duties of the respective labour inspectorates.

Labour issues have a high profile in the Netherlands, where the labour inspectorate is centrally funded (confirmed by SZW, February 11, 2000). It is therefore able to bring far more personnel into the field than the Californian Department of Labor Standards Enforcement (DLSE); namely, four hundred labour inspectors to less than a hundred in California, although its population is half the size of the US State. A quarter of the Inspectorate's labour force is expected to participate in annual summer vacation inspection, and surveys of particular types of work, such as newspaper delivery, intended to discourage illegal employment of young people. This comparison suggests that child labour inspection has a lower priority both in Britain and California, where it is treated as part of general labour standards enforcement. For instance, less than half of fines levied for child labour violations are collected by the DLSE.[13]

iv) Accountability – evaluation and justification

The inspection of children's work got no mention in a recent biennial report of the California Department of Industrial Relations (California Department of Industrial Relations, 2000). Unlike the Dutch child labour inspection reports,[14] Californian inspection data are not officially presented to Government (Confirmed by letter from DLSE, December 28, 2000), whilst no comprehensive records are available in the UK, due to the fragmentation of child labour provisions.[15] In addition, certain local authorities which issued annual reports in former years (Birmingham City Council Education Department, 1994, 1995), have discontinued the practice (Telephone conversation with Birmingham City Council Education Department, 3 December 2003).

Conclusion

Comparing the implementation of child labour provisions in the three States shows that the sole act of ratification of children's rights conventions does not, in itself, result in improved conditions for young people. The comparison confirms the importance of enforcement and accountability when dealing with any legislation intended to be more than symbolic, emphasising that it is meant to be taken seriously.

   Although the Dutch child labour law goes furthest in giving young people a choice, a serious shortcoming in all three jurisdictions is the fact that the target population was not consulted at the drafting stage. Nevertheless, recommendations have been made that children and adults should not be separated in the decision-making process (Council of Europe, 2001; Flekkøy and Kaufman, 1997: 87).

In addition, there is an argument in favour of giving more weight to the significance of efforts spent in schoolwork. Whilst the work of teachers is acknowledged as such, the effort of children is not – it is called something else. Yet study and work are not really that different, as acknowledged in the Dutch provisions for sixteen to eighteen-year-olds.

This comparison suggests that more attention may be paid to this aspect in countries with a unified policy towards the rights of children. It also draws attention to the fact that distinctions between the labour standards of young people and the rights of workers in general are as much a function of tradition as of objective need.

Generally, the prevention of exploitation of young people concentrates on restricting activities that might jeopardise their education or cause them harm. However, harmonisation with International Conventions may also lead to the adoption of positive entitlements such as Arts. 27 and 31 of the *UNCRC*[16] and 13(1)(b)[17] of the *Minimum Age Recommendation*, equalising labour standards for young people under eighteen with those of adult workers. Above all, we should begin to regard children as subjects with a voice worth listening to and entitled to participation in society rather than as objects to be protected. The *UNCRC*, in particular, shows the way to a future which values young people as persons in their own right like other members of society.

Notes

1. Having a Gross National Income per capita of over $22,000 (World Bank, *World Development Indicators* database).
2. Applicable to the *CRC*, the ILO *Minimum Age Convention, the Inter-American Convention on Human Rights* and the *International Covenant on Economic, Social and Cultural Rights*.
3. E.g. the England and Wales *Children and Young Person's Act*, 1933 and the US *Fair Labour Standards Act*, 1938.
4. *Minimum Age Recommendation*, Art. 13(1)(a), 'the provision of fair remuneration and its protection, bearing in mind the principle of equal pay for equal work'.
5. 'Current United States law and practice satisfy the requirements of Convention no. 182. Ratification of this Convention, therefore, should not require the United States to alter in any way its law or practice in this field' (Senate – August 05, 1999), *Congressional Record*, S10533.
6. Instead of contracts, UK child employment guides, such as the West Midlands Low Pay Unit leaflet (IL22 June 2000), speak of the need for permits and registration.

7. 'See how it is,' words of a fifteen-year old.
8. E.g. *SCC v Ikhya* [27 July 2001], Woking Magistrates Court.
9. Fragmented both in Belgium and Germany, communication from an official from the Dutch Department of SZW, February 11, 2002, see also a German Government Report (Deutsche Bundestag (2000).
10. Every year 70 adolescents die from work injuries in the United States and 200,000 are injured. (California Labor Code, S 6359).
11. *National Minimum Wage Regulations* 1999, SI 584, Art. 12(1).
12. Despite the UK's ratification of the ILO *Labour Inspection Convention*, securing the enforcement of the legal provisions relating to conditions of work, of 'the employment of children and young persons' (Art. 3(1)(a)), restated in ILO *Recommendation* 146, Art. 14, enforcement of the legislation is fragmented, because it is defined as a responsibility of local authorities.
13. 'Some fines stay unpaid due to businesses filing bankruptcy, relocating out of state, or are just uncollectable.' (Office State Labor Commissioner, January 8, 2001).
14. Report presented with a covering letter from the Secretary of State to the Chair of the Lower House of the Dutch Parliament, July 5, 2002.
15. House of Commons Hansard, 11 December 2000. In response to the question from Mr. Ruane, 'how many companies were prosecuted for illegally employing children in each of the last 20 years,' limited information on the number of prosecutions was available for selected years only.
16. 'Standard of living adequate for the child's physical, mental, spiritual, moral and social development', and 'right to rest and leisure.'
17. 'Equal pay for equal work.'

References

Aldridge, J. and S. Becker (1993) 'Children who care.' *ChildRight* (97), pp. 13–14.
Alston, P. (1989). 'Implementing Children's Rights: The Case of Child Labour.' *Nordic Journal of International Law* vol. 58(1): 35–53.
Beckhoven, A. P. M. v. (1991) Evaluatie richtlijnen voor het optreden van kinderen. Den Haag, Ministerie van Sociale Zaken en Werkgelegenheid, Directoraat-Generaal van de Arbeid door Regioplan Onderzoek en Adviesbureau voor Regionale Economie en Locale Ontwikkelingen.
Birmingham City Council Education Department (1994, 1995) Child Employment and Children in Entertainment: Annual Report. Birmingham, Court & Child Employment Section.
Boskey, J. B. (1990) 'Preventing Exploitation of the Child'. Children's Rights in America: UN Convention on the Rights of the Child Compared with United States Law. C. Price Cohen and H. A. Davidson, American Bar Association Center on Children and the Law and Defense for Children International-USA.: 303–314.
Boyden, J. (1997) 'Childhood and the Policy Makers: a Comparative Perspective on the Globalization of Childhood', in: *Constructing and Reconstructing Childhood*. A. James and A. Prout. London, Falmer Press: 190–229.
California Department of Industrial Relations (2000) 1998–1999 Biennial Report.
Challis, J. and D. Elliman (1979) *Child Workers Today*. Sunbury, Quartermaine House (Anti-Slavery Society Study).

Cohen, C. P. and H. A. Davidson, (eds) (1990) *Children's Rights in America: UN Convention on the Rights of the Child Compared with United States Law,* American Bar Association Center on Children and the Law and Defense for Children International-USA.

Committee on the Rights of the Child (1991) *General guidelines regarding the form and content of initial reports to be submitted by States Parties under article 44, paragraph 1(a), of the Convention*; CRC/C/5. Geneva.

Committee on the Rights of the Child (2002) *Concluding Observations*; CRC/C/15/Add.188. Geneva.

Council of Europe (2001) *Report by the Social, Health and Family Affairs Committee to the Parliamentary Assembly: Building a 21st century with and for children: follow-up to the European strategy for children (Recommendation 1286).* Geneva, Council of Europe.

Cunningham, H. (1991) *The Children of the Poor: Representations of Childhood since the Seventeenth Century.* Oxford, Blackwell.

Davies, E. (1972) 'Work out of school; the Emrys Davies report.' *Education,* 10 November 1972: i–iv.

Deutsche Bundestag (2000) *Bericht der Bundesregierung über Kinderarbeit in Deutschland* (Drucksache 14/3500).

Donnelly, P. (1997) 'Applying child labour laws to sport.' *International Review for the Sociology of Sport*: 389–406.

Employment of Children Bill-Research Paper 98/18. 1997/1998, February 3, 1998.

Flekkøy, M. G. and N. H. Kaufman (1997) *The Participation Rights of the Child: Rights and Responsibilities in Family and Society.* London: Jessica Kingsley Publishers.

Frederiksen, L. (1999) 'Child and Youth Employment in Denmark; Comments on Children's Work from their own Perspective.' *Childhood – a Global Journal of Child Research*, vol. 6(1): 101–112.

Fyfe, A. (1989) *Child labour.* Oxford, Polity Press.

General Accounting Office (1991) *Child Labor; Characteristics of Working Children*, GAO/HRD-91-83BR. Washington, General Accounting Office.

Glauser, B. (1997) 'Street Children: Deconstructing a Construct'. *Constructing and Reconstructing Childhood.* A. James and A. Prout. London, Falmer Press: 145–164.

Great Britain – Treasury (2003) *Every child matters, CM. 5860.* London: TSO.

Greenberger, E. and L. D. Steinberg (1986) *When Teenagers work: The Psychological and Social Costs of Adolescent Employment.* New York: Basic Books.

Hobbs, S., M. Lavalette, *et al.* (1992) 'The Emerging Problem of Child Labour.' *Critical Social Policy*, 12, 1(34), summer: 93–105.

van der Hoek, T. (2004) 'Growing up in poverty, while living in an affluent society: personal experiences and coping strategies of Dutch poor children' *The Politics of Childhood: International Perspectives, Contemporary Developments.* London: Palgrave Macmillan.

Human Rights Watch (2000) *Fingers to the Bone: United States Failure to Protect Child Farmworkers*, Lee Tucker, (ed.) New York: Human Rights Watch.

ILO (1996) *Child Labour: Targeting the Intolerable*; Report VI(1). Geneva, International Labour Office.

International Labour Office (2002) *A future without child labour.* Geneva, ILO.

Jenks, C. (1996) *Childhood.* London; New York: Routledge.

Khair, S. (2000) 'Child Labour Reconsidered: the Employment of the Girl Child in the Bangladesh Garment Industry'. *Gender, law and social justice: international perspectives*. A. Stewart. London, Blackstone: 119–137.

Lantos, T. (1992) 'The Silence of the Kids: Children at Risk in the Workplace.' *Labor Law Journal*, vol. 43(2): 67–70.

Lavalette, M. (1994) *Child Employment in the Capitalist Labour Market*. Aldershot: Avebury.

Mendelievich, E., (ed.) (1979) *Children at work*. Geneva, International Labour Office.

Morrow, V. (1996) 'Rethinking Childhood Dependency: Children's Contribution to the Domestic Economy.' *The Sociological Review*: 58–77.

Neve, J. H. and P. H. Renooy (1989) *Kinderarbeid in Nederland. Een verkenned onderzoek naar omvang en verschijningsvormen van kinder en jeugd arbeid in Nederland*. s'Gravenhage, Ministerie van Sociale Zaken.

Pettit, B., (ed.) (1998) *Children and work in the UK: reassessing the issues*. London: Child Poverty Action Group.

Pond, C., A. Searle, *et al.* (1991) *The hidden army: children at work in the 1990s*. Series (Low Pay Unit pamphlet, no. 55). London: Low Pay Unit.

Qvortrup, J. (2001) 'School-work, paid work and the changing obligations of childhood'. *Hidden Hands: International perspectives on children's work and labour*. P. Mizen, C. Pole and A. Bolton. London, RoutledgeFalmer: 91–107.

Raad voor het Jeugdbeleid (1990) *Jong geleerd oud gedaan?: een advies over de positie van kinderen en jeugdigen in de nieuwe arbeidstijdenwet*. Rijswijk, Raad voor het Jeugdbeleid, Ministerie van Welzijn, Volksgezondheid en Cultuur.

Save the Children (1998) 'Children's perspectives on work'. *Children and work in the UK: reassessing the issues*. B. Pettit. London, Child Poverty Action Group: 59–80.

Seymour, J. (2004) 'Entertaining Guests or Entertaining the Guests: Children's Emotional Labour in Hotels, Pubs and Boarding Houses'. *The Politics of Childhood: International Perspectives, Contemporary Developments*, London: Palgrave Macmillan.

State of California (1998) *California Child Labor Laws 1998*. Department of Industrial Relations, Division of Labor Standards Enforcement.

State of California (2000) *California Child Labor Laws 2000*. Department of Industrial Relations, Division of Labor Standards Enforcement.

Thomas, N. (2004) 'Interpreting children's needs: contested assumptions in the provision of welfare'. *The Politics of Childhood: International Perspectives, Contemporary Developments*. London: Palgrave Macmillan.

Trattner , W. I. (1970) *Crusade for the Children; a history of the National Child Labor Committee and Child Labor reform in America*. Chicago: Quadrangle Books.

Tweede Kamer der Staten-Generaal (2000–2001) *Opvang zwerfjongeren* no. 28, 265, s'Gravenhage, SDU Uitgevers.

UNICEF Innocenti Research Centre (2000) *Innocenti Report Card no. 1*, June 2000. 'A league Table of Child Poverty in Rich Nations'. Florence.

United Nations Commission for Human Rights (2002) *Guidelines regarding initial reports to be submitted by States Parties under article 12, paragraph 1, of the Optional Protocol to the Convention on the Rights of the Child on the sale of children, child prostitution and child pornography*: 04/04/2002, CRC/OP/SA/1. Geneva: United Nations.

Weisberg, D. K. (1985) *Children of the Night: a study of adolescent prostitution.* Lexington: Lexington Books.

Woll, L. (2000) *The Convention on the Rights of the Child Impact Study.* Stockholm: Save the Children.

World Congress Against Commercial Sexual Exploitation of Children (1996) *Declaration and Agenda for Action.* Stockholm.

Zelizer, V. A. (1985) *Pricing the Priceless Child.* New York: Basic Books. (Revised, 12–03–2004).

6

Entertaining Guests or Entertaining the Guests: Children's Emotional Labour in Hotels, Pubs and Boarding Houses

Julie Seymour

Introduction

Children's contribution to the labour of the household is well documented, particularly around the issues of domestic labour (Morrow, 1994; Punch, 2001), the provision of caring activities (Aldridge and Becker, 1993; Becker, Aldridge and Dearden, 1998) and income generation (see van der Hoek, this volume). Research has also shown that many children are involved in assisting in their families' work-related activities, particularly family businesses (Song, 1996; James *et al.*, 2000).[1] This chapter focuses on children's contribution to the emotional labour of family businesses by drawing on examples from interviews carried out with families living and working in hotels, pubs and boarding houses in England.[2] One striking theme that emerged from early analysis of the data was the expected involvement of children in social interaction with guests, both conversationally and in activities outside the business location. Parents and children recognised this activity as 'part of the job'; that is, as essential emotional labour connected with the workplace. Such labour involves a cognitive recognition that this is a responsibility of household members – the adoption of 'sentient activity' and 'active sensibility' as theorised by Mason (1994) – but also actual interactive activities to create a hospitable ambiance for guests. The positive outcomes which parents assert for their children carrying out emotional labour, which include the development of communication and social skills, will be contrasted with the notions of an 'ideal childhood', which include freedom for children from adult res-

90

ponsibilities and work (Scott, 2001; James *et al.*, 2002). However, it will also be noted that children show resistance to these work demands and are able to subvert their performance in order to gain personal advantage.

This chapter arises from research currently being conducted on families where business and family life occurs within the same location. Much has been made of the work-home balance (Bond *et al.*, 2002) with the assumption that this occurs in discrete spaces, but by examining accounts from family groups living in hotels, pubs and boarding-houses, this research looks at the interrelationship between these two spheres and the negotiations that take place to accommodate multiple activities in the same dwelling space. Elsewhere, I have considered issues relating to the permeability of the work/home boundary, the constructions of temporal, spatial and material practices in dual locations and discourses around 'a proper family life' (Seymour, 2001a, 2001b, 2002). However, within this chapter, I will concentrate on the contribution of children to the emotional labour of the businesses in which they are being brought up.

The data used come from a range of sources. A small scale empirical study was carried out in which fieldwork was split between two East Coast seaside resorts; one in the South and one in the North of England. Twenty in-depth interviews were carried out with families (both parents and children) currently living in hotels, pubs or boarding houses. A further six interviews were undertaken with individuals and couples who raised their families in such establishments or who grew up in them in the 1960s and 70s. Finally, secondary data analysis was carried out on fifty oral history interviews relating to participation in the tourist industry in one northern seaside town during the early and middle twentieth century.[3] Although each set of interviews provides a static snapshot of a particular era, when brought together they provide an illuminating, if imperfect, longitudinal account of combining work and home life in UK tourist locations since the 1930s from the viewpoints of the occupants of hotels, pubs and boarding houses. Admittedly, the data collected from two sets of interviewees is retrospective rather than prospective; that is, relying on memory rather than 'current attitudes or behaviour' (Arber, 2001: 275). Yet, while not following one cohort of individuals through this time period and thus allowing the consideration of changes at the micro-level or the causal ordering of variables (ibid.), this form of comparative cross-sectional inquiry (Ryder, 1965) does allow for a consideration of the temporal variations in family and work practices in this employment sector.

Children's contribution to household labour

As previously mentioned, the contribution of children to the labour of households is well established. Whether domestic labour (Morrow, 1994; Punch, 2001), caring activities (Aldridge and Becker, 1993) or financial contributions (Song, 1996; and see Heesterman, and van der Hoek, both this volume), children are no longer viewed as just consumers of household labour but also as contributors to it. It is important to note that, although there are still appropriate concerns about the exploitation of children through their labour, as Heesterman discusses in the previous chapter, the recent reconceptualisation of children as active agents has necessitated a reconsideration of the role that work has in childhood experiences. Many of the recent debates have focused on children's involvement in income-generating activities or the housework and people-care carried out by them in the private sphere. There has been far less discussion of the emotional labour carried out by children despite the rapid and considerable growth in research in this area, particularly of adults in work organisations (Barbalet, 1998; Bendelow and Williams, 1998; Bolton and Boyd, 2003).

Such discussion as there has been has focused on the area of children's emotional work (where an economic element is not involved) rather than emotional labour. Hence, emotional work has been acknowledged as an essential component in the activities of child carers within the home (Becker, Aldridge and Dearden, 1998). For example, in Dearden and Becker's 1995 study it was found that 25 per cent of the young carers were providing 'emotional support' (p. 20) for dependent relatives.

Mayall has, of course, written about children, emotions and daily life (in Bendelow and Williams, 1998) and the management of bodies. However, she deliberately atomises the arenas of the school work-place and the home, seeking to emphasise the 'distinctive social forces in play in the private world of the home and in the public world of school' (p. 150). Such spatial and social distinctions are perhaps less clear in dwellings which children occupy that are both homes and businesses. By examining the emotional labour carried out by children in such dual locations, I wish to further Sapsford's (1997) call for the established concepts of public and private to continue to be problematised.

Emotional labour

Before describing the emotional labour provided by the children in my study, I will first outline the salient features of this concept and show how it occurs in the day-to-day work of all members of families running hotels, pubs and boarding houses. Emotion work has been defined by Hochschild (1983) as 'explicit management of the emotions', both of oneself and of others. This chapter will use her definitions but adopt the phrase 'emotional labour' rather than 'emotion work' to re-emphasise that these activities occur within the context of a work arena.

Emotional labour can consist of management of oneself, that is:

'Management of feelings to create a publicly observable facial and bodily display' (Hochschild, 1983)

Data from the interviews showed that for individuals running or living in a hotel, pub or boarding house such self-management took place as part of the labour process. This would either involve falsely putting on a friendly face in front of guests or, conversely, toning down 'bad' emotions so as not to be overheard by customers. This was evidenced by the following comments on behaviours adopted by family members living in hospitality establishments:

F: You've got to learn to smile when you feel like crying.
(Hotel owner, 17[4])

F: If there was ever like a family argument or anything like that it was always 'Shush, we've got guests in'.
(Daughter of B & B owner, 15)

F: Always got to watch, always got to be on best behaviour.
(B & B owner, 12)

Emotional labour also involves the management of the emotions of others. Although talking of the domestic sphere, Delphy and Leonard's definition of emotion work as producing 'a sense of belonging (in individuals) … [it] thereby makes them feel good' (1992: 21), is easily transferable to the ambience of small hospitality establishments and in particular those who aim to provide, as one hotelier put it, 'a touch of home from home' (Hotel owner, 17).

Emotional labour consists of both cognitive and active dimensions. The former involves the 'sentient activity' described by Mason (1994) as 'attentiveness to the needs, health, well-being, behaviours, likes and dislikes ... of others' and the engagement of the 'active sensibility' through which an individual recognises that the care and welfare of another individual is their responsibility. These preliminary cognitive stages are then followed by the actual interactive part of the labour itself which, to return to Delphy and Leonard's (1992) definition, requires 'effort and skill' (p. 21) and consists of:

> Doing actual activities: talking to them about things that interest them, fetching them things that give them pleasure, smiling at them (*ibid.*) ...

Adult hoteliers in the UK, however, may draw the line at the parts of the definition which include:

> ... cuddling them and stroking their bodies and their egos (*ibid.*).

The production of emotional labour in hotels, pubs and boarding houses in the study usually occurred alongside the carrying out of more practical services, especially the provision of food and drink. Thus one owner commented that providing refreshments was usually accompanied by an expectation on the part of guests that this would also involve significant social interaction:

> M: When you've got like guests in and they want a drink, they half expect either I or Janet or both of us to come and sit with them. (B&B owner, 14)

It can be seen then that emotional labour is a key component of the tasks carried out by family workers in hotels, pubs and boarding houses. Often, such labour is interspersed with other more practical tasks such as serving drinks or a meal, and may not then be visible to either guests or family workers (Indeed, it can be argued that the best performance of emotional labour is that which is invisible).

The recognition and categorisation of emotional labour in this study is literally an academic exercise; one that emerged from the analysis of the data rather than being sought as a pre-determined area of investigation in the interview schedule. Hence in my interviews with the families it was not explicitly labelled as such, although the quotations provided above do show that there is an understanding of the labour process undertaken. However, despite not being framed in a discourse of emotional labour (either in the questions or answers which made up the interviews), I will show that the performance of such interactions was seen as a crucial contribution by children to the family business. In a preliminary analysis of the data, this did not appear to be the case as the social interaction that children had with guests was framed by their parents as the development of social skills and frequently presented as an advantage the children got from living in hospitality establishments – the opportunity to mix with entertaining guests.

Entertaining guests

When first reviewing parental responses as to what were the positive aspects of growing up in a hotel for their children, it was significant that everyone that was asked mentioned the acquisition of social skills and the ability to interact with a range of individuals. The following quotations are examples of parents' responses:

> F: Yeah, it's been good for Catherine. Catherine was very shy really before we moved in, she's a lot more confident. I've noticed her self-confidence has gone up, so it has been good for her.

> For Catherine definitely, mixing with other people has been a good thing.
> (Hotel owner, 17)

> F: I think with the girls, it's given them a lot more confidence because they speak to all types of different people from all different walks of life, different age groups and it has really gave them a lot more confidence because they speak to anybody and everybody, all age groups.
> (B & B owner, 12)

These parental descriptions of the best aspects of growing up in a hotel were accompanied in only one case with a listing of the more practical skills relating to the business and here they were interspersed with social skills. The manner in which the social and practical skills are interwoven demonstrates graphically the way that emotional and practical tasks are merged in such establishments. This account was, on the informant's request, written rather than spoken due to a hearing impairment:

> Good things about growing-up in Hotel Life
>
> You learn:
> Good manners
> Politeness
> Ability to speak to anyone
> Knowledge of Wine and Food
> Know how to lay a table for Dinner Party
> Which cutlery to use, etc.
> Learn how to cook and serve food and wine
> Not to be shy
> How to handle people and staff
> Cleanliness, Food Hygiene
> (B & B owner, Questionnaire)

When I asked children what <u>they</u> saw as the most positive dimensions of a hotel life, it again centred on social interaction. This was, as perhaps would be expected, less about the acquisition of social skills than the advantages of having guests as a source of entertainment, visits and treats. Hence nine-year-old Carrie prefers the hotel in summer rather than winter:

> 'cos sometimes guests take me places. Like Terry does, comes every year ... the one that takes me to the cinema all the time.

As with the previous written account, Carrie intersperses her comments on social interactions with descriptions of the physical labour she carries out:

> JS: What's fun about it? (living in a hotel)
>
> Carrie: 'cos you can do jobs, putting water on the table, put out the vinegar and salt and pepper.
> (Parents working in family-run hotel, 16)

While for thirteen-year-old Sophie the good bits were:

> F: Um, I don't really know, probably chatting to the visitors actually.
> (Daughter of B&B owner, 10)

Interviewees who were taking a retrospective view on growing up in a hotel, pub or boarding house also highlighted the social relations with guests, although one young adult, echoing the parental comments, did relate these interactions to the development of social skills and subsequent employment choices, as the first pair of quotations below shows:

> F: It's always been a bonus I suppose really, the amount of people that you've met.

> It probably maybe aided me to ... very much a people person.
> (Daughter of B & B owner, 15)

> F: I used to like to meet people, they used to make a fuss of you.
> (Hotel owner, 17)

Hence, while children focused on entertaining guests – i.e. those who were entertaining for them – parents mentioned the extent to which their own children were entertaining the guests. It appeared on further analysis that the social interactions described were not only a positive addition to growing up in a hotel but actually a requirement placed on the children living in such locations. This led to the consideration of the role of children's emotional labour in businesses which are also the home.

Entertaining the guests – children's emotional labour

The interview data produced numerous examples of children growing up in hospitality establishments carrying out emotional labour which is recognised by parents and considered good for business. This is either self-management (and here Goffman's (1953) concepts of impression management, developed while carrying out research in a hotel, have literal spatial enactment as 'front' management) or the management of the emotions of others to produce an appropriate 'harmonious' (Oakley, 1974) or holiday atmosphere.

Parents discussed how their children carry out front management with guests, masking their 'real selves',

> F: Barry likes older people, even when he was little he got on well with older men and older women. He's a bit of an old man in hisself. He's very polite which goes down well. I mean it's not a true reflection of him, he's an untidy so-and-so but *he's got the image bang right, which is good from our point of view.*
> (Hotel owner, 17, my emphasis)

F: [Guests say] Oh, what a charming son you've got but god, you
know, they don't know him
(B&B owner, 15)

Or when discussing their children socialising with guests, parents
noted how it contributed positively to the business:

JS: Were you aware that the children were doing that as well with
the guests?

M: Yes I mean it wasn't planned as such but they did, yes and everyone there must have thought, they're cute. When they get to be
spotty teenagers not so much. Part of the family ambience really,
being a family hotel
(Hotel owners, 7)

F: We have a guest lounge, all the family have always gone in there
with drinks for them and stayed and chatted
(B & B owner, 15)

(Of daughters interacting with guests)
F: Chat to them, say hello, have you had a good day, the odd word
in passing.
(B & B owner, 12)

Again what is noticeable is the interweaving of tasks of physical and
emotional labour in the accounts of children's contributions to the
family business, as shown by the following quotation:

(Of daughter)
F: When she's home she sort of joins in. You know, chats to the
guests and she helps in the dining room and kitchen and whatever.
(B & B owners, 14)

Indeed, in some cases, there was not only an acknowledgement of children's emotional labour on behalf of the business but an expectation
of it. The account below shows how such emotional labour with guests
has become a requirement for one (now seven-year-old) boy who, in
order to carry it out successfully, needed in his mother's view to
develop social skills. Later however, in perhaps making a virtue out of a
necessity, such skills may well be presented by his parent as a positive

benefit of growing up in a hotel, echoing the parental opinions high-lighted earlier in this chapter.

> (Of son)
> F: He knows that if there are guests in the dining room he doesn't stay in there. He'll walk through and people have remarked on how polite he is because he'll go walk through and say good morning. From three and a half, he's done that and people have remarked on it so he has learnt to do that … He's got to learn those social skills (My emphasis).
> (B & B owner, 6)

Changing demands on children's labour

It is, of course, perhaps not surprising that children growing up in hotels, pubs and boarding houses will have social interaction with the guests who frequent such establishments. Yet the emergence of such emotional labour in the contemporary accounts of family lives in the workplace stands in sharp contrast with the twentieth-century oral histories I examined, which focus on similar dual situations earlier in the century. In these accounts, although there are detailed narratives of the physical labour involved (particularly for girls, before and after school, and for boys, ferrying luggage to and from the train station), many of the respondents speak of their contribution to the business when they were children being one of absence. One woman recalls:

> I was in charge of my twin brothers and after breakfast we were packed up with sandwiches and told 'don't come home until after the visitors' tea'.

Similarly, one female hotelier who I interviewed, who was raised in a guesthouse nearly thirty years ago, described how she was often absent from the business premises/home:

> Again looking through a child's eyes, I don't particularly think I missed out on anything because I used to play out. Quite simply, I used to play out. That was my life, you know, get in, have my tea and go out and play out.
> (Hotel owner, 17)

In contrast to the above quotations, within the accounts of contemporary childhoods, the combination of a discourse of a 'proper family life' (which consists of time and activities spent together with family members, Seymour, 2002) and heightened concerns relating to 'stranger danger' (Scott *et al.*, 1998) mean that children are less likely to be sent out of the hotel, pub or boarding house unaccompanied. This obviously increases the probability of their interaction with guests. As a consequence then, emerging ideas of good parenting may, for children living in such establishments, result in increased demands for both the performance of emotional labour and the development of an accompanying active sensibility which recognises their responsibility for other's feelings. Such demands, however, are in opposition to current ideologies of childhood, in which work activities for children are secondary to play and education (Scott, 2000). There appears, then, for parents and children living in hotels, pubs and boarding houses, a tension in which contemporary models of good parenting place increasing demands on children's contribution to the business and, as a result, directly conflict with notions of an ideal childhood. In theory, this means that the 'better' the parent, the less ideal the experiences of the child.

In addition to this apparent contradiction of parent-child interests, it would also be too simplistic to present a picture of all children currently growing up in hotels, pubs and boarding houses as suffering from parental exploitation due to the family business. The children in this study do not comply with the demands made on them simply as passive recipients but show agency in the way they carry out emotional labour, as the following section illustrates.[5]

Children's resistance to emotional labour demands

The literatures on emotional labour and the social study of childhood have both developed from the initial necessary establishment of a new area of academic interest to a more detailed consideration of the complexity and fluidity of individual action and the role of agency in potentially bounded situations. The subject-defining work on emotional labour of Hochschild (1983) and Bendelow and Williams (1998) has evolved into studies of the multi-dimensional ways in which individuals may perform emotional labour to their own advantage. Bolton and Boyd (2003) show how, alongside Hochschild's 'commercialisation of feeling', which assumes that the benefit of the worker's emotional labour accrues to the organisation, the individual may evaluate the returns to themselves of such labour and adjust their behaviour accordingly. Bolton and Boyd propose a typology of emotional labour performance ranging from the pecuniary (money/commercial oriented), through the prescriptive (organisational expectations) and the pre-sentational (proper social manner) to the philanthropic (the gift – the little bit extra) which they claim individuals use to calculate the anti-cipated personal paybacks to be gained from performing certain forms of emotional labour. Such considerations allow a greater degree of agency to be revealed in the employer/employee dynamic and for sites of resistance to be examined. Drawing on the work of others in the field, Bolton and Boyd (2003: 294) state:

> 'it is the worker who calibrates how much feeling is invested into the performance. Arguably the deterministic feel that the term 'emotional labour' carries with it undervalues the vitality and inde-pendence of outlook that participants bring to organisations and neglects their ability to carve out 'spaces for resistance and misbe-haviour' (Thompson and Ackroyd, 1995).

Similarly, the research on the social study of childhood has emphasised the child as social actor and more recently focused on the performance of agency, including resistance (James and Prout, 1997; James *et al.*, 1998; and van der Hoek, this volume). In addition, the role of work in children's lives as necessarily negative and exploitative has been recon-sidered by the adoption of a less protective construction of children than simply that of emerging adults (Jenks, 1996).

In this study, then, although there was clearly an expectation by the adults in the family that children's emotional labour would be carried out, the degree and the underlying rationale for its performance showed evidence of this 'multidimensional view of [organizational] emotionality' (Bolton and Boyd, 2003: 305) by children. Some were able to exercise resistance by carrying out only the minimum required emotional labour – a prescriptive model – as shown by the example below:

> F: Some of them (guests) will chat to him and ... he's polite and then sort of makes his leave.

> He did used to chat more to them and he's polite, he talks to them but then he'll go off and do his own thing. I think probably people ask him the same questions that he's answered a thousand times before and so, it's a bit old hat to him.
> (B & B owner, 6)

Other children in the study appeared to have adopted a more philan-thropic, 'gift' approach where their emotional labour consisted of much more than just the least required to present a sociable front. Hence twelve-year-old Barry, who was described earlier in this chapter as liking old people, has voluntarily become involved in providing entertainment for such guests, particularly in relation to games of bingo. He initially sold the tickets but has also become involved as a caller of numbers, as his mother explained:

> F: One day by chance, early on in the season, he says 'Oh Mum, can I have a go?' and I was immediately about to say 'No love, I'm sorry you can't', and there was a cry of 'Oh, let him have a go' and they clapped after you see. He thought it were wonderful and the guests enjoyed it.
> (Hotel owner, 17)

Interestingly, when Barry was interviewed he considered the best part of living in a hotel was not his contacts with guests, but the constant availability of fizzy drinks. However, Barry's motives may not be wholly philanthropic and he is able to gain extra finances through his interactions with guests. The quotation below shows the complex merging of his performance of both physical tasks and emotional labour, which are a response not only to parental and guest expecta-tions but also fulfil personal social and fiscal strategies:

> F: Barry works as well on a Saturday, he brings all the bags down and takes some guest bags up and that gives him some pocket money, you know. The little old ladies like to see the kids with us so we just more or less got him to do that. He was a bit reluctant at first but I think he's found out. People give him tips you see and he likes that now so it's gelling together well.
> (Hotel owner, 17)

Other children in the study may have adopted an even more straight-forwardly pecuniary approach to the performance of emotional labour, with the monetary gain being personal rather than commercial (that is, for them rather than for the family business). For example, one woman who grew up in a boarding house mentioned the numerous presents and gifts she had received from guests. Also that:

> F: We met some really mint guests over the years, you know, that have taken me out.

... I've been to some Sergeant Messes Balls because the wife couldn't come down.
(Daughter of B & B owner, 15)

It may be then, that one form of children's resistance to the expectation of carrying out emotional labour on behalf of the family business, is to turn it to personal gain. The requirement of Entertaining the Guests can be used as a mechanism for converting them into Entertaining Guests; that is, people who provide interest, activities and sometimes goods for the children in the hotel, pub or boarding house. This may explain the focus of children's accounts on entertaining guests outlined early on in this chapter. Indeed, such guests are frequently able to provide for the children in this study the 'quality time' which their parents, precisely because of the temporal and spatial limitations of the home/workplace, are unable to offer. As such, the performance of emotional labour by children for their family business appears less of a situation of the former's passive exploitation and more one of mutual advantage (or at least mutual exploitation) for parents, children and guests alike. This study, then, illustrates the 'multi-situated systems of activity' which Bolton and Boyd (2003: 304) consider more fully describe the everyday performance of emotional labour in workplaces.

Conclusion

The three chapters making up this section of the volume all show how the reality of children's lives and labour activities contradicts the 'romanticised notions of an ideal childhood' (James *et al.*, 2002). Such constructions usually include, at least in part, freedom from the responsibilities and realities of adult life. As Scott (2000: 98) puts it, following Ariès, modern western childhood quarantines children from the world of adults so that 'childhood is associated with play and education rather than work and economic responsibility'. The evidence presented here, however, suggests that children are often involved in all four of these activities, even though some, such as emotional labour, may be less obvious than physical tasks. Although the potential for the exploitation of child labour is always present, more nuanced accounts can show how children are competent actors in these situations and able to exercise agency in producing profitable, social or even entertaining outcomes from their labour.

Notes

1. In a survey on children's use of time, James *et al.* (2000) found that 12 per cent of girls and 16 per cent of boys help in the family business.
2. A boarding-house is a small, usually family-run, establishment, often with fewer than ten guest rooms.
3. The interviews were funded by the Millenium Commission and conducted as part of the 'Looking Back, Looking Forward' project carried out by the North Yorkshire Museums Department. I am grateful to the projects organiser, Karen Snowden, the interviewers and particularly the interviewees, who allowed their thoughts and words to be passed on to other researchers.
4. These numbers refer to the interview number with the family group.
5. I am grateful to Samantha Punch for encouraging me to develop this dimension of the chapter.

References

Aldridge, J. and Becker, S. (1993) *Children who Care: Inside the World of Young Carers*, Loughborough: Loughborough University, Department of Social Sciences.
Arber, S. (2001) 'Secondary analysis of survey data', in N. Gilbert (ed.) *Researching Social Life*, London: Sage: 269–287.
Barbalet, J. M. (1998) *Emotion, Social Theory and Social Structure*, Cambridge: Cambridge University Press.
Becker, S., Aldridge, J. and Dearden, C. (1998) *Young Carers and their Families*, Oxford: Blackwell.
Bendelow, G. and Williams, S. (eds) *Emotions in Social Life. Critical Themes and Contemporary Issues*, London: Routledge.
Bolton, S. and Boyd, C. (2003) 'Trolley dolly or skilled emotion manager? Moving on from Hochschild's Managed Heart', *Work, Employment and Society*, 17(2): 289–308.
Bond, S., Hyman, J., Summers, J. and Wise S. (2002) *Family-friendly working? Putting policy into practice*, York: Joseph Rowntree Foundation.
Dearden, C. and Becker, S. (1995) *Young Carers: The Facts*, Sutton: Reed Business Publishing.
Delphy, C. and Leonard, D. (1992) *Familiar Exploitation: A New Analysis of Marriage in Contemporary Western Societies*, Oxford: Blackwell.
Goffman, E. (1953) *Communication Conduct in an Island Community*, unpublished PhD dissertation, Department of Sociology, University of Chicago.
Heesterman, W. (2004) 'Child Labour and Children's rights: Policy issues in three affluent societies', in J. Goddard, S. McNamee, A. James and A. James (eds) *The Politics of Childhood*, London: Palgrave.
Hochschild A. (1983) *The Managed Heart: Commercialization of Human Feeling*, Berkeley: University of California Press.
James, A. and Prout, A. (1997, 2nd ed.) *Constructing and Reconstructing Childhood. Contemporary Issues in the Sociological Study of Childhood*, London: Routledge Falmer.
James, A., Jenks, C. and Prout, A. (1998) *Theorizing Childhood*, Cambridge: Polity Press.

James, A., Christensen, P., Jenks, J. and McNamee, S. (2000) *Playing Out: Children's Time under Threat*, paper given at the British Sociological Association Annual Conference, York, April, 2000.

James, A., James, A. and McNamee, S. (2002) 'Children's Rights and Parenting Practices: Perspectives of Childhood from Guardian ad Litems and Family Court Welfare Officers', unpublished paper given at Children's Rights seminar, Centre for the Social Study of Childhood, University of Hull, 5th March 2002.

Jenks, C. (1996) *Childhood*, London: Routledge.

Mason, J. (1994) 'Gender, Care and Sensibility in Family and Kin Relationships'. Paper presented to the British Sociological Association Annual conference, 28th–31st March 1994, University of Central Lancashire, Preston.

Mayall, B. (1998) 'Children, emotions and daily life at home and school', pp. 135–154 in G. Bendelow and S. Williams (eds) *Emotions in Social Life. Critical Themes and Contemporary Issues*, London: Routledge.

Morrow, V. (1994) 'Responsible children? Aspects of children's work and employment outside school in contemporary UK', in B. Mayall (ed.) *Children's Childhoods: Observed and Experienced*, London: The Falmer Press: 128–143.

Oakley, A. (1974) *Housewife*, Middlesex: Penguin.

Punch, S. (2001) 'Household division of labour: Generation, gender, age. birth order and sibling composition', *Work, Employment and Society*, 15 (4) 8–3–823.

Ryder, N. (1965) 'The Cohort as a concept in the study of social change', *American Sociological Review*, 30, 843–61. (Also reprinted in Bulmer, M. (ed.) (1977) *Sociological Research Methods: An Introduction*, London: Macmillan: 138–167).

Sapsford, R. (1997) 'Endnote: public and private', in J. Muncie, M. Wetherell, M. Langan, R. Dallos and A. Cochrane (eds) *Understanding the Family* (2nd ed.) London: Sage: 317–322.

Scott, J. (2000), 'Children as Respondents: The Challenge for Quantitative Methods', in A. James and P. Christensen (eds), *Conducting Research with Children*, Falmer Press: 98–119.

Scott, S., Jackson, S. and Backett-Milburn, K. (1998) 'Swings and roundabouts: risk anxiety and the everyday worlds of children', *Sociology*, 32 (4), 689–705.

Seymour, J. (2001a) '"Treating the hotel like a home": Developing "family practices" in hotels, pubs and boarding houses', Working Paper no. 4, Centre for the Social Study of Childhood, Hull: University of Hull.

Seymour, J. (2001b) '"Dinner is at seven": Prescribing and protecting family practices in hotels, pubs and boarding houses', Working Paper no. 7, Centre for the Social Study of Childhood, Hull: University of Hull.

Seymour, J. (2002) 'Doing "Proper family life": Combining employment and home life in one location', Paper presented at BSA Annual conference, 25th–27th March 2002, University of Leicester.

Song, M. (1996) '"Helping Out": Children's labour participation in Chinese take-away businesses in Britain' in J. Brannen and M. O'Brien (eds) *Children and Families: Research and Policy*, London: Falmer Press.

Thompson, P. and Ackroyd, S. (1995) 'All quiet on the workplace front? A critique of recent trends in British industrial sociology', *Sociology*, 29 (4), 615–33.

Van der Hoek, T. (2004) 'Growing up in poverty, while living in an affluent society: Personal experiences and coping strategies of Dutch poor children', in J. Goddard, S. McNamee, A. James and A. James (eds) *The Politics of Childhood*, London: Palgrave.

7
Growing Up in Poverty While Living in an Affluent Society: Personal Experiences and Coping Strategies of Dutch Poor Children

Tamara van der Hoek

Introduction

Both political attention to, and research on, child poverty in rich countries is clearly on the increase. At the Lisbon European Union Council in March 2000, EU member states were formally invited to set 'adequate targets' for the reduction of poverty, in addition to which it was for the first time recommended that children should be one of the specific groups singled out for concern (Ruxton & Bennet, 2002). However, most of today's research on child poverty in rich countries is quantitative in nature and concentrated on determining its extent, trends and future outcomes. Much less attention is paid to the question of what poverty might mean to children themselves. This chapter aims to disclose poor children's perspectives on their own poverty on the basis of the primary results from an ongoing qualitative study on child poverty in the Netherlands. The main objective of this study has been to explore children's personal experiences and own actions (coping strategies) that follow upon the fact that they grow up in limited financial circumstances while living in an affluent society such as the Netherlands. Qualitative in-depth interviews have been conducted among six to sixteen-year-old children in the Netherlands who grow up in families with an income at the Dutch minimum benefit level. In addition, children's parents have been interviewed in order to be able to more fully understand children's answers against the background of the specific family financial circumstances that they grow up in. Altogether, interviews have been conducted among children and parents of 65 families from different ethnic backgrounds in various larger and smaller Dutch cities.

Current research on child poverty in rich countries

Children are now made much more visible within poverty statistics. By making children the unit of observation – as opposed to the more customary practice of subsuming them within the family unit – new essential information on children's conditions is emerging. Through such 'child-sensitive' poverty statistics, recent studies within the scope of comparative child-poverty research have, for instance, revealed how,

Table 7.1   Relative child poverty rates across EU countries

Country	Year	%	Rank
Sweden	1995	2.6	1
Finland	1995	4.3	2
Belgium	1992	4.4	3
Luxembourg	1994	4.5	4
Denmark	1992	5.1	5
Netherlands	1994	7.7	6
France	1994	7.9	7
Germany	1994	10.7	8
Spain	1990	12.3	9
Ireland	1997	16.8	10
UK	1995	19.8	11
Italy	1995	20.5	12

Source: UNICEF-Innocenti Research Centre. Innocenti Report Card No.1, June 2000. A league table of child poverty in rich nations. Poverty line: 50 per cent of median national income.

Table 7.2   Trends in child poverty

Country	Period	Percentage point per annum increase in child poverty
Italy	1986–95	+ 0.9
UK	1979–95	+ 0.8
Netherlands	1983–91	+ 0.4
Germany	1973–94	+ 0.2
Belgium	1985–92	+ 0.2
Luxembourg	1985–94	+ 0.1
Sweden	1975–92	0.0
France	1979–89	0.0
Denmark	1987–92	0.0
Spain	1980–90	– 0.1
Finland	1987–91	– 0.2

Source: Bradbury & Jännti (2001:19). Poverty line: 50 per cent of median national income.

Table 7.3 Child poverty rates compared to overall poverty rates

Country	Year	Poverty rate Children	All
Austria	1987	5.6	4.8
Belgium	1992	6.1	5.7
Denmark	1992	5.9	4.9
Finland	1991	3.4	3.2
France	1989	9.8	9.4
Germany	1994	11.6	8.5
Greece	–	–	–
Ireland	1987	14.8	12.2
Italy	1995	21.2	15.6
Luxembourg	1994	6.3	4.4
Netherlands	1991	8.4	6.5
Portugal	–	–	–
Spain	1990	13.1	10.3
Sweden	1992	3.7	2.9
UK	1995	21.3	15.1

Source: Bradbury & Jäntti (1999:32). Poverty line: 50 per cent of median national income.

even within the EU, relative child-poverty rates vary widely across rich countries (from below 5 per cent to over 20 per cent: see Table 7.1)

Such data also shows how child-poverty rates have increased as well as exceeded general poverty rates in various rich countries (see Tables 7.2 and 7.3)

As we can see in Table 7.3, among all age groups, children run the highest risk of living in poverty (Bradbury & Jäntti, 2001, 1999; Vleminckx & Smeeding, 2001; UNICEF-IRC, 2000; Micklewright & Stewart, 2000; Bradshaw, 1999; Cornia & Danziger, 1997).

Hence, by making children the unit of observation within poverty statistics, an important step forward has been made in illuminating their position. However, as has been stated:

> Statistics is an important, necessary, indeed indispensable research instrument to give expression to children's life conditions; politically it has even a strategic importance in that it is easily understood and grasped; on the other hand, it represents only a small part of the different sources of information which are needed to encompass the life worlds of children (Qvurtrop, 1997: 104)

In the United States – known for an extensive tradition of child-poverty research – the main focus has been on poor children's 'outcomes'. Studies within this tradition have shown that poverty correlates with lower scores on tests of cognitive functioning, lower levels of school achievement and higher prevalence of social-emotional problems such as depression, social withdrawal and low self-esteem (McLoyd, 1998; McLeod & Edwards, 1995; Felner *et al.*, 1995; Duncan, Brooks-Gunn & Klebanov, 1994; Huston *et al.*, 1994; McLeod & Shanahan, 1993; DuBois *et al.*, 1992; McLoyd, 1990). More recently, attention has shifted to the processes through which such outcomes occur (McLoyd, 1998; Huston *et al.*, 1994). Besides the neighbourhood as a process, (Brooks-Gunn *et al.*, 1997), it is processes within the family that have received considerable attention in the literature. In the analytical models evolved to examine these processes, parenting behaviour continually operates as a key element. The principal assumptions are that (a) poverty causes psychological distress in parents; (b) this distress is related to marital conflict and decrease in the capacity for skilful parenting; and (c) disrupted parenting has adverse consequences for child development. It is assumed that, rather than affecting children directly, poverty influences children indirectly through its impact on parents' behaviour toward children (McLoyd *et al.*, 1994; Conger *et al.*, 1994; McLoyd, 1990).

Connected with this, researchers have become aware of individual differences in poor children's outcomes and have started to consider which could be the issues that may diminish or worsen the negative effects on children. In this context, the influence of social support and the duration of poverty have been offered further attention. It is maintained that social support can have a 'buffering effect' on the negative consequences of poverty, directly but also indirectly: when social support is given to parents, poor children may be protected through its tempering effect on parent's psychological distress, which in turn lessens harsh parenting behaviour (McLoyd, 1998, 1990; McLoyd *et al.*, 1994; Hashima & Amato, 1994). Regarding the duration of poverty, recent research consistently reports that persistent poverty has more harmful effects on cognitive functioning, school achievement and social-emotional development than short-lived poverty, with children experiencing both types of poverty generally doing less well than never-poor children (McLoyd, 1998; cf.: McLeod & Shanahan, 1993; Korenman *et al.*, 1995; Duncan *et al.*, 1994; Huston *et al.*, 1994; Conger *et al.*, 1994).

Notwithstanding the valuable results current research on child poverty in rich countries has yielded, very little still is known about what poverty might mean in the world of children, i.e., seen through children's eyes in their present-day life as a child. In fact, the child's perspective on childhood poverty has thus far been mainly disregarded;

as a result of which, poor children's personal experiences and ways of dealing with poverty remain unnoticed. Consequently, children have been mostly regarded as playing only a passive role: they have either been reduced to numbers or have been depicted as inactive victims awaiting the eventual outcomes at the sheer end of rather static analytical models. As such, they are presented as if the poverty situation just happens to them, as if they do not reflect and act on that situation themselves. A rare and valuable exception to this is the recent work by Ridge (2002), which presents the empirical findings from in-depth interviews with 40 children living in poverty in the UK; therewith, through children's own accounts, providing us with the opportunity to understand some of the issues and concerns that poor children themselves identify as important. This chapter adds to the focus on the child's perspective and presents some preliminary results from ongoing qualitative research among poor children in the Netherlands.

Child-poverty research and the sociology of childhood

Studies within the field of the sociology of childhood have illuminated the ways in which traditional approaches to childhood (dominated by developmental psychology and socialisation theories) tend, in general, to consider children merely in terms of their future status as adults: as 'human becomings' instead of 'human beings', thereby reducing them to a primarily passive role (James *et al.*, 1998; James & Prout, 1997; Corsaro, 1997; Qvortrup *et al.*, 1994). As Corsaro states:

> Adults most often view children in a forward-looking way, that is, with an eye to what they will become – future adults. Rarely are they viewed in a way that appreciates what they are – children with ongoing lives, needs and desires. [Whereas] children are active, creative social agents who produce their own unique children's cultures while simultaneously contributing to the production of adult societies. (Corsaro, 1997: 4–7)

The above quotation makes explicit how such a focus on the future, on what children will become, obstructs a focus on the present-day experiences and actions of children living in the social world 'as a child' (James *et al.*, 1998; Corsaro, 1997). Subsequently, the novel approaches of the sociological study of childhood offer alternative views of children and childhood. These new viewpoints may prove to be significant to child-poverty research, in that the principal theoretical and methodological considerations of the sociology of childhood may further advance attempts to bring to light the meaning of childhood poverty from the viewpoint of children actually living their present-day life in poverty and, further, will capture their personal experiences and own ways of dealing with it.

Another important perspective which the sociology of childhood can bring to the field of child-poverty research is the notion that children are competent social actors, i.e., children are not only future members of society or outcomes of social processes, they are also, indeed, participating in it. As Alanen (1994: 28) puts it:

> Participation in the sense of being and acting in society does not begin first when a defined age limit or degree of adultness has been reached. In fact, it is simply impossible for children to opt out of participation in social life. (Alanen, 1994: 28)

Moreover, it is argued that childhood ought to be considered a permanent and integrated form in society (as opposed to a perspective on childhood as just a temporary phase in individual development); for even if its members change continuously, childhood itself does not disappear (James *et al.*, 1998; James & Prout, 1997; Corsaro, 1997; Qvortrup *et al.*, 1994).

Equally important, the new social study of childhood brings a methodological consideration to the field of child-poverty studies. This is explicated in the statement that children ought to be considered 'participants in' instead of 'subjects of' research (James & Prout, 1997), which implies that children are to be treated as 'knowledgeable' and that their knowledge ought be respected (Alanen, 1994: 35). According to James and colleagues (1998), it is this shift toward studying 'real' children and the 'experiences of being a child' that is to be considered the primary epistemological break from traditional to new sociological approaches to childhood. Child-poverty research can successfully integrate their call for studies which foreground children's agency in social action, in order to understand how children deal with their circumstances.

Child-poverty research and literature on children's coping

To further understand children's actions on growing up in poverty while living in an affluent society, this section briefly outlines current literature on coping processes among children in order to evaluate whether its theoretical concepts might provide a useful framework in studying the particular coping strategies of children in poverty. Although this literature is concerned with outcomes for children, there are some issue relevant to child-poverty research.

The literature on children's coping reveals that when studying children in challenging situations, at least two questions should be taken into consideration. Firstly, when the children under study are confronted with a particular stressful situation, do they themselves truly appraise this situation as stressful? For it is claimed that outwardly the same challenging situations may not be equally distressing to the individuals who are confronted by it (Lazarus, 2000; Sandler *et al.*, 1997; Shaw-Sorensen, 1993; Rutter 1988; Folkman *et al.*, 1986). Therefore, literature on children's coping highlights the importance of paying attention to children's personal interpretation of stressful events. Secondly, when children do appraise a particular situation as stressful, what coping strategies do they employ? For it has become evident that coping may operate in a positive as well as a negative manner: 'some coping strategies may serve protective functions, whereas others may exacerbate the effects of stress' (Seiffge-Krenke & Klessinger, 2000: 618). Sandler *et al.*, (1997) state:

> There is consistent evidence that dimensions of active coping [...] about a stressful situation are related to lower mental health problems [and] that use of avoidance coping strategies [...] is related to higher mental health problems in children (Sandler *et al.*, 1997:13).

However, there appears to be yet another preceding question that should be taken into account, namely: Are the children under study really confronted with the stressful experiences that tend to be associated with a particular stressful situation? For Richters and Weintraub (1990 in: Cowan *et al.*, 1996: 15) note that 'researchers can define a risk group, but individuals in a risk category may not have experienced many of the stressful experiences that tend to be associated with the risk'. In this way, in order to understand the variability in children's outcomes it is important first to determine whether children who have adjusted differently to the same stressful situation have in fact endured a similar exposure to the commonly related stressful experiences (Roosa *et al.*, 1997). It may be the case that children who show no negative outcomes in the presence of a particular stressful situation are well shielded against it (by means of effective protection mechanisms) instead of well adjusted to it.

Moreover, in trying not only to comprehend how but also why children's coping processes may differ, efforts have been made to identify the factors that might influence these processes. This has led to the search for so-called 'risk' and 'protective' factors. Early efforts were primarily focused on children's personal characteristics (e.g., age, gender and to a lesser extent ethnicity). However, researchers within this field are increasingly acknowledging that the variety in children's coping processes may also derive from factors operating in the child's social context. Accordingly, it is predominantly the family context that receives most attention (e.g., the influence of parents' perceptions of the stressful events, parent-child communication about it and parents' coping strategies), especially because of the dependent role of the child within the family. Nevertheless, it is also being recognised that the child's wider social environments (such as peer group and school life) may affect children's coping processes as well (Lindström, 2001; Slap, 2001; Luthar *et al.*, 2000; Wolchik & Sandler, 1997; Hetherington & Blechman, 1996; Shaw-Sorensen, 1993; Compas *et al.*, 1992; Garmezy, 1988).

Poor children's experiences

The following sections present the empirical findings from in-depth interviews conducted in the Netherlands among the children and parents of 65 families living at the Dutch minimum benefit level. If children's and parents' own narratives on poverty are listened to, it becomes clear that children are confronted with divergent challenging experiences due to the fact that they grow up in a poor family.

Meeting children's basic needs: healthy nourishment, sufficient clothing and access to medical care

Against what might have been expected in a rich welfare state such as the Netherlands, the present study shows that in a quarter of all families interviewed children do not receive a hot meal on a daily basis due to lack of money in the household. Daily fresh vegetables and fruit appear to be even less common – within one third of all families interviewed, they are considered to be too expensive for daily consumption. Moreover, within almost half of families interviewed, parents state that they are not able to obtain sufficient clothing for their children. This means that children in these families have to wear clothes and/or shoes that are in fact too small or worn-out, since there is no money to immediately replace these items at any necessary time. Finally, although all families interviewed can lay claim to the National Health Service (NHS), still, within fifteen of the 65 families, parents claim that their children's access to medical care has been limited due to lack of money. The limited access shows itself when medical care is needed that is not (completely) covered by the basic NHS package: certain medicines or medical treatments require own contributions or supplementary insurance or are excluded from the NHS altogether and therefore cannot be afforded.

Although children may not express themselves in terms of 'healthy' food or 'sufficient' clothing, the children's interviews make clear that they may come to realise that buying food and clothes is somehow problematic. Some, for example, claim to know that money runs out at the end of the month, for they notice that 'just bread or soup' is eaten these days or that 'the refrigerator is empty'. Others relate to the fact that they mostly 'have to wait' for new clothes.

> To us, it's a celebration when money comes in. Money came in today. So now at least our refrigerator is full. Or well, full ... Anyway, we've normal food again and we don't have to pay attention so much and go easy on it. About a week before a month's money comes in, then it starts. We've to go easy on everything. I can't do anything then and there's only what's strictly needed, bread and something to eat in the evening. Sometimes it's just soup. Or we borrow money to have a hot meal. (15-year-old girl)

> If we want something mom mostly says 'it's not possible'. If your shoes are worn out and there's no money, you have to wait. Food always comes first with our mom. (15-year-old girl)

Social contacts with peers

Children, however, do not only operate within their own family. They go to school, play in the street and visit their friends' homes. The interviews with children make clear that it is especially through social contacts with peers that the limited financial circumstances they live in acquire significance in their lives. By comparing themselves with other children, they may notice they possess fewer (and in their eyes often less attractive) material goods or do not have the latest toys and other products that are 'in'. Possessing clothes with certain brands or clothes that are in fashion is not possible. Because of that, some of the children interviewed have experienced bullying by other children.

> Those other families have very modern, new things in their houses. And we don't. Our TV broke down. Now we've one off someone else. Or for example our couch. That too is second-hand. (13-year-old girl)

> I don't think I have nice clothes. I want those clothes that are in fashion. At school there is often said something about it: 'you dress out of fashion' and 'you look stupid'. It's not nice to hear such things. (13-year-old girl)

Besides these material characteristics of poverty, living in poverty often encompasses less access to social activities as well. This is labelled 'social poverty' or 'social exclusion', which means that due to lack of money it is not possible to participate in the ordinary social life of the society that is lived in. For the children interviewed, this may imply that they do not have the possibility to become a member of a sports club, that they cannot always celebrate their birthday party or participate in school excursions or that they cannot go on holidays every year or even may have never been on holiday. In the experience of children, it is especially the absence of holidays which appears to be perceived as a problem. Here again, it is particularly through comparisons with peers that children feel excluded.

> I've never been on holidays. My whole life, never. At school, they talk about Spain, France. I've never been there. Truly, I don't like that. I too would like to go abroad once. Even if it is only once. (15-year-old girl)

Emotional pressure

Furthermore, children may be pressured emotionally by the difficult financial situation of the family they grow up in. It appears that, within more than half of the families interviewed, parental worries over money are being confided in to children. Parents, especially, share with their children those financial worries that are related to unexpected expenditures, such as unexpected bills. It seems that, already hard-pressed, parents just cannot conceal their disappointment over sudden extra expenditures and worries that go along with it. Discussions as such may vary from sometimes making a remark to very frequent and/or detailed conversation. In addition, several parents borrow money from their children (for example, money from the children's birthday or pocket money or money they earned with a sideline job).

(I: Does your mother ever talk to you about money?) Yes she does. Pretty often actually. About something she needs. Or she says 'actually I need money for this or that' or 'I can't pay that bill'. (14-year-old boy)

(I: Does your mother ever talk to you about money?) 'Yes, some-times. That we haven't got it. That the housing association is giving her a hard time. That she didn't have the money to pay for my schoolbooks. That sort of thing. The money for those schoolbooks, I had to advance. She borrowed that money from me, but I will get it back.' (16-year-old girl)

Discussion: variability in children's personal experiences

Notwithstanding the aforementioned difficult circumstances which poor children in the Netherlands may encounter, it should be noted that when children's experiences are examined at the individual level, clear differences emerge between poor children: not every child is materially or socially deprived in a similar sense and not every child is emotionally burdened with family financial problems. Children are not equally affected by poverty.

Preliminary analysis shows that when the individual experiences of children are considered within their broader social context, different factors emerge that may be of influence on the individual diversity in children's experiences with poverty. For example, though all of the children interviewed grow up in families who live at or near the min-imum subsistence level, the actual free space of expenditure appears to diverge significantly. Certain families are weighed down by debts, while other families do not have debts at all. In certain families extra informal income is generated, while in other families there is no such additional income. Certain families have extra expenses because of illness in the family, while in others families all its members are per-fectly healthy. Therefore, understandably, differences arise in the actual amount of money that can be spent on children.

Nevertheless, the way in which poverty leaves its mark on the fam-ilies interviewed for this study is not only a financial matter, but is also influenced by the way in which parents handle the poverty situation, which in turn may be influenced by the social support parents receive. The interviews with parents showed that the poverty situation is not equally constraining for every single parent: not every parent worries about this situation and not every parent who does worry about it discusses these worries with their children. A number of parents report that they attempt not to discuss their worries with their children, because they want 'their children to be able to be a child' and they do not want to burden them with their own financial problems (see also McNamee *et al.*, this volume). They try to keep their worries to themselves or seek emotional support from friends or relatives outside the family. In this way, the emotional-support network of parents can provide protection for children: if parents are able to share their worries with others, fewer burdens are laid on the child's shoulders.

Furthermore, a number of parents appear to be very creative in inventing effective solutions or inexpensive but satisfying alternatives for their children, whereas other parents succeed in this much less. Moreover, some families are supported by others in a material and financial way, while other families do not receive this support at all. Children, too, report when their parents think of solutions and successful alternatives or when they receive support from others. For example, they relate to inexpensive but still successful holidays or talk about the times that they were taken out by a friend's parents, went to the cinema with their older brother or received presents from their father living away from home. For these children, the sharpest consequences of the poverty situation seem to be diminished to some extent.

Besides parents and the family's social-support network, as we have seen before, peers also play a role in the way poor children may feel deprived. In daily contacts and communication with these peers, the poverty situation can be of major or minor importance. As has been mentioned, some children are bullied by other children because of their low-priced clothes. In this way, these children are again reminded that their parents do not have much money. However, there are also children who report that they 'actually never talk about money-related matters' with peers; that it is 'not so much an issue'.

To summarise, analysis of the interview material shows that different mediating factors emerge that may be responsible for the existing variety in children's personal experiences with poverty: the family's actual free space expenditure (i.e., the actual amount of money that can be spent on children); parents' coping strategies (i.e., the manner in which parents know how to handle the poverty situation, including parents' creativity); parent-child communication (i.e., the extent to which parents and children communicate about poverty); the family's social network (i.e., the social support received by the family: emotional, financial, material); and contact with peers (i.e., the importance of money-related matters in the interaction with peers). Some of these factors clearly resemble the mediating factors that have also been identified within the US literature on child poverty and literature on children's stress and coping processes (see above discussion).

Poor children's coping strategies

The preceding discussion foreshadows the question of how children who are confronted with challenging experiences related to poverty try to deal or 'cope' with these experiences. What is striking is that the majority of the children interviewed demonstrate reactions that involve active steps with the intention to change the difficult situation. Hence, these children clearly are not just passive victims of the poverty situation they grow up in. Quite the contrary, they actively try to do something about it. Many of the younger children, for example, report that they buy their own toys by saving up their pocket or birthday money. They also try to earn additional money by means of little jobs like washing cars or doing chores around the house. Among the older children, several earn additional money through spare time jobs, mostly a newspaper round. Moreover, some children search for very creative solutions in order to fulfil their wishes. As one ten-year-old boy, who has set his hopes on a television programme, says:

> I'm gonna write to 'The Chance of Your Life'. I still have to go to my aunt and there I'll type everything on a note. This I'll send to Ron Brandsteder [the ringmaster of the programme] and then, maybe, I'll get into 'The Chance of Your Life' and receive everything I want. (10-year-old boy)

Despite these active solutions that poor children appear to develop, they are often not in the position to change their situation in a substantial way: they cannot change the fact that they grow up in a poor family. Nevertheless, it appears that several children interviewed develop coping strategies that enable them to appraise their poverty in a more positive light. They actively try to manipulate or reframe their perception of the situation, by providing it with a positive label. In this context, children may express themselves in a rather grown-up manner and make remarks such as: 'at least we have a house' and 'other things are more important'. Or, as an eleven-year-old boy says:

> Sometimes I think: well, it's better to have food than a Play Station, cause you can't eat a Play Station. (11-year-old boy)

However, it must be noted that the children interviewed do not always react in such positive ways to the experiences they encounter due to poverty. Several children just try not to think too much about it. They seem resigned to the situation and make rather fatalistic remarks such as 'I'm already used to it' or 'there isn't any thing to do about it anyway'. However, some children say they really worry about the family's financial situation. Other children relate to feelings of shame, jealousy or exclusion when their friends or classmates can have and do so much more than they themselves can or report becoming sad or angry when the things they would like to have so much are refused over and over again by their parents. It must be noted, however, that several children do their utmost to conceal their disappointment and do not complain about the things they can not have or do, in order not to make in any harder on their parents:

> Sometimes I worry. At times that we still have to pay this and that and then we haven't got so much money and than everything is out of the ordinary. That's quite difficult sometimes. A few years ago, when she [her mother] told me something I myself got a stomach-ache out of it. (16-year-old girl)

> When I know I can't have it, I don't ask. Because then she [her mother] starts thinking, 'my children want this and that, but I can't give it to them'. (12-year-old girl)

Conclusion

One of the barely touched areas within today's mainstream child-poverty research is the life world of 'real' children that lies concealed behind the facts and figures on children in poverty. Hence, although the child evidently has come into view, the perspective is primarily directed *upon* the child, whereas little notice is taken of a perspective *from within* the child. What is to be generally opposed to this disregard of children's own viewpoints, is that it results in the fact that children are depicted as playing only a passive role in the situation they live in. Consequently, children's personal experiences and own actions remain largely unnoticed.

The main objective of this chapter has therefore been to bring to light poor children's perspectives on their own poverty. Still, how may children's perspectives contribute to our knowledge on child poverty in rich countries? First of all, children's perspectives offer an inside view what growing up in poverty means in the everyday life of a child. We have seen that it is especially through their interaction with peers that the limited financial circumstances they live in acquire significance in children's lives: by means of their social contacts with friends and classmates, the existing differences between themselves and others become apparent. In this way, they are frequently confronted with situations in which they may feel materially and socially deprived. In addition, they may also be pressured emotionally by the difficult financial situation of the family they grow up in: i.e., when their parents confide in them with their problems and worries over money. Nevertheless, it also became clear that children develop various strategies to deal with poverty. What is striking is that the majority of the children interviewed demonstrate reactions that involve active steps with the intention of changing the difficult situation. Hence, these children clearly are not just passive victims of the poverty situation they grow up in.

At the same time, however, it should be noted that when children's experiences and coping strategies are examined at the individual level, clear differences emerge within the group of children labelled as poor (children who's family income falls below a certain threshold). That is, not every child is materially or socially deprived in a similar sense, not every child is emotionally burdened with their family's financial problems and not every child copes effectively with their poverty situation. It is therefore important not to consider poor children as one homogeneous group, but rather to emphasise the individual differences within the group of poor children and to further reveal the factors that may aggravate or diminish the negative impact of poverty on children's daily lives. Clarifying these factors and subsequently making a classification of protective and risk factors may give some clear underpinnings for policy makers: factors that prove to be protective should be strengthened, whereas factors that seem to exacerbate the negative impact of poverty on children should be tackled.

References

Alanen, L. (1994) 'Gender and Generation: Feminism and the "Child Question"'. In: Qvortrup, J. *et al.* (1994) *Childhood Matters. Social Theory, Practice and Politics.* Ashgate Publishing: Avebury: 27–42.

Bradbury, B. & Jäntti, M. (2001) Child poverty across the industrialised world: evidence from the Luxembourg Income Study. In: Vleminckx, K. & T. Smeeding (eds) *Child well-being, child poverty and child policy in modern nations. What do we know?* Bristol: The Policy Press: 11–32.

Bradbury, B. & Jäntti, M. (1999) *Child poverty across industrialized nations.* Innocenti Occasional Papers, Economic and Social Policy Series, no. 71. Florence: UNICEF International Child Development Centre.

Bradshaw, J. (1999) Child poverty in comparative perspective. In: *European Journal of Social Security.* vol. 1 (4): 383–406.

Brooks-Gunn, J., Duncan, G. J. & Aber, J. L. (eds) (1997) *Neighborhood poverty. Context and consequences for children.* New York: Russel Sage Foundation.

Compas, B. E., Worsham, N. L. & Ey, S. (1992) 'Conceptual and developmental issues in children's coping with stress'. In: Greca, A. M. La, L. J. Siegel, J. L. Wallander & C. E. Walker (eds) *Stress and Coping in Child Health,* New York: The Guilford Press: 7–24.

Conger, R. D., Ge, X., Elder, G. H., Lorenz, F. O. & Simons, R. L. (1994) 'Economic stress, coercive family process, and developmental problems of adolescents'. *Child Development:* 541–561.

Cornia, G. A. & Danziger, S. (eds) (1997) *Child poverty and deprivation in the industrialised countries, 1945–1995.* Oxford: Clarendon Press.

Corsaro, W. A. (1997) *The Sociology of Childhood.* Thousand Oaks, California: Pine Forge Press.

DuBois, D. L., Felner, R. D., Brand, S., Adan, A. M. & Evans, E. G. (1992) 'A prospective study of life stress, social support, and adaptation in early adolescence'. *Child Development:* 542–557.

Duncan, G. J., Brooks-Gunn, J. & Kato Klebanov, P. (1994) Economic Deprivation and early childhood development. *Child Development:* 296–318.

Felner, R. D., Brand, S., DuBois, D. L., Adan, A. M., Mulhall, P. F. & Evans, E. G. (1995) 'Socioeconomic disadvantage, proximal environmental experiences, and socioemotional and academic adjustment in early adolescence: investigation of mediated effects model'. *Child Development:* 774–792.

Folkman, S. & Moskowitz, J. T. (2000) 'Positive affect and the other side of coping'. *American Psychologist:* 647–654.

Folkman, S. *et al.* (1986) 'Appraisal, Coping, Health Status, and Psychological Symptoms'. *Journal of Personality and Social Psychology:* 571–579.

Garmezy, N. (1988) 'Stressors of Childhood'. In: Garmezy, N. & M. Rutter (eds) *Stress, Coping, and Development in Children* Baltimore: The John Hopkins University Press. Reprint. Originally published: New York: McGraw-Hill, 1983: 43–84.

Hashima, P. Y. & Amato, P. R. (1994) 'Poverty, Social Support, and Parental Behavior'. *Child Development:* 394–403.

Hetherington, E. M. & Blechman, E. A. (eds) (1996) *Stress, Coping and Resiliency in Children and Families.* New Jersey: Lawrence Erlbaum Associates.

Huston, A. C., McLoyd, V. C. & Garcia Coll, C. (1994) 'Children and poverty: issues in contemporary research'. *Child Development:* 275–282.

James, A., Jenks, C. and Prout, A. (1998) *Theorizing Childhood*. Cambridge: Polity Press.

James, A. & Prout, A. (1997) *Constructing and Reconstructing Childhood: Contemporary Issues in the Sociological Study of Childhood*. Second Edition. Routledge Falmer: London.

Korenman, S., Miller, J. E. and Sjaastad, J. E. (1995) 'Long-term poverty and child development in the United States: results from the NLSY'. *Children and youth services review*: 127–155.

Lazarus, R. S. (2000) 'Toward better research on stress and coping'. *American Psychologist*: 665–673.

Lindström, B. (2001) 'The meaning of resilience'. *International Journal of Adolescent Medicine and Health*: 7–12.

Luthar, S. S., Cicchetti, D. & Becker, B. (2000) 'The construct of resilience: a critical evaluation and guidelines for future work'. *Child Development*: 543–562.

McLeod, J. D. & Edwards, K. (1995) 'Contextual determinants of children's responses to poverty'. *Social Forces*: 1487–1516.

McLeod, J. D. & Shanahan, M. J. (1993) 'Poverty, parenting, and children's mental health'. *American Sociological Review*: 351–366.

McLoyd, V. C. (1998) 'Socioeconomic disadvantage and child development'. *American Psychologist*: 185–204.

McLoyd, V. C. (1990) 'The impact of economic hardship on black families and children: psychological distress, parenting, and socioemotional development'. *Child Development*: 311–346.

McLoyd, V. C., Epstein Jayaratne, T., Ceballo, R. & Borquez, J. (1994) 'Unemployment and work interruption among African American single mothers: effects on parenting and adolescent socioemotional functioning'. *Child Development*: 562–589.

Micklewright, J. & Stewart, K. (2000) *The welfare of Europe's children. Are EU member states converging?* Bristol: The Policy Press / UNICEF.

Qvortrup, J. (1997) 'A voice for children in statistical and social accounting: a plea for children's rights to be heard'. In: James, A. & A. Prout (1997) *Constructing and Reconstructing Childhood: Contemporary Issues in the Sociological Study of Childhood*. Second Edition. RoutledgeFalmer: London: 85–106.

Qvortrup, J. *et al.* (1994) *Childhood Matters: Social Theory, Practice and Politics*. Ashgate Publishing: Avebury.

Richters, J. & Weintraub, S. (1990) 'Beyond diathesis: Toward an understanding of high risk environments'. In: J. Rolf *et al.* (eds) *Risk and protective factors in the development of psychopathology* Cambridge, UK: Cambridge University Press: 67–96.

Ridge, T. (2002) *Childhood Poverty and Social Exclusion From a Child's Perspective*. The Policy Press: Bristol.

Roosa, M. W., Wochik, S. A. & Sandler, I. N. (1997) 'Preventing the negative effects of common stressors. Current status and future directions'. In: Wolchik, S. A. & I. N. Sandler (eds) *Handbook of Children's Coping: Linking Theory and Intervention*. New York/London: Plenum Press: 515–533.

Rutter, M. (1988) 'Stress, Coping, and Development: Some Issues and Some Questions'. In: Garmezy, N. & M. Rutter (eds) *Stress, Coping, and Development in Children*. Baltimore: The John Hopkins University Press. Reprint. Originally published: New York: McGraw-Hill, 1983: 1–41.

Ruxton, S. & Bennet, F. (2002) *Including Children? Developing a coherent approach to child poverty and social exclusion across Europe.* Euronet – The European Children's Network.

Sandler, I. N. *et al.* (1997) 'Developing Linkages between Theory and Intervention in Stress and Coping Processes'. In: Wolchik, S. A. & I. N. Sandler (eds) *Handbook of Children's Coping: Linking Theory and Intervention.* New York/London: Plenum Press: 3–40.

Seiffge-Krenke, I. & Klessinger, N. (2000) 'Long-term effects of avoidant coping an adolescents' depressive symptoms'. *Journal of Youth and Adolescence*: 617–630.

Shaw-Sorensen, E. (1993) *Children's Stress and Coping. A Family Perspective.* New York/London: The Guilford Press.

Slap, G. B. (2001) 'Current concepts, practical applications and resilience in the new millennium'. *International Journal of Adolescent Medicine and Health*: 75–78.

UNICEF-IRC: Innocenti Report Card no. 1 (2000) A league table of child poverty in rich nations. Florence, Italy: UNICEF-Innocenti Research Centre.

Vleminckx, K. & Smeeding, T. (eds) (2001) *Child well-being, child poverty and child policy in modern nations. What do we know?* Bristol: The Policy Press.

Wolchik, S. A. & Sandler, I. N. (eds) (1997) *Handbook of Children's Coping: Linking Theory and Intervention.* New York/London: Plenum Press.

Part Three
Children at School

8
Mobilising Family Solidarity? Rights, Responsibilities and Secondary Schooling in Urban Mexico

Maribel Blasco

Introduction[1]

Rights-based approaches to social development have gained increasing currency in recent years. Their attraction lies partly in the fact that they recast the poor and other marginalised groups as active subjects in their own development rather than passive beneficiaries of welfare and aid or, at the other extreme, as empowered consumers exercising 'choice' (DFID, 2000: 13, in Cornwall, 2002: 55; Subrahmanian, 2002). In Mexico, the focus of this chapter, social rights have been increasingly linked to the notion of responsible citizenship and social participation (Gordon, 2001). These developments have implications for children, who depend on their parents, guardians or other adults to enforce their social rights.

This chapter takes a critical look at these implications by focusing on the example of schooling. Secondary schooling became a constitutional right and was made compulsory in 1993 and parents were simultaneously rendered constitutionally 'co-responsible' for assuring it (Secretaría de Educación Pública, 1993: 25). This took place in the context of reforms aimed at encouraging the participation of private actors, including families, in assuring children's access to public education. The chapter examines how the right to secondary education is negotiated in families from a low-income urban neighbourhood in Guadalajara, Mexico, and raises some problems that can arise when parents are made responsible for guaranteeing their children's rights.

It is argued that the devolution to parents of responsibility for assuring their children's right to schooling assumes the *a priori* existence of

127

specific types of affective relations and economic capabilities in families that can be mobilised through appeals to parents' sense of responsibility towards their children. As will be seen below, however, the right to secondary schooling is neither articulated in law nor perceived by poorer families as an unconditional right. Rather, it takes on the character of a moral obligation that is ultimately negotiated and reinterpreted by parents attempting to reconcile their children's right to schooling with the economic hardship that can make complying with this extremely difficult. One result of this is that the right to schooling meshes with family norms and strategies of reciprocity in complicated ways that are not always favourable to children. The enforcement of children's right to schooling thus comes to lie squarely within the private sphere (see also Blair, this volume, for reflections on implications of the way that private-public boundaries are drawn in education).

Toothless rights?

The increasing influence of rights is a global trend that has had a profound impact on Mexico, as on the rest of Latin America. Popular awareness of the 'right to have rights' has intensified among many different groups – children, women, the elderly – as a result of increasing political pluralism, democratisation and the impact of international human rights discourse (Levinson, 1998; Salles, 2001; Fox, 2000: 184; Grindle, 2000; Kersting and Sperberg, 1999). Rights have become part of a language intelligible to all: a discursive field with a 'shared vocabulary and a shared ethic' (Rose, 1999: 28). They have likewise become a fundamental building block in political legitimation – a political driving force in their own right.

Paradoxically, however, in Latin America popular awareness of and demands for social rights is finding heightened expression at precisely the moment that government commitment to guaranteeing them is waning and the functions of government are becoming increasingly dispersed and decentralised (Silva, 1999). Despite the growing rights consensus and the progress made in terms of political rights in the region, this has not been matched by the consolidation of social rights, a contradiction that has been described as the growing divide between social citizenship and political citizenship (Sperberg, 2001: 138; Kersting and Sperberg, 1999: 133–4). In Mexico, as in the rest of Latin America, the major structural reforms of the 1980s and 1990s, and the ensuing austerity, severely reduced governments' capacity to guarantee social rights.[2] Governments obliged to 'do more with less', and follow-ing a global neo-liberal political logic,[3] refocused welfare provision from a universalist approach, offering basic universal subsidies, towards compensatory programmes targeted at the very poorest groups and often subject to conditions such as participation in certain activities, such as health checks and ensuring children's school attendance[4] (Martin, 1998; Gilbert, 1997). This restructuring marks the further erosion of a social protection system that has *always* been scanty and inadequate: the social rights that emanated from the 1910 Mexican Revolution and were enshrined in the 1917 Constitution – for instance, to education, health and housing – have never guaranteed effective protection for the poor (Gordon, 2001). Social rights have been effectively toothless: their provision is inadequate and there are no sanctions for their non-fulfilment.

An important shift has nonetheless occurred in the *meanings* associated with social rights in official discourse (Mesa-Lago, 1992). From being portrayed as a State responsibility, social rights have been reframed in terms of self-help, shared responsibility and the need for an active, participatory role for society in individual and social development. The notion of citizenship thus also becomes recast as contingent upon responsibility, involvement and personal choice, to be enacted in an array of different arenas and practices ranging from the political act of voting to sending one's children to school. This shift both opens up new opportunities for inclusion and democratic participation whilst simultaneously ushering in new forms of exclusion and control.

How do these forms of inclusion and exclusion affect children? Also, through what kinds of apparently free choices – and whose – do they manifest themselves in everyday practices? According to Kabeer (2002: 21), citizenship is 'a particular way of defining personhood that is in contradistinction to definitions based on status within hierarchical social relationships. It seeks to replace claims based on norms, charity, benevolence or patronage with rights guaranteed by the state'. These relationships include the family, where, in principle, ascriptive hierarchies of authority are replaced by relations of contract guaranteed by law (Dolgin, cited in Strathern, 1996: 42). These ideas of human rights in international agreements such as the UN Convention on the Rights of the Child merge with the notion of compulsory formal schooling that ushers in a prolonged period of childhood (Hart, 1991: 345). Education is seen as a fundamental 'empowerment right' for children in the sense that it facilitates the realisation of other key citizenship rights, such as freedom of expression and association, and access to employment, food and health (Coomans, 1996).

The following sections examine how the 1993 Education Act reframes the above-mentioned meanings of social rights, responsibilities and citizenship, and discuss how they are refracted and negotiated in families over the issue of secondary education. The Act effectively grants children the right to schooling, but at the same time places both enforcement of and accountability for this right in the hands of their families. The rights of children thus come to depend on the goodwill, capabilities and choices of the adults, typically parents or other family members, who are responsible for them.

Recasting educational policy: the 1993 reform

The context of austerity and the changes in the conceptualisation of social rights, described above, shaped the 1993 Educational Modernisation Act (Piester, 1997: 469; Trejo, 1996: 156).[5] The Act was the product of a situation where devolving centralised power and improving the quality of education were essential for political and economic reasons, but resources were scarce.[6]

A key change introduced by the Act was that secondary education was simultaneously made compulsory and a right.[7] This step was accompanied by an emphasis on the co-responsibility of parents/guardians and the State for children's education, with the former made responsible for ensuring attendance (SEP, 1993: 14).[8] Education is depicted in the Act both as an individual right and as a duty to society, where the development of the self becomes the means to develop society through its transformation into 'human capital'. At the same time, though, the Act emphasises that no sanctions will be imposed for failure to attend school and that lack of schooling must not be used as an excuse for discrimination in employment or other spheres:

> Education ennobles the individual and improves society ... [it] is a social duty whose reward is individual and collective progress, and the only sanction for not attending school is the person's more limited development. (Secretaría de Educación Pública, 1993: 20–21)

Making secondary schooling both compulsory and a right undoubtedly has positive dimensions inasmuch as it puts greater pressure on governments to universalise access to this level of education, something that still falls far short of reality.[9] However, the emphasis on family responsibility for ensuring school attendance has a number of less favourable implications. Chief among these is that educating oneself is portrayed not as a right or a duty to society but as a personal choice entirely devoid of legal repercussions. Failure to do so, on the other hand, is depicted as a *moral* transgression towards oneself and, by extension, towards society. When transposed into the family arena this means that the compulsory side of the right to schooling is left to parents to enforce, with the implicit message that non-compliance will truncate their *children's* opportunities.

In this way, secondary schooling is 'universalised' as a right but also simultaneously and paradoxically turned into a commodity, access to which, in poorer families, depends not on parents' free choices, as the Act implies, but on their economic capabilities. Significant private contributions to public schooling are nothing new in Mexico (see e.g. Bracho and Zamudio, 1997). Despite the constitutional premise that basic education is free (SEP, 1993),[10] the state actually provides only the school building and the teachers' salaries; all other outlays must be met by parents through so-called 'voluntary' enrolment contributions (*cuotas*), added to the cost of books, uniforms and other occasional expenses that are often far beyond the means of poorer families (Calvo, 1998; González de la Rocha *et al.*, 1990; Martin, 1996a; see also Tremlett, this volume). The opportunity costs of schooling can also be prohibitively high for poorer families, where a child in school is a potential worker lost[11] (World Bank, 1999: 51).

The lack of sanctions for non-attendance means that the right to schooling is articulated as a moral duty, not a legal absolute. In modern, liberal democratic regimes, plans, policies and programmes cannot merely be imposed upon micro-locales such as families and schools, but must be linked up with these different authorities through a process of conviction (Rose, 1999: 48). Under the 1993 Education Act, parents are, in theory, harnessed to the task of universalising basic education through a rights discourse that appeals to their moral obligations towards their children and the latter's expectations of them. Educational decisions and outcomes thus take on a private character (see also Blair, this volume). Ultimately, however, it is children who suffer the consequences if their parents fail to 'participate' in assuring their schooling.

Parents in this study had been informed at parent-teacher meetings of the changes in their role demanded by the introduction of compulsory secondary schooling. The school is the key arena in which information about policy changes, such as those described above, is

mediated. The way in which such information is mediated and received thus also comes to be shaped by the nature of the teacher-parent
relationship. In many schools, including the one studied here, an
authoritarian tradition exists between teachers and parents, where
teachers make no attempt to hide the fact that they consider parents to
be the key culprits in school failure and drop-out, owing to their low
educational levels, apathy and sometimes direct sabotage of their children's schooling (Blasco, 2001; see also Calvo, 1998). In this way, a
sense of blame is often directly transmitted to parents through their
relationships with teachers.

For their part, children also learn in school[12] that basic education is
their right, both according to Article 3 of the Mexican Constitution
and Universal Declaration of Human Rights; and that it is the obligation and responsibility of their 'parents/families' and 'society' to guarantee this right (De la Barreda, 1999: 64–66). How this awareness plays
out in practice, however, looks somewhat different. The following
section looks at how families recast their children's right to schooling
and their obligation to ensure their attendance into a *favour* that they
bestow upon them, with the explicit aim of reinforcing reciprocity in
the immediate present and in the future.

Parents: using schooling as a bargaining counter

Arguably, the transformation of secondary schooling into a right
enables children potentially to make new claims of their parents and
legitimately to protest if they fail to assure their schooling. New spaces
for appeal and reproach are, thus, opened up within the family.
Education is highly valued in Mexico as a route to personal progress
(*superación*) and a better future, and access to secondary schooling,
specifically, has become a key 'make or break' issue in Mexican education, both in terms of work and life opportunities.[13] Parents who do
not support their children's schooling thus risk being seen as failing;
both as parents, for denying their children's rights and limiting their
individual development and as citizens, for failing to assume their
responsibility to produce well-educated human capital. Following this
reasoning, the conversion of secondary schooling into a right means
that parents ought, in theory, to lose some of the leverage vis-à-vis
their children that supporting (or threatening to withdraw support for)
their secondary schooling afforded them before it was made compulsory, when poorer parents could and did frame their support for
secondary schooling as a *favour* they bestowed on their children.

However, as others have pointed out, students' awareness of their rights is a fairly recent phenomenon in Mexico (Levinson, 1998). For parents, too, it is a new situation. This study found that far from the right to schooling being perceived as unequivocal in families, it is instead deployed as a bargaining counter in family negotiations of different kinds, with parents reframing the right to schooling in the language of family rights and obligations.

Why do they do this? A key point in this connection is that children are an important resource for low-income families in Mexico, both in terms of their immediate contributions to the household economy and with respect to the 'promise' of future support to their parents. Studies from Mexico City and Guadalajara indicate that reciprocal exchange mechanisms among family and neighbours are a key survival strategy in areas where few families have access to social security benefits or insurance of any kind (Lomnitz, 1993: 26; Martin, 1990: 126). This reciprocity can take various forms: it is not necessarily just a short-term strategy, but can also operate over longer periods with, for instance, favours done to children 'repayable' when elderly or infirm parents need support (see e.g. Varley and Blasco, 2001). In this context, schooling may be conceptualised not only as an investment in children's futures but also in parents' own futures. By supporting their children's education, parents improve their children's life chances and, simultaneously, their capacity to take care of them in later life.

In this study, expectations of reciprocity explicitly underpinned the way parents talked about schooling their children. Students reported how their parents described the future 'payback' they expected from their educated children: 'They tell me not to leave them, and to work hard at my studies because if I want a great future the only way is to study'; 'They say "if you study you'll be able to achieve the profession you always wanted in life, and then you'll be able to help your parents"'. Parents reinforced their children's gratitude to them for supporting their schooling by emphasising the sacrifices that this implied for them. The link between parents' emphasis on sacrifice and their expectations of filial loyalty and help in return has been noted by others working in comparable sectors of Guadalajara. Martin (1996b: 198) notes that sacrifice is a key feature of the 'moral economy' of 'self-regulating' households, where the parent-child relationship is characterised by 'mutual sacrifice and reciprocal rights and duties in a hierarchy of authority' (Martin, 1996b: 199).[14] However, parents' sacrifices were not gratuitous,. Children had to earn the privilege of going to school by studying hard, getting good marks, and helping out and behaving properly at home (see also Martin, 1990; 1994; 1998a). Students and teachers confirmed that it was not uncommon for students to be withdrawn from school because of bad marks. Mothers in particular[15] emphasised the sacrifices they had to make to be able to send their children to school, often despite their husbands' indifference or opposition, an endeavour requiring many hardships.

In fact, mothers' and fathers' attitudes towards schooling and other matters of child rearing diverged substantially in the area studied. The very different upbringings brought to the same household by each partner at marriage do not necessarily dissolve into a shared and harmonious worldview or a jointly worked-out child rearing strategy, but instead can be a source of friction and conflict between parents.[16] The notion, implicit in the 1993 law, that 'parents' constitute a consensual and supportive unit when it comes to their children's schooling was thus found to be questionable in this study. It is also belied by literature documenting the many fissures and fractures that can characterise marital relations in low-income sectors such as that studied. Parenting is not necessarily consensual, and household members are not always altruistic or self-abnegating. Both decision-making and the distribution of resources in the family are likely to depend on its internal power-relations, with gendered and generational hierarchies shaping decision-making, which can be characterised by vigorous negotiation and conflict (González de la Rocha, 1995; Chant, 1985; Varley and Blasco, 1999; Benería and Roldán, 1987).

The right to schooling was thus translated into terms intelligible in the language of family norms of reciprocity, and re-interpreted as contingent upon the *student's* behaviour, not upon parents' willingness or capacity to send them to school. In this way, the notion of parental sacrifice is used to bargain over schooling, helping to secure children's compliance with parents' demands in the immediate present *and* appealing to an ethic of family solidarity with a view to assuring their own personal security in old age. Schooling thereby becomes a bargaining counter: concrete proof of sacrifices undertaken and favours owed. In this way, parents indirectly devolve responsibility for assuring the 'right' to schooling to their children. In theory, since secondary schooling is now a right, parents should no longer be able to condition their children's school attendance in this way. But since non-attendance is not sanctioned by the authorities, and since schooling does in fact involve many expenses and hardships that parents cannot afford (something that they take pains to ensure that their children realise), parents can continue to make schooling conditional upon compliance with present and future family obligations.

Children, adolescents or adults?

In this connection, it is also pertinent to discuss how differences in students' and their parents' perceptions of life stages influenced family negotiations over rights and responsibilities vis-à-vis schooling. As numerous scholars have noted, both experiences of childhood and adolescence and the boundaries and meanings attributed to these categories differ tremendously according to social and geographical context (Ariès, 1962; Caputo, 1995; Postman, 1994; Kett, 1977; Corsaro, 1997; James, Jenks and Prout, 1998). Assumptions about child development cannot, therefore, 'be borrowed wholesale by other cultures' (Hart, 1998: 27). In Mexico among poorer sectors, childhood, in the sense of a carefree period unburdened by adult responsibilities, ends far earlier than in Europe and the US. Children are involved in domestic and productive work from early on and 'in reality one of the few times when they behave (or are required to behave) like children in the conventional sense that the school takes for granted is, precisely, when they are pupils' (Tedesco, 1983: 140).

Similarly, the notion of 'adolescence' is relatively new among poorer sectors in Mexico and is differently understood among students and their parents. The secondary school has been a key element in precipitating the use of this term, particularly since it was made a compulsory level of basic education in 1993 (see also Levinson, 1999). Most parents interviewed for this study had never been to secondary school and some were, in fact, not even quite sure what an adolescent was or were ambivalent about its implications (see Blasco 2001: 311–312). To them, their offspring were beyond an age where they could be considered children; yet their being in school and unable to engage in productive activities rendered them child-like. At the same time, parents demanded more responsible behaviour from their children precisely because they had received a lengthier education than themselves: in other words, their greater knowledge should render them capable of making their own decisions.

Conversely, students were explicitly confronted at school[17] with a notion of adolescence framed in terms of a 'liberal modernist emphasis on an adolescent's development towards autonomy, individual rights, and freedom of choice in pursuing career issues' (Levinson, 1999: 157). Their life choices are not presented, at school, as bound or constrained in any way by family obligations (see Blasco, 2001: 311–312 for further details). Students at La Colina struggled to reconcile their school identity as adolescents – people-in-the-making – working towards their own individual advancement, with home demands upon them to be fully-formed, productive and responsible household members. Liberal discourses of self-development and individual rights thus merge at secondary school with discourses of adolescence, with perceptions of childhood and adolescence often varying tremendously between children and their parents who have never been to secondary school.

The net result of the above contradictions was that parents tended to leave decisions about schooling, explicitly or implicitly, up to their children, either by conditioning school attendance upon various types of domestic demands or simply through non-interference – a kind of *laissez faire* approach (see Blasco 2001 and 2003). Not wishing to be blamed for depriving their children of opportunities, yet unable to support their schooling adequately because of the hardship entailed, this is an understandable reaction. A key point here is that in a context where schooling decisions are largely in their hands, students' experiences of the school can greatly affect their willingness to persist with their studies or not. Currently, the hierarchical organisation and authoritarian nature of Mexican secondary schools means that, in practice, many students experience the school environment as rather harsh and offputting; and in practice they certainly enjoy few 'rights' there (Calvo, 1998; Blasco, 2003). At the same time, on the home front they are painfully aware that their school attendance is a drain on a hard-pressed family economy and in some cases also a source of controversy between parents. The paradoxical result of these push and pull factors is that if the decision is left up to them, students may well choose not to exercise their right to schooling, making life, in the short term at least, easier for all concerned.

Conclusion

The chapter argues that in contexts where governments cannot guarantee the social right to schooling, shifting this responsibility to the family is not a viable alternative. The Mexican 1993 Education Act presupposes that the right to schooling will be assured through mobilising parents' sense of moral obligation towards their children, but this cannot be guaranteed, particularly given marked differences in mothers' and fathers' attitudes to their children's education. Not only does children's right to schooling then became contingent upon parents' consent and economic capabilities, but accountability and 'sanctions' for non-fulfilment of this right may also come to be located in the realm of the family, with children potentially blaming parents for denying them opportunities. Parents can hold schooling hostage to their children's compliance with certain demands, e.g. for good marks and behaviour. In other words, they must 'earn' the right to study. Responsibility for schooling is thus indirectly ultimately shifted to children, those least capable of assuming it.

A broader conclusion to draw from this is that in contexts where the failure to guarantee children's rights is not subject to sanctions, it must be expected that these rights will be negotiated and accommodated within local circumstances, in which the meanings associated with categories such as 'children' or 'parents' may not correspond at all with legal definitions or assumptions. In this connection, discussions of rights to and responsibilities for education must strive to be sensitive to how the perceived boundaries between childhood, adolescence and adulthood can differ tremendously in different geographical and social contexts, and between the different actors involved; in particular, teachers, mothers and fathers, and students.

The chapter also highlights the potentially exclusionary consequences of prevailing political discourses of participation and responsible citizenship. Once a social right like schooling is articulated in terms of *choices* it becomes fundamentally inequitable, since poorer families often cannot make the right choices – those deemed morally right and conducive to promoting their children's futures. Thus, socioeconomic differences, which should be attenuated through the 'equality of abstract rights' that is an integral part of citizenship, are, instead, reproduced by these rights (García Canclini, 2001: 15).

Notes

1. The paper takes as its point of departure the author's PhD dissertation: '*In loco parentis?* Students, families and secondary schooling in urban Mexico'. The data resulted from a year's fieldwork employing mainly qualitative methods, including in-depth biographical and group interviews with students, staff and parents, observation, and a survey of 84 students. Supplementary data were collected from other nearby secondary schools, including interviews with school counsellors. Data are also included from research carried out with Dr. Ann Varley of the Department of Geography, University College London, from 1997 to 1999, on the ESRC-funded research project: 'Gendered Housing: Identity and Independence in Urban Mexico'. I am grateful to Ann for permission to draw on empirical data from the project for the purposes of this article.

2. Between 1980 and 1995, social spending on housing, social security and welfare, and education fell substantially, with spending on health unchanged (Grindle, 2000: 27).

3. These changes were part of larger packages of economic reforms supported by international agencies such as the World Bank and the International Monetary Fund, and implemented through structural adjustment programmes (SAPs). The reforms increased the influence of markets on economic decision-making, reduced that of national governments, and promoted trade liberalisation, tariff reductions on imports, privatisation and decentralisation (Gwynne and Kay, 1999: 14 and 68).

4. In Mexico, the PROGRESA poverty-alleviation programme (reframed as *Oportunidades* under the current Fox administration), introduced during the government of President Ernesto Zedillo, is one example. Families received nutritional supplements and cash payments as long as they complied with certain 'conditions', such as regular health checks for women and sending their children to school. However, such targeted programmes only attend a very small percentage of the poor population and barely begin to address the severity of difficulties experienced by families in, for example, schooling their children (Martin, 2000: 8).

5. The reform was also partly instigated by preparations for the imminent signing of the North American Free Trade Agreement (NAFTA) and the pressing need to produce better-skilled workers to facilitate Mexico's insertion into the global economy (Martin, 1993: 2). At the same time, it formed part of a political project aimed at shoring up the legitimacy of the (then) ruling party, the PRI, by providing at least a facade of political opening and a sharper focus on equity.

6. Key specific aims of the reform included: to decentralise and to involve the states to a greater extent in educational planning; to promote teacher training and incentives; to restructure the powerful and volatile teachers' union, the SNTE; and to promote 'social participation' in education (Rodríguez, 1997: 83). See Blasco (2001); Government of Mexico (1992); Martin (1998); Quiroz (1990 and 1995); SEP (1993) for further details concerning the changes ushered in by the reform.

7. Primary schooling was made compulsory under the 1917 Constitution.

8. The 1993 amendment to paragraph 1 of Article 31 of the Constitution reads that 'it is the duty of all Mexicans to ... ensure that their children or tutees attend public or private schools, in order to receive primary and secondary education ...' (SEP, 1993: 30). However, in much of the document, parents are named as solely responsible for children's school attendance, e.g. 'Parents are made co-responsible for ensuring that their children exercise their right to education' (SEP, 1993: 25; see also pp. 35; 45; 21); and in regard to other school-related duties, such as attendance at social participation councils and parents' associations (SEP, 1993: 81).

9. Statistics from 2000 show that only 76.1% of children starting secondary school completed it (70.3% in Jalisco where the present study was carried out). If primary schooling is included in this calculation, one finds that of 100 children starting primary school only 65 complete their secondary education (61 in Jalisco), i.e. their compulsory basic education (www.inegi.gob.mx).

10. In July 2002, a single secondary school text book from one of the cheapest publishers certified by the Education Ministry, Santillana, cost 90 pesos – around two days' minimum wage.

11. See also World Bank (1998: 83). Work may mean income from a job, or it may mean help in the home, especially in the case of girls, who are responsible for looking after younger children to release their mothers for work outside the home (Martin, 1994: 8; Moore, 1994: 23). The OECD (1998: 360) notes that: 'From the individual's point of view, costs correspond to direct costs of tuition fees, educational materials, student living costs and forgone earnings during the time of study'.

12. Until 1993, students were informed of this during a class called Educational Guidance (*Orientación Educativa*); in 1999 this subject was replaced by Civic Education (*Formación Cívica*), which devotes a section in its textbooks to children's rights, including the right to basic education.

13. It is widely acknowledged that primary education alone is no longer sufficient to ensure an adequate income or to improve a young person's chances of social mobility (Reimers, 2001; Martin, 1990; 1992; Blasco, 2001).

14. In Mexico, such relations of reciprocity have been documented as permeating many areas of social life, in various forms. They are present in networks among kin or neighbours, ritual bonds of reciprocity such as *compradrazgo*; they can be horizontal, i.e. among equals, or vertical within an established hierarchy of authority; and they exist in the political system, the unions, and both the public and the private sectors (Mantilla, 1999; Lomnitz, 1993; Lomnitz, 1982). 'Traditional kinship and social exchange ties' are an 'integral part of political institutions' (Carlos and Anderson 1980 in Lomnitz 1982: 65). Lomnitz and Pérez-Lizaur's (1987) study of a *Mexican Elite Family* over several generations shows how 'patron-client relations permeate both family and enterprise' (see also Lomnitz, 1982: 60; Vangstrup, 1999).

15. Self-sacrificing motherhood is a powerful ideal in Mexico that can secure children's sympathy and loyalty. This ideal has an important inbuilt 'welfare' function, as among many low-income families children are often women's only future safety net (under Mexican Social Security legislation, the spouse, children, siblings and parents of a contributor (government employee) have the right to health cover). Many women in such contexts do not have jobs that could provide them with social security cover in old age (or husbands who do) and some form of support from their children in later life is crucial for them, especially given that they are more likely to be widowed than men (Varley and Blasco, 2001).

16. Interviews with mothers showed that they drew heavily upon their recollections of their own upbringings when discussing the way they brought up their own children, often stressing how different their own perspectives and upbringing had been from their husbands'. Their reference for how to bring up their own children was their own upbringing ('*mi casa*'), not a consensus they had reached together with their husbands (Blasco, 2001).

17. In e.g. their Civic and Ethic Education classes (*Formación Cívica y Etica*).

References

Ariès, P. (1962) *Centuries of Childhood*. New York: Alfred A. Knopf.

Benería, L. and Roldán, M. (1987) *The Crossroads of Class and Gender*. London: University of Chicago Press.

Blasco, M. (2001) In loco Parentis? Students, Families and Secondary Schooling in Urban Mexico. PhD dissertation, International Development Studies: Roskilde University (Denmark).

Blasco, M. (2003) 'Los maestros deben ser como segundos padres'? Escuela secundaria, afectividad, y pobreza en México', *Revista Mexicana de Investigación Educativa*, 8 September–December.

Bracho, T. and Zamudio, A. (1997) 'El gasto privado en educación. Mexico, 1992', *Revista Mexicana de Investigación Educativa*, 2 (4) July–December: 323–347.

Calvo, B. (1998) 'The policy of modernisation of education', in: Zou, Y. and Trueba, H. (eds), *Ethnic Identity and Power: Cultural Contexts of Political Action in School and Society*. Albany: State University of New York: 159–185.

Caputo, V. (1995) 'Anthropology's silent 'others': a consideration of some conceptual and methodological issues for the study of youth and children's cultures', in: Amit-Talai, V. and Wulff, H. (eds), *Youth Cultures: A Cross-Cultural Perspective*. London: Routledge: 19–42.

Chant, S. (1985) 'Family formation and female roles in Querétaro, Mexico', *Bulletin of Latin American Research*, 4 (1): 17–32.

Coomans, F. (1996) 'Core contents of the right to education', in: Erazo, X., Kirkwood, M. and De Vlaming, F. (eds) *Academic Freedom 4 Education and Human Rights*. London: Zed Books.

Cornwall, A. (2002) 'Locating citizen participation', *IDS Bulletin*, 33 (2): 49–58.

Corsaro, W. (1997) *The Sociology of Childhood*. London: Sage.

De la Barreda, J. (1999) Formación Cívia y Etica 1. México: Santillana.

Finch, J. (1989) *Family Obligations and Social Change*. Cambridge: Polity Press.

Fox, J. (2000) 'State-society relations in Mexico: historical legacies and contemporary trends, *Latin American Research Review*, 35 (2): 183–215.

García Canclini, N. (2001) *Consumers and Citizens*. Minneapolis and London: University of Minnesota Press.

Gilbert, A. (1997) 'Poverty and social policy in Latin America', *Social Policy and Administration*, 31 (4) December: 320–335.

González de la Rocha, M., Escobar, A., and Martínez, M. (1990) 'Estrategias versus conflicto: reflexiones para el estudio del grupo doméstico en época de crisis', in: De la Peña, G, Durán, J. M., Escobar, A. and García De Alba, J. (eds), Crisis, Conflicto y Sobrevivencia: Estudios sobre la Sociedad Urbana en México, Guadalajara: Universidad de Guadalajara/Centro de Investigaciones y Estudios Superiores en Antropología Social (CIESAS): 351–367.

González de la Rocha, M. (1995) 'The urban family and poverty in Latin America', *Latin American Perspectives*, 85, 22 (2) Spring: 13–31.

Gordon, S. (2001) 'Ciudadanía y derechos sociales: ¿criterios distributivos?', in: Ziccardi, A. (ed.), Pobreza, Desigualdad Social y Ciudadanía: los límites de las políticas sociales en América Latina. Buenos Aires: CLACSO: 23–36.

Grindle, M. (2000) 'The social agenda and the politics of reform in Latin America', in: Tulchin, J. and Garland, A. (eds), *Social Development in Latin America*. Boulder and London: Lynne Rienner: 17–52.

Guttman, M. (1996) *The Meanings of Macho*. London: University of California Press.

Gwynne, R. and Kay, C. (1999) 'Latin America transformed: changing paradigms, debates and alternatives', in: Gwynne, R. and Kay, C. (eds), *Latin America Transformed: Globalisation and Modernity*. London: Arnold: 2–29.

Hart, S. (1991) 'Children's rights in education: An historical perspective', *School Psychology Review*, 20 (3): 345–359.

Hart, R. (1998) 'The developing capacities of children to participate', in: Johnson, V., Ivan-Smith, E., Gordon, G., Pridmore, P. and Scott, P. (eds), *Stepping Forward: Children and Young People's Participation in the Development Process*. London: Intermediate Technology Publications: 27–31.

James, A., Jenks, C. and Prout, A. (1998) *Theorizing Childhood*. Cambridge: Polity Press.

Kabeer, N. (2002) 'Citizenship, affiliation and exclusion: perspectives from the South', *IDS Bulletin*, 33 (2): 12–23.

Kersting, N. and Sperberg, J. (1999) 'Pobreza urbana, sociedad civil y ciudadanía en Chile y Brasil', *Nueva Sociedad*, 164: 133–145.

Kett, J. (1977) *Rites of Passage*. New York: Basic Books.

La Jornada (14.08.02a) 'El presidente Fox creó un millón 300 mil pobres'.

La Jornada (14.08.02b) 'En la pobreza, 53.7% de mexicanos; fijan nuevos parámetros de medición'.

Lehmann, D. (2000) 'Female-headed households in Latin America and the Caribbean: problems of analysis and conceptualisation'. Mimeo.

LeVine, S. with Sunderland Correa, C. (1993) Dolor y Alegría: Women and Social Change in Urban Mexico. Madison: University of Wisconsin Press.

Levinson, B. (1998) 'The moral construction of student rights', *Journal of Contemporary Ethnography*, 27 (1): 45–66.

Levinson, B. (1999) 'Una etapa siempre difícil': concepts of adolescence and secondary education in Mexico', *Comparative Education Review*, 43 (2) May: 129–161.

Lomnitz, L. (1975/1993) Como Sobreviven los Marginados. Mexico: Siglo Veintiuno Editores.

Lomnitz, L. (1982) 'Horizontal and vertical relations and the social structure of urban Mexico', *Latin American Research Review*, 22 (2): 51–74.

Lomnitz, L. and Pérez-Lizaur, M. (1991) 'Dynastic growth and survival strategies: the solidarity of Mexican grand-families', in: Jelin, E. (ed.), *Family, Household and Gender Relations in Latin America*. London and Paris: Kegan Paul and UNESCO: 123–132.

Mantilla, L. (1999) 'Familia y familiaridad en el mundo público'. Paper presented at the Department of Educational Studies, University of Guadalajara.

Martin, C. (1990) 'To hold one's own in the world': issues in the educational culture of urban working class families in West Mexico', Compare, 20 (2): 115–138.

Martin, C. (1992) 'The dynamics of school relations on the urban periphery of Guadalajara, Western Mexico', *European Review of Latin American and Caribbean Studies*, 53 December: 61–81.

Martin, C. (1993) 'On the cheap: educational modernization at school level in Mexico', in: Allsop, T. and Brock, C. (eds), *Key Issues in Educational Development*. Cambridge: Cambridge University Press/Triangle Books: 145–166.

Martin, C. (1994) 'Let the young birds fly: schooling, work and emancipation in rural west Mexico', *Compare*, 24 (3): 259–276.

Martin, C. (1996a) 'Economic strategies and moral principles in the survival of poor households in Mexico. An urban and rural comparison', *Bulletin of Latin American Research*, 15 (2): 193–210.

Martin, C. (1996b) 'Personal and social development in post-compulsory education in the UK and Mexico', *Compare*, 26 (2) June: 133–152.

Martin, C. (1998) 'More for less: the Mexican cult of educational efficiency and its consequences at school level', in: Buchert, L (ed.), *Education Reform in the South in the 1990s*. Paris: UNESCO: 165–190.

Martin, C. (2000) 'Reform and educational development: current thinking on school improvement in Mexico'. Paper presented at the 2000 meeting of the Latin American Studies Association (LASA), Miami, March 16–18.

Melhuus, M. (1990) 'A shame to honour – a shame to suffer', *Ethnos*, 55 (1–2): 5–25.

Mesa-Lago, C. (1992) 'Protection for the informal sector in Latin America and the Caribbean by social security or alternative means', in: Tokman, V. (ed.), *Beyond Regulation: the Informal Economy in Latin America*. Boulder and London: Lynne Rienner Publishers: 169–206.

Moore, H. (1994) 'Is there a crisis in the family?', Occasional Paper no. 3, World Summit for Social Development. Geneva: United Nations Research Institute for Social Development.

MOST-FLACSO (1997) Modernización Institucional de las Políticas Sociales en América Latina: El Caso de Chile, Brasil, Argentina y México. Santiago: MOST-FLACSO.

Nickson, A. (1998) 'Educational reform and decentralisation in Latin America'. Paper presented at the Efficiency and Equity Social Policy Study Group Seminar, Institute for Latin American Studies, University of London, 30 October.

OECD (1998) Education at a Glance: OECD Indicators. Paris: OECD.

Palacios, J. (1990), 'La economía subterránea de América Latina ¿alternativa obligada de supervivencia o mecanismo ilegal de producción?', in: De la Peña, G., Durán, J. M., Escobar, A. and García De Alba, J. (eds), *Crisis, Conflicto y Sobrevivencia: Estudios sobre la Sociedad Urbana en México*. Guadalajara: Universidad de Guadalajara/Centro de Investigaciones y Estudios Superiores en Antropología Social (CIESAS): 119–138.

Piester, K. (1997) 'Targeting the poor: the politics of social policy reform in Mexico', in: Chalmers, D. *et al.*, (eds), *The New Politics of Inequality in Latin America: Rethinking Participation and Representation*. Oxford: Oxford University Press: 468–488.

Postman, N. (1994) *The Disappearance of Childhood*. New York: Vintage Books.

Quiroz, R. (1990) 'Los nuevos planes y programas no resuelven los problemas actuales de la secundaria', Documento DIE no. 18, México: Departamento de Investigaciones Educativas (Centro de Investigación y Estudios Avanzados del Instituto Politécnico Nacional (DIE/CINEVESTAV).

Quiroz, R. (1995) 'Los cambios de 1993 en los planes y programas de estudio en la educación secundaria', Documento DIE no. 40, México: Departamento de Investigaciones Educativas (Centro de Investigación y Estudios Avanzados del Instituto Politécnico Nacional (DIE/CINEVESTAV).

Reimers, F. (2001) 'Educación, exclusión y justicia social en América Latina', in: Ornelas, C. (ed.), *Investigación y Política Educativas: Ensayos en honor de Pablo Latapí*. México, Santillana: 187–230.

Rodríguez, V. (1997) *Decentralisation in Mexico*. Boulder: Westview Press.

Rose, N. (1999) *Powers of Freedom*. Cambridge: University of Cambridge.

Salles, V. (2001) 'Familias en transformación y códigos por transformar', in: Gomes, C. (ed.), *Procesos Sociales, Población y Familia*. México: FLACSO/ Porrúa: 103–126.

Selby, H., Lorenzen, S., Murphy, A., Morris, E. and Winter, M. (1990/1994) 'La familia urbana mexicana frente a la crisis', in: De la Peña, G., Durán, J. M., Escobar, A. and García De Alba, J. (eds), *Crisis, Conflicto y Sobrevivencia: Estudios sobre la Sociedad Urbana en México*. Guadalajara: Universidad de Guadalajara/Centro de Investigaciones y Estudios Superiores en Antropología Social (CIESAS): 369–388.

SEP (1993) Artículo 3° y Ley General de Educación. México: Secretaría de Educación Pública.

Silva, P. (1999) 'The new political order in Latin America: towards technocratic democracies?', in: Gwynne, R. and Kay, C. (eds), *Latin America Transformed*. London: Arnold: 51–65.

Sperberg, J. (2001) 'El significado de la sociedad civil para los pobres urbanos en Chile', *Nueva Sociedad*, 171: 133–145.

Stevens E. (1973) 'Marianismo: the other face of machismo in Latin America', in Pescatello, A. (ed.), *Female and Male in Latin America*. London: University of Pittsburgh Press: 89–101.

Strathern, M. (1996) 'Enabling identity? Biology, choice and the new reproductive technologies', in: Hall, S. and Du Gay, P. (eds), *Questions of Cultural Identity*. London: Sage: 37–52.

Subrahmanian, R. (2002) 'Citizenship and the 'right to education': perspectives from the Indian Context', *IDS Bulletin*, 33 (2): 74–81.

Tedesco, E. (1983) 'Pedagogical model and school failure', *CEPAL Review*, 21: 131–146.

Trejo, G. (1996) 'La reforma educativa en México: ambivalencia frente al cambio', in: Roett, R. (ed.), *El Desafío de la Reforma Institucional en México*. Mexico: Siglo Veintiuno Editores: 155–180.

Vangstrup, U. (1999) 'Collective efficiency or efficient individuals? Assessment of a theory for local industrial development and the case of regional industrial clusters in Mexico', PhD dissertation, Department of Geography and International Development Studies, Roskilde University, Denmark.

Varley, A. and Blasco, M. (1999) '"Reaping what they sow?" Older women, housing and family dynamics in urban Mexico', in: INSTRAW (ed.), *Ageing in a Gendered World*. Santo Domingo: United Nations INSTRAW (Institute for Research and Training on Women): 153–178.

Varley, A. and Blasco, M. (2000) 'Exiled to the home: masculinity and ageing in urban Mexico', *European Journal of Development Research*, 12 (2) December: 115–138.

Varley, A. and Blasco, M. (2001) '¿Cosechan lo que siembran? Mujeres ancianas, vivienda y relaciones familiares en el México urbano', in: Gomes, C. (ed.), *Procesos Sociales, Población y Familia*. México: FLACSO/Porrúa: 301–322.

World Bank (1998) *World Development Indicators*. Washington: World Bank

World Bank (1999) *World Development Report 1998/99: Knowledge for Development*. New York: Oxford University Press.

Young, M. (1958) *The Rise of the Meritocracy 1870–2033: An Essay on Education and Equality*. London, Thames and Hudson.

9

'Gypsy Children Can't Learn': Roma in the Hungarian Education System

Annabel Tremlett

Introduction

The motivation for writing the paper on which this chapter is based came from my first year spent in Hungary as a 'Youth Action' volunteer with VSO (Voluntary Services Overseas), in a town in the middle of the Hungarian Great Plains, working in an office of a non-governmental organisation (2000–2001). I started to help out, twice a week, in a mainstream school that had become unofficially segregated. It was known as 'the gypsy school' and I was told that I was crazy to go there because the children would be wild and violent. So it was with slight trepidation and laden with balloons and sweets (for bribery) that I entered the gates of the school, noticing on my way in that someone had scrawled 'bolondok háza' ('mad house') on the outside wall.[1] In the school, I found there to be – children. Boisterous, shy, intelligent, lazy, sharp, slow, happy, sad, excitable ... children. The two things they all had in common was that their families were often very poor, and that people (including, sometimes, the children themselves) used the word 'cigányok' (gypsies) to label them, often as if it were a swear word or a disease.[2] The account that follows[3] came about as a result of my interest in why these children so often failed at school.[4]

In early summer 2002, a year after I wrote the original paper, I was sitting with some Roma children at a Saturday morning club in the local Gypsy Minority Cultural Centre. I was talking with two young sisters, Zsuzsa and Kati, about how Kati, aged five, was just about to start school.

'What school will you go to?' I asked,
'The one on Nyíri street', she replied.

145

'Huh!' intervened her older sister who attends a local mainstream school, 'that's the *special* school, only stupid crazy people go to the *special* school.'

I frowned at Zsuzsa and looked back at Kati.

'How come you're going to that school?', I asked.

'I did a test and I failed', said Kati with a shrug of her shoulders.

Zsuzsa was fidgeting, 'Tell Annabel what you said! Tell her what you said!'

Kati looked at me wide-eyed and said:

'They asked me what I did in the mornings ... and so I said ... I wake up, I go outside, I play with my friends ...' – her voice trailed off.

'DUH!' scorned Zsuzsa, 'you're meant to say: "I get up, I get dressed, I eat breakfast, I brush my teeth, I go to the toilet."'

'But Zsuzsa,' protested Kati, 'I don't *do* that!'

'*I* know that,' replied Zsuzsa, 'But you *know* what you're meant to say, I *told* you!'

She looked distastefully at her little sister and rolled her eyes:

'See? ... you *are* crazy.'

This anecdote illustrates some of the many complex processes involved in a child's access to education in Hungary and shows the fundamental cultural expectations of schools prior to their even accepting a child. This cultural divide has been seen as a problem to be addressed and the trend in 'dealing' with Roma pupils has firmly focused on their 'socialisation'. This is evident in a report written in 2000, to show how the Hungarian state was improving the situation of its largest minority:

> Besides arranging pre-school schooling and organising various forms of halls of residence adjacent to schools, the programme also considers the formation – where demand for such is apparent on the part of the Roma minority – of new educational centres. Particular attention is paid to the introduction of various special educational forms: here the programme endeavours to reduce deficiencies but in such a way as to avoid educational segregation (Doncsév 2000)

Although 'deficiencies' are elsewhere vaguely defined as 'the social inequalities of opportunity' (p. 6), the solution is far more precise: 'pre-school schooling'. This follows a common representation that depicts the Roma child as someone who needs to be 'pre-socialised' – i.e. someone without social habits. This stereotype is hardly a new one and has a well-researched history of its own (see Willems, 1998; Hancock, 2002). As well as repeating offensive and harmful representations, it does not offer any satisfactory explanations for the perceived failure of Roma children in the Hungarian education system.

The focus of this chapter is on the Hungarian government's failures to ensure the implementation of policies aimed at Roma people. This is evident in the reports and policies commissioned by the Hungarian State and the European Union (especially the accession process, which came to fruition in May 2004), not only in terms of what these documents say, but also how they choose to say it. The perceived 'failure' of Roma children cannot be laid solely at the feet of the Hungarian government, however, since this is part of wider processes that illustrate how a society can be structured for the dominant majority (not just ethnic, but also cultural and social) and how a focus on 'failure' can stagnate debates about the education of minority groups.[5]

The chapter will look at the history of the segregation of Roma children in the Hungarian education system and explore how this has been sustained and exacerbated in recent times, becoming a more intense, visible and openly debated issue in recent years. It will then consider other issues that may contribute to the 'failure' of Roma children in school and look at how Roma compare with their peers in the education system in Hungary.

Segregation in education

A Hungarian government report in 2000 states: 'the situation of the Roma in Hungary stands at the forefront of world attention' (Doncsév: 2000). Indeed, in European institutional discourses their situation has had increasing prominence since 1993, when improving the situation of Roma minorities became one of the criteria to be met by candidate countries wishing to join the EU. However, although the Hungarian government was at first complimented on its efforts to introduce a comprehensive strategy towards tackling Roma poverty and exclusion, in the 1998 EU Regular Report,[6] more recently there has been criticism that has focused on poor implementation of the policies.[7]

It is also evident, however, that segregation is the outcome of the Hungarian school system itself, with Roma minorities receiving substandard education. During his term in office, the Minorities Ombudsman of the Hungarian Government, Mr Jenő Kaltenbach, repeatedly voiced his concerns at the continuation of the segregation of the Roma in education.[8] Therefore, despite the fact that Hungary has freely committed itself to eliminating racial discrimination in all its forms,[9] the experience of Roma students in mainstream education is one of discrimination, segregation and marginalisation, and reports commissioned by international bodies, as well as by the Hungarian Government itself, identify segregation of the Roma in education as a focal point of criticism.[10]

'Collective Dustbins' and 'Mass Warehouses': Roma in Special Schools

Perhaps one of the most disturbing illustrations of segregation is the method through which Roma children in Hungary have been systematically and purposefully removed from mainstream education and placed into *Speciális Iskolák* (special schools) reserved for children with mental or physical learning difficulties. There are reportedly 678 such schools in Hungary, 659 of them being called *Gyógypedagógiai Iskola* (school for handicapped children), the remainder being specialist schools for children with specific learning difficulties (for example, deafness or blindness) (Kaltenbach, 1996). Over 40 per cent of the students in special schools are estimated to be Roma (see Table 9.1 below). Special schools have been described as a space where 'children with similar problems can further their education using specialised equipment' but it is also argued that sending children to such schools will be to the benefit of mainstream schools since 'it is also good for the school the children leave behind as they will be more homogenous and able to learn at a faster pace'.[11]

This move to homogeneity of perceived learning skills also, however, parallels an increase in ethnic homogeneity in different school settings. According to research, there should be the same rate of disabled children in every population,[12] yet, in Hungary, a Roma child is much more likely to be placed in a special school than a non-Roma child. This is clearly seen in Table 9.1. The percentage of Roma people in Hungary is roughly 5%[13], yet from 1992–1993, over 40 per cent of children in special schools are reported to be of Roma origin. A 1998 government study revealed 90 per cent of pupils in special schools in Borsod county were Roma (Kadét, 2001). Two years later, in 2000, research undertaken by the European Roma Rights Centre (henceforth called ERRC) in the eastern Hungarian town Hajdúhadház also revealed that around 90 per cent of the special school population were Roma.

Whereas in some countries (such as Bulgaria) separate education is primarily rooted in residential segregation,[14] in Hungary the placing

Table 9.1 Roma learning in Special Schools

School Year	Total Number Learning	Out of this, number of Roma	Percentage of Roma
1974–75	29,617	7,730	26.1%
1977–78	31,666	9,753	30.8%
1981–82	33,079	12,107	36.6%
1985–86	39,395	15,640	39.7%
1992–93	32,099	13,662	42.6%

Source: Cigány tanulók az alsó-és középfokú oktatásban (Gypsies learning in primary and secondary education) Budapest, TÁRKI, 1986 (the first four lines); MKM Statisztikai Föosztály (last line).

of Roma children in special institutions is based on a government-sponsored test assignment system that claims to provide special assistance to (mostly Roma) students with special needs. The nursery or primary school teacher decides whether the child needs to take this test, according to their personal experience of the child. The child is then referred to a local committee of experts which uses various visual and written tests as well as measuring for a minimum IQ. This test is orientated towards the dominant majority and thus requires a good understanding of Hungarian language, culture, and spelling (Human Rights Watch Report, 1998). As a consequence, many Roma children fail this initial test and hence are directed to special schools. A Roma researcher for the ERRC reported that a Roma child undergoing the test in Budapest was asked to draw a triangle – 'háromszög' in Hungarian, which literally means 'three nails'. The child immediately drew three nails and was consequently told that due to this error, she would need a specialised education in a special school [personal communication, 2001].

Other Roma children may pass the test, but during the school year are put in separate 'catch-up classes', where they are told that they do not fulfil the requirements of the school and are hence recommended for relegation to the special school (see quote below). In Hungary, there are also financial incentives for parents with children in special schools, as well as for the special schools themselves. In the current economic climate in Hungary, in which 60–80 per cent of Roma are unemployed, such payments for special schooling provide another mechanism for the perpetuation of separate, substandard schooling for Roma (Cahn *et al.*, 1999). One Roma mother told of how three of her six children were moved into a special school from their primary school in Kecskemét, a town in central Hungary. When asked why her children were sent to the special school she replied:

> The problem was with the headmaster [of the mainstream school]. The reason was simply discrimination. He didn't like the gypsies, but he had to accept the gypsy students because it was law, that is the children lived near the school so they had to attend that school. This school has got a 'special needs class' that just produces children for the mentally handicapped school[15]

This mother was so concerned about her children being placed in the special school that she organised a meeting with the head teacher of the special school, who admitted to her that between 60–70 per cent of his pupils were perfectly capable of mainstream education and did not need to be there at all.

In Hungary, legislation stopping children who had graduated from special schools from continuing in anything other than a parallel system of substandard secondary schools was changed in 1992, when the stamping of identification papers with 'special needs' was outlawed. Although this has stopped the 'official' labelling, however, it is well known in every region which are the special schools and who attends them, so once a child has been recorded as attending such a school, it remains an unofficial stamp for all to see. According to ERRC research, therefore, children graduating from special schools in Hungary are still unable to cross the line from special primary education into mainstream secondary education (Petrova, 2002).

The rules governing the transfer of children to special needs classes have been repeatedly tightened (for example, there is now the right to have an expert external examination), but these changes have failed to prevent the use of such classes as 'massive deposits', 'collective dustbins', or 'mass warehouses' for Romani children.[16] The high numbers of children in such classes are not, however, an indication of the intellectual unsuitability of the Roma but of the discrimination that is practised against them and of the pedagogical failure of the institutions of State education. The consequence of such failure for the many Romani children in these types of institutions is that their chances of further study or employment are drastically reduced.

Segregation within mainstream schools[17]

The past forty years in Hungarian history has seen a continuing increase in the segregation of Roma minorities in mainstream education. In 1961, the Hungarian Socialist Workers Party, which at that time had a monopoly on political life, created the category of 'hátrányos helyzetü ('socially deprived') into which Roma children were placed. From 1962, so-called 'C-classes' were established for these 'socially deprived' children, 'C' being the lowest level on a scale of A–C. This also became synonymous with 'C' for 'cigány' (gypsy) (Cahn *et al.*, 1999) and in 1971, Kemény *et al.* reported that these classes were predominantly Roma. Between 1962 and 1971, the number of these classes more than doubled, from 70 to 181 (Kemény *et al.*, 1976). A subsequent report by Radó (2001) found that in 1995, in 132 of 840 mainstream schools surveyed there were separate classes made up predominantly of Roma children. If we extrapolate from this figure, it would suggest that, given that there were 3,809 mainstream schools in Hungary at the time of the survey, as many as 16 per cent of primary schools were practising racial segregation in the everyday schooling of their pupils.[18]

Two examples illustrate the nature of such discrimination. In the town of Bogács, in northern Hungary, Romani children are taught in separate classrooms, use separate toilets and are even made to drink from separate plastic cups in the canteen and are called by their non-Roma classmates 'bushmen'.[19] This school received 1.5 million HUF (61,000 euros) as an 'ethnic quota' for the catching-up and identity strengthening and cultural programmes.

Similar discriminatory practices led fourteen young Roma to bring a law suit against the local government of Tiszavasvári in 1997. The school had separate classes for Romani children, who were not allowed to enter the gym or the cafeteria and had to hold a separate graduation ceremony. On December 1, 1998, the City Court of Nyíregyháza brought a verdict in the case of the Romani children of Tiszavasvári. The court declared that the children's personal rights had been violated at the segregated graduation ceremony and ordered the local government to pay 100,000 HUF (about 400 euros) to each child in damages. This same school has been awarded 250 million HUF (approximately 1 million euros) of European Union Phare Programme contributions costs (Vadász *et al.*, 1998).

Hungarian schools are funded both by the state and the local education authorities. There is also financial support given to minority education and the government has confirmed that 'The single largest amount of specified minority-targeted budgetary support goes on supporting education for the minorities' (Doncsév, 2000). In a report commissioned by the government, Gábor Havas, a leading Hungarian sociologist, confirms that in the last few years, the trend of separating the Roma children in the primary school has risen, and the government's policy which provides money for the minority programmes only serves to exacerbate the situation' (Havas, in an interview with Kadét 2000). Often, the extra funds are used to segregate the Romani children even further, setting up or maintaining special 'gypsy classes', not unlike the 'C' classes from the 1960s.[20]

The Havas report argued that such improper uses of funding combined with the poor quality of the education the Roma children receive means that 'in those schools where the rate of the Roma children reach a certain percentage, extra classes are provided which cost more money and produce worse educational quality' (Kadét, 2000). The report goes on to point out that, rather than getting the 'specialised' teaching and support one might expect from 'special classes', Roma children actually receive teachers of inferior experience and knowledge.

This is illustrated by Ms Anna Orsós, Romani mother of two pupils at an eight-grade primary and music school in Hidas, who told the ERRC:

> When my children began school this year in September they realised that they had been separated from the other children. They were attending a Romani special needs programme whilst the others were learning German. I take regular care of my children and I help them with their studies. So far they have always come home with the best grades and there have been no problems with them in school. I don't understand why they need to attend the Romani special needs programme. Maybe it's true that there are some Roma children in Hidas who are behind, but the fact that my children are attending the Romani special needs programme proves that they put all the Roma children into one group. When I asked the teachers to move my children into the other, Hungarian group they said that it was out of the question. (Pickup and Mohácsi, 1998)

Examination results show that more Roma students learn Russian language than the other non-Roma students. This is because Roma children are used to offer opportunities for those teachers who were not retrained after the collapse of the communist system, in which every child had to learn Russian as a second language. Further evidence of this comes from a primary school in Borsod, where the Roma students learned Russian whilst the other classes were taught English (Kadét, 2000). An English language teacher I interviewed also reinforces this idea that the Roma don't 'deserve' the same education as non-Roma:

> I have no Roma in my class. I think the reason is that I teach only the best children, only the cleverest children, so I don't have to teach the Roma children. The Roma always receive the lowest grades {...} To tell you the truth. I don't really like them, we have a lot of problems, they are very very different[21]

Along with this feeling that the Roma should not be given the same advantages as other students, they are also often taught by unqualified teachers. One school in Borsod county is reported to employ seven people, none of whom has a teacher qualification (*Roma Rights,* 2002). Approximately one third of the schools examined for the Havas investigation employed untrained teachers, yet the percentage of schools employing untrained teachers nationwide is extremely low (Kadét, 2000).

Within an ethnically mixed classroom, Roma pupils may also receive differential treatment:

> My first time at school there were three Roma in the class. After two weeks of school, in a short break between two lessons, the teacher asked me and the two other Roma to go and clean the shit off the walls. The teacher didn't ask who had done it, we just had to clean the shit. My parents found out and then I moved schools[22]

This man's son, now 10 years old, has also been singled out by the teacher in his primary school, a different school to the one his father attended. 'I had a bad experience with the boy's teacher' the father said. His son was forced to sit at the back of the classroom until his father went into school to speak to the teacher. He now sits with the rest of his class.

An interesting feature of the Hungarian education system is an arrangement called 'private schooling'. Although this was reportedly initially introduced to allow especially talented students to be excused from mandatory school attendance, in the wording of the 1993 Hungarian Education Act, 'it is justified by the student's abilities, disabilities or his or her special situation.' Subsequently, there have been widespread reports of the abuse of this provision to allow the removal of Roma children from schools. 'Private students' are children who, under this particular legal provision, by agreement of the school and the parents, are no longer required to attend classes and only come to school to take exams. My own research in a central-Hungarian town revealed that 10 per cent of a majority-Roma primary school were private students. The headteacher admitted that: 'the students who learn in this way {...} are not successful. It is almost impossible to learn individually'[23] ERRC research in the eastern Hungarian village of Berettyóújfalu revealed that, as of March 2000, all nine private students at the Toldi Miklós school were Romani and many of these were repeatedly failing exams. There were no other 'private students' at any of the other five schools in Berettyóújfalu as of that time (Kóczé 2000).

As one female special school teacher in Hungary told the ERRC:

> I had a Romani boy in my class who was very disruptive. First we tried transferring him to another class in which the teacher was a male and stricter than I am. But the student was still very disruptive, in a class where there had already been quite a number of students with behavioural problems. So in the end the child became a private student. Once every month he comes to school. We decided on a day when he sits down with his teachers, and the teachers explain to him what to study, and he takes exams. I know the results of his last exams and all I can say is that becoming a private student has not meant any good results for the student concerned (Cahn *et al.*, 1999).

According to a study by Girán and Kardos, out of 85 schools in Hungary in which the percentage of Romani students was 10 per cent or more, there were 50 per cent with 'private students' who were affiliated to but not attending the schools. These 'private' students were all Roma (Girán and Kardos, 1997).

Creating de facto segregation

According to the school statistics for the academic year 1992–93, the proportion of Roma students in Hungarian general education was 7.12 per cent. Residential segregation differs between towns and regions, with the result that the proportion of Roma students can vary considerably between educational institutions. Thus, in 1992, over 70 per cent of Roma children studied in a school where they comprised more than 10 per cent of the children in the school and, within this, 42 per cent went to schools where their proportion exceeded 22 per cent (Aáry-Tamás 1998). Segregation within the school system has deteriorated since then, the subsequent Havas report revealing that the 193 schools studied had a Roma student population of above 50 per cent. It is these schools that have a lower standard of education, and also suffer from a lack of funds and fewer qualified teachers (Kadét, 2000).

A combination of lower standards, together with the introduction of an Act allowing parents to send their children to schools of their choosing, even if this is not necessarily in the local area,[24] has exacerbated the problem. Non-Roma parents have been 'voting with their feet', taking their children out of schools with a high percentage of Roma children and spending extra time and money taking their children elsewhere, even to neighbouring towns or villages.[25] This situation, which has been labelled 'the white flight',[26] has resulted in steadily worsening segregation in many schools.

As a consequence of such pressures, in the village of Jászladány (Szolnok County) the mayor István Dankó announced in November 2000 that the local government intended to transform the recently constructed public elementary school into a private one, where students would be required to pay for their education. It was reported at the time that the mayor wanted to 'lure back' non-Roma pupils whose parents had chosen to send their children to schools of a higher educational standard outside of the village.[27] This announcement was made in the full knowledge that the poorer Roma families would not be able to afford such fees. A hunger strike amongst the Roma ensued in protest and, in response, the local assembly withdrew its contribution to the operating expenses of the Gypsy minority self-government.[28]

The difference between saying and doing

Funding issues

As part of the medium-term package, the Ministry of Education has pledged almost 700 million forints (approximately 2.7 million euros) for the development of Roma education. Research shows that very little of this money has been spent and it is difficult to monitor exactly what it has been spent on (Kadét, 2001). However, evidence referred to above documents what the Minorities Ombudsman has concluded – that several local authorities 'only organise Romani minority education in order to obtain supplementary normative support, and they exploit this form of education to segregate Romani pupils' (Kaltenbach, 1996), a practice that has led to Roma pupils receiving an inferior quality of education.

There is also concern about whether the funding arrives at its target destination at all. A headteacher from a primary school with 90–100 per cent Roma pupils told me the following:

> From one side we get money from the Hungarian government, plus the local government funds the rest. This covers the whole budget. We do not get any extra funding for the ethnic minority children, because we should be a gypsy school {...} The parents don't want this to be a gypsy school, and neither does the leader of the local gypsy government, he does not want this to be a gypsy school either, they think this will be discrimination. Officially it's not a gypsy primary school, but actually it is.[29]

This confusion of identity and the stigma attached to being a 'Gypsy school' (in other words, a mainstream school in which most pupils are Roma), illustrates the fact that, because of the tensions between societal rejection and 'official' status, some schools are not always accessing the extra funds available. In fact, under the Data Protection Act, registration of Roma in schools is forbidden, since ethnic identity is seen as a private and personal affiliation.[30]

On the other hand, the government has allocated specific funds to Roma students and headteachers therefore have to state the 'percentage' of Roma children in a school in order to obtain funding. The headteacher is then put in the position of determining the ethnic identity of children, in the paradoxical situation in which a high percentage of Gypsy students could stigmatise the school locally but could also bring in extra funds. In the end, this situation raises funding distribution and monitoring issues, as it becomes virtually impossible to tell whether the extra funds ever meet their intended target. ERRC research has also shown that there are schools which do not ask for this extra funding because of the additional work involved in creating an effective minority education, such as the greater involvement with pedagogical services.

As a result, measures that are intended to improve the situation and reduce discrimination fail because of the government's lack of control and monitoring of the use made of the funds that are made available for the education of Roma children. As the Minorities Ombudsman reported, 'the minority education of Gypsies still lacks the appropriate professional and legal background. This makes it excessively difficult to examine and control the appropriate utilisation of the supplementary per capita normative allowance for Gypsy minority education' (Aáry-Tamás, L. 1998).

Curriculum issues

The current Hungarian education system does little to include Romani language or culture in the curriculum. Literature used in Hungarian classrooms either ignores the history and culture of Roma[31] or identifies it with negative stereotypes. In the year 2000, the Hungarian Ministerial Commissioner for Education Rights, Lajos Aáry-Tamás, requested that the Hungarian Ministry of Education remove a text book containing prejudiced statements about Roma from the official list. The fifth grade text book 'Humans and Society' (published in 1998) stated that a 'major part of the Roma could not or would not lead a European lifestyle', and 'the life of a part of the Roma is marked by crime.' The book also alleges that the Roma spied for the Turks during Turkish rule in Hungary (after the 16th century) and that they acted as henchmen at the execution of Hungarian historical figures (*Roma Rights* no. 3, 2000).

In October 1995 the long-awaited new National Curriculum was approved by the government, which gave three years for schools to create their own local curriculum. This change came as a shock to teachers whose lifetime experience had revolved around the teaching from one book and one method. Local education authorities were also not prepared for, and did not have the experience to implement, a successful curriculum based on local needs,[32] not least because the national curriculum in Hungary is, in spite of changes that have been made, still deeply embedded in the monolithic education system introduced in 1948 based on Soviet models of education. This authoritarian and conservative pedagogy left little room for minorities.

A senior lecturer from a Teacher Training College in Central Hungary spoke to me of the difficulty of creating a specialised curriculum:

> Many Hungarians had a very special socialisation process in the communist era, and people used to have a very comfortable situation. In the centre was a big brain, the communist party. The government and the state decided what we should do and we did it. No options, just one handbook, and just one curriculum we had to follow. It was very comfortable for people, because nobody questioned it {...} When people were asked to make their own pedagogical programme and curriculum in the school, nobody was able to do it, because it is not daily pedagogical work, it is something different.[33]

Thus although institutions now have full, autonomous control over their own affairs, it seems that most institutions are at a loss over what to do, having no extra training in minority education, particularly with regards to the Roma.

Ignorance and misrepresentation of the Roma are also perpetuated in the classroom by some teachers. On February 21, 2001, The Roma Press Center (RSK) reported that a biology teacher in the primary school in Erdőtelek, northeast Hungary, forced eighth grade Romani pupils to write down that 'the Gypsies can be characterised by high rates of unemployment and by their special odour' and taught them that 80 per cent of the prison population is Romani. The local mayor refused to accept any responsibility for the events, adding that the teacher's comments about the special odour of the Roma was not equivalent to saying that they smelt unpleasant (*Roma Rights*, 2001/1). The Minorities Ombudsman launched an investigation into the incident and the Parliamentary Commissioner on Education Rights is expected to follow suit.

Similar concerns led to more than seventy parents and teachers of the local primary school in Halmajugra (North-East Hungary) demonstrating, on July 12th 2001, in protest against the continued employment of the then head teacher of the primary school. The only primary school of the village with 50 per cent Romani inhabitants is attended almost exclusively by Romani children, while the director's and other non-Roma families' children attend a school in the neighbouring village. Roma parents regarded the director as holding racist views and complained of physical and verbal abuse directed at Roma children.[34]

Outcome: exclusion

Segregation of Roma children in schools reflects scepticism and antipathy from teachers and governing bodies who do not believe that Roma children can actually learn. In my interviews with teachers and specialists in and around a central Hungarian town, this theme comes up again and again – that Roma people do not see the 'value' of learning or school work.[35] Yet in ERRC interviews and my informal conversations with Roma parents of young children in Central Hungary, education has consistently been a theme that was brought up as a matter of concern to the families. This is also substantiated for the country as a whole in the 1998 Ombudsman's Report (Aáry-Tamás, 1998). In other research, factors used to explain the high drop-out rate of Roma from education do not include the educational motivation of Roma students or their parents, but rather point to the issues identified above – of segregation of schools (including an exodus of non-Gypsy students from certain schools) and school selection procedures (Kállai, 2000: 41–43).

The dire economic situation of Roma families has also been used to explain the low educational standards of Roma children and, indeed, the widespread poverty of Roma families cannot be ignored. A recent Hungarian household survey revealed that, whilst they made up only 4 per cent of the total sample (corresponding to the overall ratio in society), the Roma constituted 33 per cent of the long-term deprived (Mészáros *et al.*, 2000). This economic inequality between Roma and non-Roma has been linked to inequality in education, since children in Hungary have to purchase their own school equipment and many Roma parents are simply unable to buy their children the things that the majority can afford. Even in the areas where local councils give grants to Roma parents for their children's school books, the grants are normally not given until September of the new school year, yet the books must be bought at the end of the previous summer term. Similarly, Roma parents cannot afford to let their children progress to secondary education, as poverty levels mean that as soon as they are old enough, they must often work in order to sustain the family's income.[36]

However, economic hardships are only part of the problem faced by Roma students in the Hungarian education system – from curriculum content to new government initiatives, discrimination and alienation are widespread and the combined effect of these pressures is to exclude children from the classroom.

Conclusion – widening the gap

The two major surveys published on the state of Romani education were carried out in 1971 and 1993. A comparison of the statistics shows an increase in the proportion of the Roma attending school – according to 1971 data, 26 per cent of 25–29 year old Roma had completed eight classes in primary school, in 1981 36.5 per cent had completed eighth grade, whilst the 1993 study showed that this proportion had increased to 77 per cent among the identical age group. This appears to indicate a marked improvement of educational participation of Roma children in Hungary. However, the same research shows that although a higher percentage of Roma children may now be attending school, the distance between the educational attainments of Roma and non-Roma pupils has continued to increase, further widening the imbalance between the two groups (Kertesi, 1998).

Running parallel with this increasing education divide, the Roma minority have become the most economically disadvantaged group within Hungarian society, with deprivation among the Roma having been shown to be more prevalent and sustained than in any other group in Hungary.[37] This is reflected clearly in the situation of Roma in the Hungarian education system, which shows that any improvements that the government may boast of as evidence of the effectiveness of its minority policies are dwarfed by the bigger and ever increasing gap between the educational standards of Roma and their non-Roma peers. Once again, however, Hungary is changing and Roma are losing out. Segregation is becoming the norm and society is increasingly excluding Roma children through educational segregation so that when they finally reach adulthood, no one will want to employ them. The government calls this 'a more favourable situation'.[38]

The Hungarian Government regards its policies for the education of the Roma as effective. In reality, however, unequal distribution of funding, lack of proper monitoring, commissioning of reports that are neither published nor closely examined, and ill-defined funding opportunities are all denying the Roma the right to an effective education[39] – even the government's own Minorities Ombudsman has criticised its policies for being 'professionally chaotic and legally hazy.' (*Roma Rights,* summer 1998). So why do Roma children fail so often in school? As with many such questions, the answers are often complicated, confusing and contradictory. One simple answer came up again and again, however: 'Gypsy children ...' the teacher/social worker/man in the pub would say to me with a roll of the eyes, 'well ... Gypsy children, they just *can't* learn'. The evidence is clear, however, that this is not the answer.

Notes

1. This was to be continually removed and sprayed back throughout my year there.
2. However, I have noticed that many people in Hungary, including the Roma themselves, use the word 'cigány' (gypsy) to describe the Roma population, which is, in fact, made up of many different groups with a variety of backgrounds. In official literature, to detract from 'cigány' being used in a negative way, the word 'Roma' is often used, which I am told comes from the Romani word 'Rom' meaning 'person'. I have chosen mainly to use the term 'Roma' here, but I want to make it clear that for me, 'cigány', or 'gypsy' is never a negative word.
3. It is based on a report written in 2001 as a part of a Youth Action Learning Project, which involved interviewing local teachers and education authorities and looking through various state and independent reports. I interviewed people I came into contact with, both Roma and non-Roma, and I am grateful to them for talking to me. I am also grateful to the European

Roma Rights Centre (ERRC) in Budapest for allowing me unlimited access to their experience and resources.

4. According to a study carried out by the Hungarian Institute for Educational Research (IER), in the 1998/1999 school year, only 19 per cent of Roma students went on to take up a place at a technical, middle or grammar school after finishing eighth grade primary school (Gypsy segregation, Hungarian Institute for Educational Research, 2000, quoted in Kállai and Törzsök, 2000: 40–41). Out of these 19 per cent, data are not available on actually how many go on to obtain the *érettségi* qualification possible from technical or grammar school, a qualification that can lead to better job prospects and a chance of entry into higher education. Without an *érettségi* qualification, only unskilled or low-skilled employment opportunities are available. Elsewhere, it has been estimated that less than 1 per cent of Roma students in Hungary go on to study at university level (Evans, 1996).

5. These debates have become more apparent since I embarked on an MPhil/PhD course after writing this paper, at the Education and Professional Studies Department at King's College London (funded by the ESRC).

6. The first Regular Report for Hungary, in 1998, complimented the government on its 'Medium-term Measures' put forward in 1997 (later modified in 1999), saying that these measures 'form a good basis for continued dialogue between the Roma, the government and society' (Regular Report, 1998: 11).

7. 'Roma policy is not well integrated into general social development strategies and exists as a separate and parallel project' (Regular Report, 2002: 33).

8. See: Aáry-Tamás, L (ed.) 1998; a press conference held on September 6th, 1999 held jointly with the Hungarian minister of Education, Mr Zoltán Pokorni, where it was stated that segregation exists in the Hungarian education system. See also *Roma Rights* No. 4, 1999.

9. See Convention on the Elimination of Racial Discrimination, 1966, Article 2 in conjunction to article 5. Hungary ratified this Convention on May 1, 1967; and in Hungarian law, see Paragraph four of Article 4 of Act LXXIX of 1993 on Education, about the prohibition of negative discrimination in education.

10. See, for examples: EC's 2000 Progress Report by Gusztáv Koszolányi in Central Europe Review (web journal) available at http://www.ce-review.org/00/39/eu39hungary.html [accessed 18/12/03]; Human Rights Watch World Report 1999; International Helsinki Federation for Human Rights Annual Report 1999.

11. Comments made by Yvonne Csányi (Head of the Department for Hearing Impaired at Eötvös Loránd University in Bárczi, Hungary) in 'Az együttnevelés fontosabb tényezõi, feltételei' ('The important factors and conditions of integrated education') available at http://pizza.barczi.hu/szaszok/CSANYI.htm [accessed 10/2001] Unofficial translation used.

12. See *Jelentés a Magyar Közoktatásról* 2000 (Report from Hungarian Public Education 2000), also mentioned in the article in a Hungarian national newspaper 'Százszor annyi a fogyatékos gyerek, mint Új-Zélandon?' ('We have a hundred times more disabled children than New Zealand?') *Magyar Hirlap*, 30. November 2000.

13. Source: *ERRC Factsheet on Roma in Hungary*, available on website http://errc.org/publications/factsheets/hungary.shtml [accessed 10/2001]

14. 'About 70 per cent of school age Romani children in Bulgaria attend all-Romani schools located in segregated Romani neighbourhoods throughout the country' (Rorke, 2002: 6)
15. Author's own Interview with Mrs K., 16 May 2001, central Hungary.
16. 'Mass deposit' used in the Minorities Ombudsman report from Hungary. Source: Report by the Ombudsman in Charge of Minority Affairs Regarding the Comprehensive Survey of the Education of Minorities in Hungary, 1998 (Aáry-Tamás: 1998).
    'Collective dustbin' used in ERRC publication *Roma Rights* Summer 1998.
    'Mass warehouses' used in Radó 2001.
17. It should be noted that there are also a number of private initiatives or non-governmental schools for Roma, such as the Ghandi School in Pécs, Hungary.
18. As for higher education, in the Act on the budget for 2000, Parliament approved a 100 million HUF supplementary fund to provide young Roma with scholarships. Although information on the number who have successfully applied for these scholarships was not available at time of writing, in the 1998/1999 academic year, 37 million Hungarian forints was spent on a total of 643 Roma students in further education (Doncsév 2000). This amounts to a tiny fraction of the 85.1 per cent of Roma students who did finish primary school (IER study, 2000).
19. Reported In the Roma Press Center (RSK) 27 August 2000 (also reported in: *Népszava*, and *Magyar Hirlap*, 28 August 2000).
20. 'In those schools where the rate of the Roma children reach a certain percentage, extra classes are provided which cost more money and produce worse educational quality. It's quite ironic that the majority of the community thinks that even if it costs more they should segregate the Roma'. (Kadét, 2000)
21. Author's own interview with Ms M. H., an English teacher at a primary school in Central Hungary, 17 May 2001.
22. Author's own interview with Mr T., a social worker for a NGO in Central Hungary.
23. Author's own interview with Mrs T. M., headmistress of primary school with majority Roma, in central Hungary, May 15, 2000.
24. Education Act of 1993, Article 79, 'The Act affirms the right to schooling, free education and the free choice of schools.'
25. 'The non Roma parents vote with their feet and they prefer to go to another village even if this means additional costs and energy.' (Kadét, 2000).
26. 'Segregation is basically caused by three reasons: (1) prejudice induced "white flight" of non-Roma student from schools where their parents perceive the number of Roma to be increasing or detrimental to their children. Since the threshold triggering the "white flight" depends on the school's socio-cultural environment, it can lead to "quality segregation". (2) The increased ease of socio-geographic mobility for the more highly educated non-Roma population leads to increased concentrations of Roma regions with high unemployment rates. (3) Roma migration within Hungary is primarily directed towards the developing city ghettos, thus increasing the proportion of Roma in these areas.' (Radó, 1997).
27. For full report and background see Roma Press Center (RSK) June 11, 2001; and for the latest situation: *Roma Rights* 2003 'Controversial Segregated

Private School Approved after Election of Non-Romani Minority Representatives in Hungary' (Nr 1–2).

28. Hungarian Law on the Rights of National and Ethnic Minorities (1993) includes the rights of a nationwide network of representative Roma institutions (the minority self-government system). For further explanation see Kovats, 2001 (333–350).

29. Author's own interview with the Ms T. M., headmistress of a primary school with majority Roma pupils in central Hungary, May 15, 2001.

30. See Article 2 of Act LXIII of 1992 on the Protection of Personal Data and the Disclosure of Data of Public Interest (abbreviated in this chapter as: Data Protection Act).

31. 'Neither the media nor the educational system act as if Hungary is a multilingual, multicultural country. This is especially applicable to the Roma population which, on a reading of the textbooks, simply do not exist at all.' (Radó, 1997).

32. 'The new curriculum started five years ago and it has been reformed many times. It has normal requirements and minimal requirements in each subject, but teachers are not well prepared to do it. I think it is a real problem in the Hungarian schools'. Author's own interview with Prof. H. (Pro-Rector of Teacher's Training College in central Hungary), 15 May 2001.

33. Author's own interview with Prof. H. (Pro-Rector of a Teacher's Training College) Central Hungary, 15 May 2001.

34. Roma Press Center (RSK) 16 July 2001.

35. For example: 'Generally the parents don't have this qualification, they don't even have the primary school certificate, they don't finish it, and that's why they thought "oh, well. It's not really important because really we have lived without school and our children can live without the school"'. Author's own interview with Mrs T. M. (headteacher of a primary school in central Hungarian town with a majority of Roma children), 15 May 2001.

36. These observations came from my own experience talking to teachers and Roma families in Hungary, although poverty is seen in reports as grounds for disadvantage in the education system (for example see Kállai *et al.* (ed.), 2000 (29–45).

37. In 1994, 63.8 per cent of the total male population receiving supplementary income support (allocated by local municipalities) was Roma (according to 1995 research carried out by the National Prison Administration's Methodology Department).

38. 'According to sociological surveys conducted in 1971, 39 per cent of the Roma population above the age of 14 was illiterate, while among the non-Roma population there were practically no examples of over-14s being unable to read and write. Comparable data for the year 1993 show a more favourable situation in this regard, and the proportion of those who had never been to school was down to 9 per cent.' (Doncsév, 2000).

39. Article 26 of the Universal Declaration of Human Rights (1948) states 'Everyone has the right to education.' The right to education is elaborated in a number of international laws and instruments, including the Convention of the Rights of the Child.

References

Aáry-Tamás, L. (ed.) (1998) 'Report by the Ombudsman for national and ethnic minority rights regarding the comprehensive survey of the education of minorities in Hungary', Budapest: Dr. Jenő Kaltenbach Parliamentary Commissioner for the National and Ethnic Minorities Rights.

Kadét, E. (2001) 'Creative accounting: State spending on programmes for Roma in Hungary' in *Roma Rights 2001* No. 2–3, Budapest: European Roma Rights Centre.

Cahn, C., Chirico D., McDonald C., Mohácsi V., Peric, T. and Székely, A. (1999) 'Roma in the Educational Systems of Central and Eastern Europe', in *The Roma Education Resource Book vol. 1*, Budapest: Institute for Educational Policy.

Danbakli, M. (2001) *Roma, Gypsies: Texts issues by International Institutions*, UK: University of Hertfordshire Press.

Doncsev, T. (ed.) (2000) *Measures taken by the state to promote the social integration of Roma living in Hungary*, Budapest: President of the Office for National and Ethnic Minorities.

Evans, S. (1996) Separate but Superior? (published on internet website Patrin at: http://www.geocities.com/Paris/5121/edu-hungary.htm)

Human Rights Watch (1998) 'Rights denied: Roma children in Hungary' in *Database of NGO Reports presented to the UN Committee on the Rights of the Child*, Helsinki: Human Rights Watch Children's Rights Project.

Girán, J. and Kardos, L. (1997) 'A cigány gyerekek iskolai sikertelenségének háttere' (What is behind Gypsy children's lack of success at school). Az Iskolakultúra, 10, 1997.

Hancock I. (2002) *We are the Romani people Ame sam e Rromane dzene*, Great Britain: University of Hertfordshire Press.

IER Study (2000) 'Roma Segregation', Budapest: Hungarian Institute for Educational Research.

Kadét.E. (2000) 'Alig van kiút a cigányosztályból' ('There is No Way Out from the Gypsy Class'), interview with Gábor Havas, *Népszava*, 17th October 2000. Unofficial translation used.

Kadét E. (2001) 'Creative Accounting: State spending on programmes for Roma in Hungary' *Roma Rights* 2001, Budapest: ERRC.

Kállai, E. and Törzsök, E. (2000) *A Roma's Life in Hungary*, Budapest: BECMR.

Kaltenbach, J. (1996) 'A kisebbségi ombudsman a Cigány Gyermekek Speciális (kisegitő) Iskolai Oktatásával Kapcsolatos Vizsgálati Jelentése' ('Report of the Minorities Ombudsman's Examination Concerning Gypsy Children in Special Schools') Budapest: Parliamentary Commissioner for the National and Ethnic Minorities Rights.

Kemény, I., Kálmán, R., Csalog, Zs., Havas, G., Havas, Zs. (1976) *Beszámoló a magyarországi cigányok helyzetével foglalkozó 1971–ben végzett kutatásról* (Report on Research Conducted During 1971 into the Position of the Gypsies in Hungary), Budapest: Hungarian Academy of Sciences, Sociological Research Institute.

Kertesi Gábor (1998) 'Cigány gyerekek az iskolában, cigány felnőttek a munkaeröpiacon' ('Gypsy children in school, gypsy adults in the workforce') In: Mihály, A. (ed.): *Iskola és társadalom – Iskola- és oktatásszociológiai szöveggyûjtemény.* Wesley János Lelkészképző Főiskola – Budapest: Újj Mandátum Kiadó, 389–435.

Kóczé, A. (2000) 'Romani children and the right to education in Central and Eastern Europe' in *Roma Rights: Rights of the Child*, nr 3 2000, Budapest: ERRC.

Kovats, M. (2001) 'Hungary: politics, difference and equality' in Guy, W. (ed.) *Between past and future: the Roma of Central and Eastern Europe*, Hatfield: University of Hertforshire Press, 333–350.

Ladányi, J. and Szelényi, I. (2000) Adalékok a Csenyétei cigányság Történetéhez, in Horváth Á.-Landau E.-Szalai J. (eds) *Cigánynak születni. Tanulmányok, dokumentumok.* ('To be born a Gypsy: studies, reports') Budapest: Új Mandátum, 507–530.

'Medium-term package of measures for the improvement of the living conditions and social situation of the Roma population' – created in 1997, appendix written in 1999, Appendix to Government resolution No. 104711999 (V. 5).

Mészáros, A. and Fóti J. (2000) 'A cigány népesség jellemzõi Magyarországon' (The Gypsy Population's Characteristics in Hungary'), Horváth Á.-Landau E.-Szalai J. (eds) Cigánynak születni. Tanulmányok, dokumentumok. ('To be born a Gypsy: studies, reports') Budapest: Új Mandátum, 285–313.

Petrova, D. (2002) 'In Defence of Desegregation' in *Roma Rights* no. 3–4 2002, Budapest: ERRC.

Pickup, A. and Mohácsi, V. (1998), 'Primary education of Roma: the case of Hidas, Hungary' in *Roma Rights*, Autumn 1998, Budapest: ERRC.

Radó, P. (1997) 'Report on the Education of Roma Students in Hungary: Expert study for the Office of National and Ethnic Minorities', Budapest: Open Society Institute.

Radó, P. (2001) 'Roma Students in the Hungarian Educational System', in *Ethnic Minority and Inter-Ethnic Relations in Context: A Dutch Hungarian Encounter* edited by Phalet, K. and Örkény, A., UK/USA: Ashgate Publishing Company.

Roma Rights Autumn 1996, Budapest: ERRC.

Roma Rights: Racially motivated violence against Roma Spring 1998, Budapest: ERRC.

Roma Rights: Roma and the Rights to Education Summer 1998, Budapest: ERRC.

Roma Rights: Romani Media/Mainstream Media 1999/4, Budapest: ERRC.

Roma Rights: Rights of the Child 2000/3, Budapest: ERRC.

Roma Rights: Access to Justice 2001/1, Budapest: ERRC.

Roma Rights: Segregation and Desegregation 2002/3,4, Budapest: ERRC.

Roma Rights: Personal Documents and Access to Fundamental Rights 2003/3, Budapest: ERRC.

Rorke, B. (ed.) (2002) *Roma Participation Program Reporter. Social desegregation issue*, Budapest: Open Society Institute.

Stewart, M. (2001) 'Deprivation, the Roma and "the underclass"' in Hann, C. (ed.) *Postcolonialism: Ideas, Ideologies and Practices in Europe and Asia*, UK: Routledge, and shorter Hungarian version in Beszélõ, July/August 2001.

Willems, W. (1998) *In Search for the True Gypsy: From Enlightenment to Final Solution*, translated from German by Dan Bloch, UK: Frank Cass.

Vadász *et al.* (1998) 'Roma sue school in northeastern Hungary: The submission against the principal of the Ferenc Pethe Primary School, Tiszavasvári, Hungary' in *Roma Rights: Racially motivated violence against Roma*, Spring edition, Budapest: ERRC.

10
The Invisible Child in Education Law

Ann Blair

Introduction

Other chapters in this part of the collection look at the effectiveness of the right to education and equal treatment in education. This chapter is concerned with children's right to have a voice in decisions that affect them and looks at the gulf between law and practice in the participation of children in decisions that affect their education. In light of the findings of McNamee, James and James elsewhere in this volume it might be considered surprising that here the principal criticism is that participation rights are absent from the education law of England and Wales, whereas children are often active participants in decisions that affect their education and the ascertaining and consideration of pupil's views is increasingly recognised as desirable in Department for Education and Skills (DfES)[1] guidance.

Inevitably, once children's participation is invoked as a 'right', the question arises as to how far it is legitimate for the State to interfere with parental autonomy. This question is particularly acute in the field of education law, where parental rights have prevailed. There is little or no scope for interventions by public authorities in private decisions affecting children's upbringing, as long as the threshold at which it is necessary to intervene to deal with abuse or neglect has not been crossed (Steutal and Speiker, 1999). Prout notes that the idea that children are the responsibility of their parents unless some serious problem such as abuse arises is especially marked in the UK, where this view has been embedded historically (2000: 110).

Once courts and public authorities have to make decisions that affect a child, however, *sections 1(3)* and *22* of the *Children Act 1989* will often come into play. These impose obligations on the courts and local education authorities (LEAs), in certain circumstances, to have particular regard to 'the ascertainable wishes and feelings of the child concerned (considered in the light of his age and understanding)'.[2] This reflects the rights in Article 12 of the UN Convention on the Rights of the Child (UNCRC).[3] However, it is now recognised as a fairly commonplace reality that the rights of the child as laid out in the UNCRC have been almost entirely absent from education law in England and Wales. Most significantly, for these purposes, the right of the mature child to have her wishes ascertained and taken into account in decisions that affect her has been conspicuous by its absence (see for example Eekelaar, 1986; Freeman, 1996; Furniss and Blair, 1997; Harris, 2000; and Meredith, 2001).

Adopting a socio-legal methodology, this chapter contrasts the invisibility of the child in the decision-making process in formal legal terms with the reality, reflected in official guidance, that often children's wishes cannot be ignored. It begins by looking at the absence of the child in various areas of education law but goes on to show that children can be found behind the mirror of education law that renders them invisible. Finally, it looks at the reasons for the differences. A significant question is the extent to which the different decisions that are taken in respect of education can be characterised as having a private rather than a public character and what the impact of this is.

The chapter will also seek to explain why the law, as it stands, needs reform. By way of introduction, it is important to establish why children's participation is a right that demands adequate recognition and protection. The traditional adult justification for excluding children from decision-making is that this is for their own good. Children are not fully formed and, as such, they are intrinsically different from adults and autonomy is harmful in a dangerous world (Schlater and Piper, citing Roche: 426). However, there are good examples of cases where children are not only seen to be capable of taking decisions but, given the right circumstances, can be extremely effective in negotiating for themselves (see, for example, Cairns: 2001). It is not always clear why it is important that children speak for themselves rather than have parents or other adults speak for them, but Sclater and Piper identify its significance as the intrinsic importance of children exercising their own power and initiative:

> If hearing children's own voices and assessing their individual needs are pre-conditions for guaranteeing basic human rights for children, we can do nothing but conclude that our present systems, through

their reliance on a discourse of welfare, actually militate against the achievement of rights for children. Without giving children opportunities to talk to those who make decisions about them they can neither reveal situations against which they need protection nor have a significant influence on the outcome. The use by decision-makers, of generalised assumptions about children's welfare cancels out both possibilities. In other words we appear to be excluding children by the very means we seek to use to protect their interests. (2001: 425)

In education law, the discourse of welfare that militates against children's participation in other areas of family life is replaced by a discourse of parental rights. In such circumstances, the task of protecting children's participation rights becomes more acute. Obviously, as McNamee, James and James point out, it is not sufficient to establish rights in law that are ineffective in practice. Nevertheless, the question of assessing how effectively children's participation rights are protected in the education system can barely begin until they are firmly established in legislation.

Children and participation in law

Three areas have been chosen to illustrate how education law in England and Wales fails to recognise children's participation rights – Special Educational Needs (SEN), Home-School Agreements and Sex Education – but the principles discussed in relation to these apply equally elsewhere. Later, these same areas will be used to show that law does not always reflect reality.

Special educational needs

The meeting of SEN is an area where the rights of the child are comparatively strong, yet participation rights remain weak. Arguably most important is the right to be educated in a mainstream school. *Section 316* of the *Education Act 1996* provides that, subject to certain conditions, a child who has been formally assessed with SEN 'must be educated in a mainstream school unless that is incompatible with … the wishes of his parent'. Parents cannot insist on a place at a special school paid for by the LEA where this is not justified, but, other things being equal, if parental preference is for a special school the LEA cannot refuse it. Rights to inclusion were strengthened by the Special Educational Needs and Disability Act 2001 (SENDA), but parental supremacy on this point was not altered and in legal terms the child's opinion continues to count for nothing.

If a child's right to inclusion is contingent upon her parents' preferences, the legal rights of pupils to participate in other SEN decisions that affect them are also extremely limited. The only area where the views of the child are recognised in the Education Acts is in relation to a child's wish to have the existence of a disability they have treated as confidential; this was introduced by SENDA. Until recently, the position in the secondary legislation (i.e. the regulations made under the Education Acts) was similar; the law failed to guarantee children a voice. However, the most significant recognition of the child's independent status in education law in England and Wales came with amendments to the *Special Educational Needs Tribunal Regulations* in 2001. Where parents appeal against a LEA decision to the Special Educational Needs and Disability Tribunal (SENDT), these regulations give the child qualified rights to attend, to give evidence and to address the appeal tribunal. Further, in SEN appeals the LEA must include in its statement of case the views of the child concerning the issues raised by the appeal or the reason why the authority has not ascertained those views.[4] This seems promising, but does not go so far as to recognise the mature child as a party to the claim or give the child a right to have views taken into consideration in the original decision (Blair and Lawson, 2003).

Home-School agreements

It has been suggested that home-school agreements or contracts have origins, at least in part, in the types of 'contract' drawn up to deal with the individual needs of the pupil with behavioural problems (Blair and Waddington, 1997). In these cases, the child is a key participant in the process of deciding what the content of the agreement should be. By the time we arrive at home-school agreements as established by *sections 110* and *111* of the *School Standards and Framework Act 1998*, however, the child or pupil has become an object of the agreements rather than a participant in the process of formulating them. *Section 110(5)* states that the school **may** invite a pupil of sufficient understanding to sign the agreement to acknowledge and accept the school's expectations of its pupils as set out in the agreement. This is hardly a strong recognition of children's agency, however; and the duty to consult on the content of the agreement is a duty to consult only with the parents. The child is almost irrelevant to the process of agreement, even though the agreement is as much or more concerned with the behaviour of the pupil as with that of the parent.

Sex education

Another important area where child rights are eclipsed by parental rights is sex education. Schools must provide a basic curriculum and in secondary schools this must include sex education. However, *section 405* of the *Education Act 1996* gives all parents an unconditional right to withdraw their child from sex education. Again, the child is absent from the picture the law presents.

This limits not just children's rights to participate in decisions that affect them, but also potentially denies their right to have their health protected through access to basic information about sexual health. The parental opt-out from sex education is limited by the fact that it does not apply to those parts of sex education that form part of the National Curriculum in Science. However, until recently the Science Curriculum was required by law to exclude aspects of human sexual behaviour other than biological aspects, AIDS/HIV and other sexually transmitted diseases. At the time of writing, this exclusion was still in effect. Thus children have a right, through the science curriculum, to knowledge of the biological basics of reproduction but through the right of withdrawal, parents might keep from them knowledge of other aspects of human sexuality that schools are encouraged to teach to all pupils. The welfare principle plays no part in this decision and children are altogether denied a voice in it. Indeed, the position is so firmly in favour of parental autonomy that a parent could refuse permission for a pupil over the age of 18 to receive sex education!

Illusion and reality

Having shown that the child is all but invisible in education law it is time to re-examine the position of the child in two ways to demonstrate how artificial this reflection of the child is. First, children are far from passive recipients of the outcomes of decisions taken for their benefit. Second, official guidance on how law should be put into effect increasingly recognises the practical importance of involving children in decisions that require their participation to be effective. However, these fall short of a right to participate.

Children and agency

Monk has observed that children should be viewed as subjects, not objects, and that regardless of legal or adult recognition they are social agents and active participants in the education system (2002: 45). The participation right in Art. 12 UNCRC recognises this and protects it. However, legal recognition on its own is not enough. Elsewhere in this volume, McNamee, James and James acknowledge the lack of a firm commitment to listening to children's views even within court processes that are subject to *section 1(3)* of the *Children Act 1989.* Nevertheless, they observe that:

> It is only when children are older that their voices are heard and lis-tened to – that is they are accorded agency – and this is because they actually *have* agency. They can 'vote with their feet' in respect of any decisions made for them ... The older a child is, in fact, the nearer to adult status the child is, the more agency they are accorded. But this is not, we would argue, done from any kind of children's rights perspective, but rather from the understanding that you cannot over-rule the wishes of older children. (McNamee, James and James, 2002: 5)).

According to Prout (2000), research from economics, marketing, psy-chology and sociology shows that children, in the private sphere of family decision-making, have become a group of consumers in them-selves. Children have a high degree of influence over family purchases and develop many techniques of persuasion to achieve this. In a mar-ketised education system, one of the most significant family 'pur-chases' is education and children can have a significant influence on choice of school (see, for example, West, 1992). Children's influence in other areas of education is also clear. First, the role of children in rela-tion to schools' behaviour policy:

> A localised initiative which is becoming increasingly popular in Britain and the United States is the idea that children, particularly children in primary schools, can become more active in regulating their own behaviour collectively. The introduction of peer media-tion and peer counselling would seem to work against the norm of adult-centredness by giving pupils more ownership of the education process. It also, importantly, assumes that pupils have a degree of social competence. (Wyness, 2001: 363)

Second, in relation to sex and drugs education:

> Notions of cuteness, naiveté and innocence have been used to exclude children from the world of work and politics. These characteristics of

childhood make it difficult to think that children can be consulted in matters that directly affect them. Yet, debates around the introduction of sex education and anti-drug initiatives in primary schools bring to the fore questions about whether educationalists can afford to sustain notions such as childhood innocence ... The key frame of reference here is not the home or the schools, but the notion of the informed child with 'responsible' adult agencies providing the information. (Wyness, 2001: 365)

And third, Smith, contesting official and received wisdom that in the case of homework more is always better, states that:

Whilst [children] are admittedly in a relatively powerless position, there is available to them a range of strategies for resistance and avoidance ... Books get lost or eaten by the dog; illnesses manifest themselves; and plagiarism occurs ... [As does] lack of commitment, for example to producing homework of any quality, rather than just 'getting it done'. (2000: 322)

Even the received wisdom since the Plowden Report (1966) that parents should act in partnership with schools, where developments have taken place without much consideration for children's views on parental involvement in their education, is not immune from children's influence. Edwards and David (1997) found that as children became older they did not necessarily welcome their mother's involvement in school activities (p. 196), and that children may desire and actively work towards separations between their school and home lives.

Guidance: recognising the reality

Official guidance issued to help implement law and promulgate good practice demonstrates the impossibility of making informed decisions without the input of the child. So, for example, as we have seen, the use of peer mentoring and counselling is recognised as a reflection of children's agency. This is reflected in government guidance, where involving pupils is suggested as a key principle in anti-bullying and harassment policies (noted by Harris, 2000: 33). In relation to all three of the areas considered in section 2 (above), the view adopted by DfES guidance is significant in recognising the need to involve children in decisions that affect them.

Before looking at how guidance recognises the importance of obtaining children's views, however, it is worth considering the legal status of such guidance. Guidance is not law and does not need to be followed precisely. Nevertheless, it has an indirect legal effect through the doctrine of relevant considerations. This means that the decision-maker – e.g. a school, headteacher or appeal panel – should use it to guide the use of their discretion. It may not be ignored, but equally it should not be followed slavishly and it is an important and often decisive factor in most cases. If the guidance is ignored, a court could declare the decision 'ultra vires' and require the decision-maker to reconsider, this time giving the guidance the weight that the decision-maker considers proper in all the circumstances.[5] If guidance states that views should be obtained where a child is of sufficient maturity and understanding one would anticipate that this will happen unless the decision-maker can provide sound reasons for having departed from it. Nevertheless, as the law stands, the school, professional or appeal panel that digests this guidance and then carries on regardless may do so with scant risk of successful legal challenge.[6]

Special educational needs

The law on SEN has never provided for children to be consulted during the assessment and statementing process.[7] Guidance issued in the form of a Code of Practice (DfE, 1994) went only as far as to state that a number of things should be appended to the statement, including 'other advice, such as the views of the child, which the LEA or any other body from whom advice is sought consider desirable.' Clearly there was no expectation that the child should participate in the process as a matter of course, except as the subject of assessment.

A new Code of Practice (DfES 2001) issued to accompany SENDA could not be more different. It emphasises an extra-statutory duty on the part of LEAs and schools to involve pupils in decisions about their own education and statementing. The call to ascertain the child's views now permeates every part of the process of identifying, assessing and meeting needs. This is a great step forward. However, it results in a curious state of affairs where parents can ignore their child's views on inclusion in mainstream education because this decision belongs only to the parent, yet LEAs cannot make a decision on the assessment and identification of SEN without taking the child's views into consideration.

Home-school agreements

With home-school agreements, the law treats the child as, at best, accepting someone else's agreement and, at worst, an irrelevance.

Clearly, however, the DfES does not consider pupils' views irrelevant to the success of home-school agreements. DfEE guidance (DfEE 1998) cited OFSTED (Office for Standards in Education) research as showing that pupils are keen to sign and that many will take the agreement very seriously. The guidance goes on to state that 'pupils' commitment is very important to the success of the home-school agreement' and in the summary of best practice it states that 'Agreements work best where they are: – a product of genuine discussion between all parties concerned, including the pupil'. The Parental Involvement pages of the DfES Standards web-site suggest to schools that pupils should be involved in drawing the agreement up as a means of giving them ownership. It is also suggested that if the document is to work it must be a working and evolving document where all partners have active roles. The agreement should be actively supported not only by parents, but also by pupils, and the monitoring process should be informed by pupils' views of its effectiveness.[8]

Sex education and rights of withdrawal

A similar picture emerges in relation to sex education. In law the rights of the parent eclipse the rights of the child, but DfES guidance on sex and relationships education explicitly recognises the need to equip young people with the information and skills that they will need to negotiate relationships as they grow older and become sexually active. The guidance recognises that young people do have sex and that the first priority must be to protect their health. The fear that their child might obtain contraceptive advice and abortion advice without their knowledge is a frequently expressed parental concern and is perhaps one of the reasons that parents would wish to withdraw their child from sex education. Nevertheless, the guidance recognises the child's right to confidentiality and autonomy over the rights of the parents in some cases (DfEE, 2000).

Pale reflections in an adult world

If the views of pupils are clearly identified as essential in all three of these areas we have examined and children are social agents within the family and within the school, why does legislation not make the mature child a formal partner in these processes? Why do law and practice seem to be separated by such a gulf? And why is education law out of step with mainstream child law in this respect?

On the first question, education rights generally belong to the parent and have been characterised as having a private rather than a public character (Monk, 2002). Despite the fact that education is regulated and most often provided by the State, parents retain much choice. In areas such as choice of school, parental autonomy is extensive. Admission to a state school that still has places available is within the absolute discretion of the parent provided certain conditions are met. Once parental autonomy is compromised, however, these decisions take on a public character. So, for example, if the school is has no place available for the child, an admissions authority and its appeals panel will become involved in the decisions. Similarly, if the child has SEN, the LEA will be required to make decisions, again subject to certain limits and to the right of appeal, and if the pupil is excluded from school, subject to the right of appeal, the decision is taken by the head teacher under statutory authority. In all of these situations the decision of a public authority will prevail, yet the public authority has no duty to listen to the child and to balance the views of the child with those of the parent. Rights of appeal and rights to be heard during the appeal process belong to the parent and the child has few rights to be heard.

One analysis that has been used to explain this divergence is that the approaches of child law and education law actually complement each other and present a consistent whole, despite their different approaches. Monk suggests that it is the role of schools and education law to construct ideal children, and the function of the rest of the law to deal with the children who fail to conform to this ideal. So, for example, the ideal child is non-sexual, but health law deals with children who are by giving them access to services such as contraception advice:

> ... it is children's failure to live up to the ideal, and parents' failure to ensure this or comply with their duties, that triggers the attempt to ascertain the child's views. In this way, despite the apparent conflict, they serve complementary functions ... The contingency of rights, which is to say their dependence on parental or child failure, suggests that the answer may have far more to do with a desire to control or attend to the needs of the problematic or disadvantaged children, than with a principled belief in acknowledging children's subjectivity and autonomy (Monk, 2002: 54).

On the second question, it has been suggested that here too the lack of child rights in education is less inconsistent with other areas of child law than is immediately apparent. This is because, firstly, education law is more similar to the private elements than the public elements of child law in which, in practice, the child has fewer opportunities to be listened to and rights to be represented (Monk, 2002; Freeman, 1996); and secondly, paradoxically, because in child law the formal importance placed on ascertaining the mature child's wishes and feelings is not always reflected in practice. Although children have rights in child law, research has shown that in both private and public proceedings under the *Children Act 1989*, the impact of children's views is often minimal or even non-existent:

> Because the statutory requirement in the Children Act 1989 is to 'ascertain' and to 'have regard to' the child's views, children's wishes and feelings can be elicited, but not necessarily followed. If what the child wants and what is perceived to be in the best interests of that child coincide, the decisions will reflect the child's wishes: where they do not coincide, the judge's view prevails. In the latter case, the paramouncy of welfare may cause the child to see doubly excluded. Therefore, in jurisdictions where ascertaining the child's views is part of a welfare checklist, particular constructions of the child's best interests, based on abstract images of children as vulnerable, legitimate the view's of children being inadequately sought or their views being overruled. (Sclater and Piper, 2001: 418: see also McNamee, James and James elsewhere in this volume; Monk, 2002; Smart and Neale, 2000 and Piper, 1999)

Now you see her, now you don't

The only legal reflections of the child's right to participate in decisions about their education are the qualified right to participate in SENDTs and the recognition of the child's independent desire for confidentiality in the new law on disability discrimination in schools. In addition, DfES guidance has come to reflect the view that children should be able to participate in decisions that affect them, but this does not have a direct legal effect. In the *Education Act 2002* there are further developments, particularly a new duty in *section 176* concerning consultation with pupils.

At first sight this might seem to undermine much of the preceding argument, but this is not the case. The precise nature of the s. 176 duty, which came into force in September 2003, is for LEAs and governing bodies to 'have regard to any guidance given from time to time by the Secretary of State [...] about consultation with pupils in connection with the taking of decisions affecting them'. The commitment is not a com-prehensive duty to ascertain the child's wishes in all matters that affect them, as seems to be required by Art 12 UNCRC, but to have regard to guidance. The extent of the guidance that will be covered by the duty is as yet uncertain and, further, how closely schools will feel they have to follow this will of course depend on the nature of that guidance. However, in strict legal terms this goes little further than the present law does. It may be that this has a symbolic importance that should not be minimised or, more cynically, it might be seen as the minimum response possible following further criticism from the Committee on the Rights of the Child following the UK's second periodic report under requirements of the UNCRC.[9] Whatever significance is attached to this, in legal terms the child remains barely visible and parental rights have retained formal and political supremacy. The practical reality that chil-dren need to be recognised as active participants in educational decisions as well as in education itself remains to be recognised by the law.

One might ask why, if the mirror of the law reflects only part of the reality of a situation where children are social agents and where official guidance often acknowledges this explicitly, we should worry about changing the law? There are three important reasons for this. First, because the child isn't always heard. New statutory guidance which may emerge in future may be scarcely more effective, if at all. As Harris has noted following his research into school exclusions:

> The guidance on exclusion appeals... now says the panel should permit the child to attend and speak on his/her own behalf unless there is a good reason to refuse. I would argue that neither of these statements goes far enough in stressing the importance of hearing the child's own version of events. It is disappointing that as yet there are no plans to place the panel under comparable duties to those being introduced in the field of special educational needs appeals, to ensure at least some guarantees that the child's view will be heard. (2000: 41)[10]

Second, children experience the effects of child law and education law in similar ways, yet it is difficult for children and their families to make sense of the different departmental structures and professionals involved in their lives and more difficult to understand their rights in different statutory procedures. (Lloyd, 1997)

Third, children should have their agency acknowledged, not just because they can 'vote with their feet' but also through recognition in law, because it is their right. In Scotland recent legislative change has drastically altered the legal status of children's views in education. *Section 2(2)* of the *Standards in Scotland's Schools etc. Act 2000* provides that

> ... in carrying out their duty [...] an education authority shall have due regard, so far as is reasonably practicable, to the views (if there is a wish to express them) of the child or young person in decisions that significantly affect that child or young person, taking account of the child or young person's age and maturity.

Meredith (2001: 6) describes this as 'unique in education legislation within the UK as a positive assertion of a right to education on the part of children ... A cultural shift of considerable importance'. It certainly goes much further than the *Education Act 2002* which, in giving guidance statutory force, only strengthens it marginally.

The lack of a right to participate in education decisions in England and Wales focuses attention on children as citizens. Classical liberalism limits social membership to those who are considered rational and responsible. Although there are places where the agency of the pupils is recognised, the education system generally presumes that children are 'logically absent and socially incompetent' (Wyness, 1999). However, in the education law of England and Wales there is also a new Citizenship curriculum to make sense of. The possible purposes of this and its potential effects are open to argument (Wyness, 1999: 364), but it does highlight the contradictions in the present law:

> We encounter the irony of a prescriptive curriculum requiring children to learn citizenship skills based on democratic values of equality, mutual responsibility and independent decision-making ... Being encouraged to behave as 'active and responsible' citizens, but being denied the opportunity to exercise rights and responsibilities in school is bound to be experienced as inconsistent and frustrating, if not hypocritical, by children themselves. (Smith, 2000: 323–324).

Conclusion

Throughout this chapter, reflections and mirrors have been used as analogies for the dissonance between law and reality and children have been characterised as silent and invisible. This is not the first use of the metaphor of invisibility to describe children in education law (Piper,

1999) and in Jeffs (1995) Acton is quoted describing the child as being 'the ghost at every meeting'. The pupils described in this chapter, however, are more like vampires than like ghosts – the law is the mirror in which their reflection cannot be seen, but if you turn your back to its shiny surface, or look behind it at the real world of education, children are plain for all to see.

As noted earlier, Monk has observed that the role of schools and education law is to construct ideal children and the function of the rest of the law is to deal with the children who fail to conform to this ideal. These idealised children have been subjected to a marketised system of education in which their parents' status as consumers leaves the children out of the picture. Meanwhile, less-than ideal children have been medicalised, as in the case of SEN, demonised where they are unruly, as in exclusions law, or inappropriately sexualised, as in sex education. Absent from the mirror of education law, these children exist in the real world and are recognised in child law and, increasingly, in guidance. It remains to be seen whether developments in the *Education Act 2002* will bring these children into focus and give their views substance. At present their image, as reflected in legislation, remains ghostly and incomplete.

Notes

1. To make sense of abbreviations it is worth pointing out that there have been many incarnations of the government department responsible for education in recent years. The Department was formerly known as the Department for Education and Employment (DfEE) and prior to that the Department for Education (DfE).
2. Section 1(3) applies where courts are considering making a section 8 order that is opposed by any of the parties to the action, or an order for care or supervision. Section 22 imposes a similar duty in respect of decisions affecting children who are 'looked after' by a local authority.
3. Article 12 states;
   1. States Parties shall assure to the child who is capable of forming his or her own views the right to express those views freely in all matters affecting the child, the views of the child being given due weight in accordance with the age and maturity of the child.
   2. For this purpose, the child shall in particular be provided the opportunity to be heard in any judicial and administrative proceedings affecting the child, either directly, or through a representative or an appropriate body, in a manner consistent with the procedural rules of national law.
4. *Regulations 30* and *13* of the *Special Educational Needs Tribunal Regulations 2001 SI 600/2001* and *Regulation 30* of the *Special Educational Needs and Disability Tribunal (General Provisions and Disability Claims Procedure) Regulations 2002 SI 1985/2002*.

5. *APP v Wednesbury Corporation* [1948] 1KB 223 and *Gillick v West Norfolk and Wisbech Health Authority* [5] [1986] AC 112.
6. More detail than there is space for here can be found in any administrative law textbook see for example P. P. Craig (1999) *Administrative Law* (4th ed.) Sweet and Maxwell: London or P. Leyland and T. Woods (2002) *Textbook on Administrative Law* (4th ed.) Oxford University Press: Oxford.
7. *Education (Special Educational Needs) Regulations 1994* SI 1994/1910 replaced by *Education (Special Educational Needs)(England)(Consolidation) Regulations 2001* SI 2001/3455.
8. http://www.standards.dfes.gov.uk/parentalinvolvement/hsa/
9. Committee on the Rights of the Child, Thirty-first session. CRC/C/15/Add.188, 4 October 2002.
10. Harris's research showed that, although children are allowed to attend if parents wish them to, the child was present in only 40 per cent of the hearings observed. In half the child's view was not presented at all to the panel, in spite of the fact that 80 per cent of all excluded children are in the 12–15 age group and most would be well able to contribute. (p. 40).

References

Blair, A. and Furniss, C. (1995) 'Sex Lies and DfE Circular 5/94' *Education and the Law*.

Blair, A. and Lawson, A. (2003) 'Disability Discrimination Reforms in Education – Could do Better?' *Child and Family Law Quarterly* vol. 15: 41–55.

Blair, A. and Waddington, M. (1997) 'Home-school "Contracts": Regulating the Role of Parents' *Education and the Law* vol. 9: 291–305.

Cairns, L. (2001) 'Investing in Children: Learning How to Promote the Rights of All Children' *Children & Society* vol. 18: 347–360.

DfE (1994) Code of Practice on the Identification and Assessment of SEN.

DfEE (1998) 'Home School Agreements: Guidance for Schools' Now published at DfES http://www.dfes.gov.uk/hsa/index.shtml.

DfEE (2000) Sex and Relationships Guidance. Circular 116/2000.

DfES (2001) Special Educational Needs Code of Practice 2001 DfES/581/2001.

Edwards, R. and David, M. (1997) 'Where are the Children in Home-school Relations? Notes Towards a Research Agenda'. *Children & Society* vol. 11: 194–200.

Eekelaar, J. (1986) The Eclipse of Parental Rights. *Law Quarterly Review* vol. 102: 4.

Freeman, M. (1996) 'The Convention: An English Perspective' in Freeman, M. (ed.) *Children's Rights: a Comparative Perspective* Dartmouth: Aldershot.

Furniss, C. and Blair, A. (1997) 'Sex Wars: Conflict in, and Reform of, Sex Education in Maintained in Secondary Schools' *Journal of Social Welfare and Family Law* vol. 19: 189–202.

Harris, N. (2000) 'Education Law: Excluding the Child' *Education and the Law* vol. 12: 31–46.

Jeffs, T. (1995) 'Children's Educational Rights in a New Era.' In Freeman (ed.) *The Handbook of Children's Rights*.

Lloyd, G. (1997) 'Can the Law Support Children's Rights in School in Scotland and Prevent the Development of a Climate of Blame?' *Pastoral Care* September 1997: 13–16.

McNamee, S., James, A. and James, A. (2002) *Family Law and the Construction of Childhood in England and Wales.* Original seminar paper given at the Politics of Childhood Conference, University of Hull, September 2002.

McNamee, S. James, A. and James, A. (2004) 'Family Law and the Construction of Childhood in England and Wales' in Goddard, J., McNamee, S. James, A. and James, A. (2004) *The Politics of Childhood: International Perspectives, Contemporary developments.*

Meredith, P. (2001) Editorial Comment: The Child's Right to Education. *Education and the Law* vol. 13: 5–8.

Monk, D. (2002) 'Children's Rights in Education – Making Sense of Contradictions. *Child and Family Law Quarterly* vol. 14: 45–56.

Piper, C. (1999) 'Barriers to Seeing and Hearing Children in Private Law Proceedings' Family Law: 394–315.

Prout, A. (2000) 'Children's Participation: Control and Self-realisation in British Late Modernity' *Children and Society* vol. 14: 304–315.

Sclater, S. and Piper, C. (2001) 'Social Exclusion and the Welfare of the Child' *Journal of Law and Society,* vol. 28: 409–429.

Smart, C. and Neale, B. (2000) '"It's My Life Too" – Children's Perspective on Post-divorce Parenting.' *Family Law:* 163–169.

Smith, R. (2000) 'Whose Childhood? The Politics of Homework' *Children and Society* vol. 14: 316–325.

Steutal, J. and Speicker, B. (1999) Family Education, State Intervention and Political Liberalism, *Journal of Philosophy of Education* vol. 33: 337–352.

West, A. (1992) 'Choosing Schools: Why do Parents Opt for Private Schools or Schools in Other LEAs?' *Clare Market Papers No. 1.* Centre for Educational Research, LSE: London.

Wyness, M. G. (1999) 'Childhood, Agency and Education Reform.' *Childhood* vol. 6: 353–368.

Part Four
Children, Power and Decision-making

11

Placing Children on the Political Agenda: New Zealand's Agenda for Children

Maree Brown and Jaleh McCormack[1]

Introduction

There's a common saying in New Zealand: 'This is a great place to bring up your kids'. But what do children think about this? Is it a great place for children? Children throughout New Zealand were asked these questions as part of the development of New Zealand's Agenda for Children (hereafter, the Agenda) (MSD, 2002a). Published in June 2002 by the Ministry of Social Development (MSD), the Agenda is an over-arching government strategy to improve outcomes for children in New Zealand. It consists of a vision: that 'New Zealand is a great place for children: we look after one another', a set of guiding principles to inform all government policy and service developments relating to children, a new 'whole child' approach to developing policies and services for children, and seven key action areas for further policy work.

The Agenda was developed through an open consultative process. It began with a public seminar on children's policy, drew on the knowledge and skills of a reference group of community experts, and involved nationwide consultation with children and adults.

A companion strategy for youth, called the Youth Development Strategy Aotearoa, was developed concurrently by the Ministry of Youth Affairs (Ministry of Youth Affairs, 2002). This strategy focuses on policies and services for young people aged 12–25, while the Agenda focuses on children (as defined by the United Nations Convention on the Rights of the Child, hereafter UNCRC) aged 0–18 years. Officials from the Ministry of Youth Affairs and MSD worked collaboratively to develop these as companion documents and developed a joint work programme to oversee their implementation.

This paper focuses on the Agenda. The first part describes the context and key drivers that led to its development and shaped its content. The second part briefly outlines the core components of the Agenda, including discussion of the consultation process used in its development. The final part reflects on the work undertaken to date. It concludes that the Agenda has been successful in bringing new perspectives on childhood into the policy arena, in making progress on some priority issues for children, and in supporting a range of related initiatives. However, fully realising the potential of the Agenda and keeping children's interests, rights and needs at the centre of policy development will be an ongoing challenge.

Context and impetus for placing children on the political agenda

The development of child welfare policy is inextricably linked to the broader social, political and economic environment. It is, therefore, useful to briefly outline the key changes in New Zealand social and economic policy over the past few decades. Welfare expenditure in New Zealand began to increase significantly between the early 1970s and early 1980s, as a result of a range of generous, largely non-means-tested social security initiatives introduced by successive governments (Boston, 1999). However, as Blaiklock *et al.* (2002) note, a combination of New Zealand's deteriorating agricultural export market, the international energy crises in the 1970s and soaring inflation and unemployment levels in the early 1980s led to increased pressure for economic reforms.

The country was struggling to meet its welfare commitments. The Labour Government elected to power in 1984 concluded that 'the costs of maintaining the welfare state meant that New Zealand could no longer compete in the international marketplace, and that taxation and government spending needed to be reduced and individual and family responsibilities promoted' (Blaiklock *et al.*, 2002: 7). The new Government embarked on a substantial programme of market deregulation, tax reductions, privatisation of state-owned enterprises and increased targeting of social assistance. From 1990, the newly elected National Government made further radical reforms; notably a substantial reduction in benefit levels and tightening of eligibility criteria for welfare assistance.

By the mid 1990s, there was growing concern about how children were faring under these policies and particular concerns about the incidence of poverty (Stephens, 1999). Various social services initiatives to target at-risk families were introduced. However, with the ageing of the population, the health and superannuation needs of older people tended to be given more political prominence (Blaiklock *et al.*, 2002).

In the lead-up to the 1999 General Election, the Labour Party (then in opposition) announced in its manifesto its intention to 'put in place policies that ensure New Zealand is the best country in the world to be a child' (New Zealand Labour Party, 1999: 10–11).[2] The Labour Party came to power with a coalition partner, the Alliance Party. The manifesto statement for the latter had stated that 'the best interests of children in New Zealand will be the first priority of all actions undertaken or advocated by an Alliance Government' (New Zealand Alliance Party, 1999: 1).

Changing perspectives on children and their position in society

The Agenda was strongly influenced by the work of New Zealand academics and child advocacy groups. Foremost among these is the Children's Issues Centre,[3] a research and advocacy unit that has published extensively and hosted numerous conferences on children's rights issues. In addition, the 1990s had given rise to many new advocacy groups for children, including 'Action for Child and Youth Aotearoa' and the 'Child Poverty Action Group'. Their concerns about the deteriorating economic position of children in New Zealand, expressed in media statements and in numerous publications, including reports to the UN Committee on the Rights of the Child, provided an important context for the Agenda.[4] Another strong advocacy group, 'Children's Agenda', had been calling since the early 1990s for improved representation of children's interests in the political process, including greater resources and independence for the Commissioner for Children.[5]

Central to the work of these academics and advocates was recognition of the cultural shift in thinking about childhood that was occurring in New Zealand (and elsewhere) by the 1990s. This shift was influenced both by the growing children's rights movement and by the academic discourse on the sociology of childhood, which challenged views of a universal childhood. Proponents of this discourse argued that childhood is socially constructed, and that the meaning and experience of childhood varies over time and place and is linked to other social categories such as class, gender and ethnicity (James and Prout, 1990: 3).

This argument is important in the policy context, as policy-makers both contribute to and are influenced by constructions of childhood in the approach they take to developing policies and services for children. The New Zealand government's decision to develop a strategy for children's policy was, at least in part, prompted by recognition that policy-making had not kept pace with changing perspectives on children and childhood that were emerging from academic discourse.

Children and families

One of these changing perspectives was the relationship between children and families. In New Zealand, as elsewhere, many policies and services aim to meet the needs of children via support for their families. However, the experiences and needs of children often differ from those of other family members, leading to calls for policymakers to consider the impact of policies on children as a separate group (Jamison and Gilbert, 2000). Furthermore, in New Zealand, persistent poor child outcomes across a number of indicators by the late 1990s suggested a need to look beyond family policy and services as the primary vehicle for investing in and improving the wellbeing of dependent children (see 'How children are faring' section below for discussion of key child indicators).

It was clear that the Agenda needed to balance the crucial role of families in children's lives, and children's inherent dependency on families in their early years, with children's developing capabilities and autonomy. Achieving this balance was complicated by the fact that there are diverse understandings of family and of children's roles and positions within them. For example, while many western academics working within the sociology of childhood paradigm acknowledge the crucial role of families in children's lives, they also promote childhood as an independent social category and children as having their own agency. However, in the New Zealand context the Agenda also needed to recognise that the wellbeing of Maori children is seen by most Maori, the indigenous people of New Zealand, as fundamentally linked to the wellbeing of their whanau[6] (extended family), hapu (sub-tribe) and iwi (tribe) (Matahaere-Ataariki, 2000; Te Puni Kokiri, 2000) because these are the structures that perpetuate Maori cultural values and practices and provide ongoing nurturing and protection to Maori children (Blaiklock *et al.*, 2002: 12).

The Agenda needed to support parents and families as the primary sources of nurturing, protection, support and guidance for children but also recognise that sometimes children have different needs and issues from other members of their family.

Vulnerable dependents, passive recipients

In addition to subsuming children within families, child policies and services have often focused on children as passive recipients, or as vulnerable dependents that are in need of adult protection, control and guidance. Many children consulted in the development of the Agenda said that adults viewed and treated them as if they were incompetent, immature, or of less importance than adults:

> People don't value your opinion as much as if you were an adult. You are in some ways not valued as a person, but as a possession.
> (Submission from girl aged 12, cited in MSD, 2002a: 20).

Bird (2003: 37) provides an example of how the view of children as passive recipients was reflected in the 1989 'Tomorrow's Schools' education reforms in New Zealand:

> ... while the stated purpose of the reforms was to improve schools and thus to cater for student's 'learning needs', the diverse voices of New Zealand children were largely silent in the policy debates through this period. It now seems surprising that students, the objects of all this attention, were seldom considered to be 'stakeholders' in the reform process ...

Many academics have called for the recognition of children's agency and capabilities and for an understanding of children as competent social actors who are shaped by and shape the world around them. For example, Corsaro states: 'children are active, creative social agents who produce their own unique children's cultures while simultaneously contributing to the production of adult societies' (1997: 4).

There have also been specific calls for children's voices to be heard in policy-making (Prout, 2002; Jamison and Gilbert, 2000: 186). In New Zealand, Smith and Taylor note that within the legal system children are still commonly viewed as objects, with a lack of capacity to participate in decision-making (2000b: 9). Given this context, it was important that the Agenda challenged some of the traditional, rather reductionist, views of children as vulnerable dependents and as passive recipients of services. A key focus of the Agenda was to promote the view of children as competent social actors and, indeed, as key stakeholders in the policy development process. One of the most important steps in developing the Agenda – and an effective means, in itself, of raising the profile of children as stakeholders – was to conduct national consultations with children to find out what their concerns were and what suggestions they had for improvements (see 'Children's involvement in developing the Agenda', p. 196).

Adults in development

Developmental theory, which views children as moving through a series of stages on their way to adulthood – or to becoming 'the whole person' – has traditionally dominated academic and lay discourses (Alderson, 2000). Many areas of policy-making are also future-focused: investing in helping children become healthy, competent, law-abiding productive adults. However, future-focused strategies can risk losing sight of the interests and needs of children in the present, as citizens in their own right with knowledge and insight into their own situation and views on how policies and services for them might be made more effective. Corsaro notes that present-focused policy will enrich children's lives, 'produce better adults and will enable our children to participate actively and fully in their own childhoods and to contribute to the quality of our adult lives' (1997: 277).

While not losing sight of what children need to achieve healthy development as they move towards adulthood, the Agenda called for a greater focus on children's interests, rights and needs in the present.

Other key drivers

There were also a number of other legal, social and economic imperatives behind the development of the Agenda. This section describes three of the key drivers, namely: legal imperatives to improve the status of children, concerns about how children are faring, and international policy developments. Further discussion of the broader context behind the Agenda is found in the published strategy.

Legal responsibility to uphold children's rights

Over the past decade or so, there has been growing international recognition of the rights of children as citizens and social actors. The United Nations Convention on the Rights of the Child (UNCRC) has done much to encourage this focus on children's rights. Such rights are commonly grouped into the three 'p's – provision, protection and participation (Lansdown, 1994).

The New Zealand government's ratification of the UNCRC in 1993 established a legal obligation to uphold children's rights. The government is required to report, every five years, on the implementation of the UNCRC.[7] In 1997, the UN Committee on the Rights of the Child was concerned that New Zealand had no overarching policy or plan of action to incorporate the principles and provisions of the UNCRC. The Committee recommended that the Government 'prepare and adopt a comprehensive policy statement with respect to the rights of the child, incorporating the principles and provisions of the Convention, that could provide guidance to all those involved in support services delivered or funded by Government' (Ministry of Youth Affairs, 2000: 7). It is important to note that New Zealand is not alone in facing criticism for not making children's rights part of the national agenda. Rayner (2002) gives a critical appraisal of the state of children's rights in Australia since it ratified the UNCRC in 1990.

There had also been a concomitant demand from parents and families, children's advocacy groups and other community organisations for better co-ordination of government policies and services for children (See Ludbrook, 2000: 115). Ian Hassall, New Zealand's inaugural Commissioner for Children (from 1989–1994), stated:

[Children] have no special place in public policy. There is no children's policy, and yet they are frequently the purported objects of public spending and public policy areas, such as education, health, and welfare. Yet children's interests are not explicitly at the centre of these policies and are surprisingly often overlooked.
                (Hassall, 1998: 42 cited in Jamison and Gilbert, 2000: 181).

The Agenda was intended, in part, to attend to these calls for an overarching framework. It is underpinned by the articles of the UNCRC and promotes a co-ordinated approach to child policy and service development.

Concerns about how children are faring

The Agenda was also driven by real concern about how children in New Zealand were faring across a number of key indicators. In some areas, the situation for children has clearly worsened over the past few decades. For example, in the period 1987–88, 16 per cent of dependent children were living in families categorised as 'poor'. In this chapter 'poor' families are defined as those with incomes below 60 per cent of the median, adjusted for housing costs. By 2000/01, this figure had risen to 29 per cent, or almost 3 out of every 10 children (MSD, 2003a: 67). Additionally, one fifth (21 per cent) of New Zealand children born in 1993 spent at least five of their first seven years of life in a family whose main form of income was an income-tested benefit (Ball and Wilson, 2002).

In other areas, while there has been improvement over time, there are still significant concerns about the current circumstances of children. For example, while the proportion of school leavers with higher qualifications increased during the 1980s, there was little improvement during the 1990s (MSD, 2003a: 42). Child abuse rates are another area of significant concern: between 1998 and 2002, for every 1,000 children, around seven children were assessed each year as being abused or neglected (MSD, 2003a: 100). Also, while infant death rates dropped sharply during the 1960s and 1970s, the pace of decline has since slowed (Ministry of Health, 2003). There are particular concerns about the rates of infant mortality for Maori and Pacific children, which are still much higher than the rates for the rest of the infant population (Ministry of Health, 2003). In terms of progress, New Zealand has been overtaken by many OECD countries that were once well behind on this key indicator of child well-being.

International policy developments

The Agenda was developed within a broader international context and drew on the policy developments and work of other nations (including academics and advocates) to increase the profile of children and improve the co-ordination of child policy and services. For instance, in November 2000 the Republic of Ireland released its National Children's Strategy. In the United Kingdom, a Cabinet Committee on Children and Young People's Services was established in July 2000 and a Minister for Children and Young People was appointed in 2003. Plans for an overarching strategy for children and young people were published in late 2003.[8]

What does the Agenda contain?

This section summarises the core components of the Agenda for Children, including the vision and principles, 'whole child' approach and key action areas. It also outlines the process for consulting children in the development of the Agenda and some of the key findings from this exercise. As noted earlier, New Zealand's Agenda for Children is an overarching government strategy to improve outcomes for children in New Zealand. It is intended to inform all child policy and service developments in New Zealand and is targeted at people who develop policies and provide services that affect children in the public service, local government, and community and voluntary sector.

Vision and principles

The Agenda's vision, 'New Zealand is a great place for children: we look after one another', was developed and refined through a public consultation process. The vision re-casts the old saying 'New Zealand is a great place to bring up your kids'. In the Agenda, the focus is firmly on children and how they experience life in New Zealand. The second part of the vision is based on the Maori concept of 'manaakitanga'; that is, providing reciprocal care and support.

At the heart of the Agenda is a set of principles to guide government policy and service development. The first principle is that policies and services should recognise children's rights as set out in UNCRC. The other principles are also rights-based. 'Child-focused' means that the interests of the child will be the most important consideration and children should have the opportunity to have their views taken into account, in accordance with their ability and level of understanding. The principle that government policies and services should be 'family and whanau oriented' affirms the importance of government services to families as a key way of meeting children's needs, and that children should be seen in the context of family and/or whanau.

The whole child approach

A key feature of the Agenda for Children is the promotion of a new approach to child policy and service development – the 'whole child' approach. This approach has been mandated by the New Zealand Cabinet as the basis for child policy and service development in conjunction with the youth development approach, which is outlined in the Youth Development Strategy Aotearoa. Table 11.1 briefly outlines the meaning of taking a 'whole child' approach to policy and service development.

Table 11.1   Whole child approach

Focusing on the big picture	• focusing on the complexity of children's lives, rather than just isolated problems or issues.
	• recognising the linkages between issues and how issues in one area are likely to impact on other aspects of a child's life.
Focusing on what children need for healthy development	• early and sustained investments in children's well-being, so that they enjoy the cumulative effect of positive opportunities and experiences, rather than government just reacting when problems arise.
Looking across the whole public service	• agencies working together across different sectors, to see what can be done to support children's healthy development, and to collectively deliver the outcomes they are responsible for rather than focusing on single-sector solutions.
	• considering the effectiveness of government interventions in the different settings of a child's life and whether multi-level interventions are needed.
Seeing children as having views on issues that affect them and ideas to contribute	• recognising children's right and desire to be involved in decision-making on issues that affect their lives, rather than viewing children as passive recipients of government policies and services.
	• gaining the benefits of involving children in the development or review of policies and services.

Key settings model

One of the foundations of the whole child approach is a key settings model. The model draws on the work of Urie Bronfenbrenner, in that it takes an ecological approach to human development (see Bronfenbrenner, 1979). The whole child approach recognises that children cannot be separated from the 'key settings' in which they live and grow. The settings focused on in the Agenda include parents, families and whanau, friends and peers (Figure 11.1).

The key settings model also reflects the view that 'children's voices and experiences are embedded not only in their own particular family, school and neighbourhood contexts, but in the context of the wider society' (Smith and Taylor, 2000a: p. ix). The different shades in the figure signify the interactions between the different settings. This model recognises that children are shaped by, but also help to shape, the settings in which they live.

The whole child approach recognises that a child's development may be profoundly affected by interactions that occur between the settings

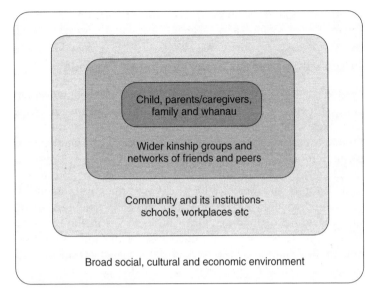

Figure 11.1 The key settings model (MSD, 2002a: 14)

in which they live. For example, how well they do at school may be influenced by their own personal temperament, by the kind of friendships they have with their peers and also by how much time and support they have at home to do their homework. A child's life might also be affected by external factors such as the conditions and hours of their parent's work, or by social attitudes towards things such as drug use or corporal punishment. Child policies and services need to work within and across each of these settings and to recognise the links between them if they are to support healthy child development and minimise the risk factors in children's lives.

Action areas

The Agenda also outlines seven key areas of action for government and government agencies, in partnership with other key stakeholders, including, of course, children themselves. The seven action areas are:

- Promoting a whole child approach
- Increasing children's participation
- An end to child poverty
- Addressing violence in children's lives, particularly bullying
- Improving central government structures and processes

- Improving local government and community planning for children
- Enhancing information and research collaboration relating to children

Children's involvement in developing the Agenda

In April 2001, the Agenda team embarked on a national consultation process to provide children with an opportunity to tell government and policy makers what issues were important to them. This was the first time that the New Zealand government had undertaken a consultation process with children on such a large scale. While in this paper we only discuss the children's consultation, the process also provided opportunities for interested adults and organisations to have input into shaping the Agenda. Children and young people were able to contribute in a variety of ways, including: responding to the Children's Discussion Pack (which contained a response sheet and other ideas for making a submission); sending in their views and ideas through a designated website; contributing to group discussions and submissions, either at school or in other groups; and participating in a facilitated session.

The Ministry received 3490 submissions and of these 3141 were from individual children and 298 from groups of children. In addition, the Ministry ran 51 facilitated sessions. Children and young people involved in these specially convened sessions brought the total number of individual submissions to 3441, and the total group submissions to 321. These submissions incorporated the views of more than 7,500 children (Agenda for Children team, 2002).

Most submissions came from primary and intermediate school students (ages five to 13). More girls participated than boys. A quarter of submissions were from Maori and six percent were from Pacific children (MSD, 2001). The following paragraphs provide a brief summary of the key findings and a selection of quotes as published by MSD (see MSD, 2001, 2002a; Agenda for Children team, 2002).

The first part of the consultation asked children to consider what they liked about being a child in New Zealand. The most common responses focused on freedom from responsibility, including not having to support themselves financially, being able to have fun, play sport and relax. Children also liked having good schools, friends and families who love them, and a safe and environmentally-sound country to live in. For example:

> You can live without the worries and responsibilities of an adult. You can enjoy and learn and develop healthily and easily.
>
> (Female, 15 years old)

Asked what they didn't like about being a child, the most common responses were: being told what to do, not being taken seriously or listened to by adults, and not being able to make their own decisions. Young people also voiced concerns about bullying and peer pressure and not having enough to do:

> I stay with my Uncle and he is the type that doesn't like to listen just likes to be listened to. What he says goes, and that's that.
>
> (Member of a mixed age and gender group)

Finally, children were asked to consider what would make life better for them in New Zealand. The most common suggestions included:

- Providing children with more to do! Especially places to go that are cheap or free like playgrounds, skateboard parks, libraries and leisure centres
- Improvements to schools and education
- Giving children more responsibility
- Trusting, listening to and respecting children
- Stop bullying, child abuse and other crime and violence generally, and
- Families should have enough money to buy the things they need.

Two young women summed up their views in the following ways:

> If people trusted young people more then I think we would behave better than we do. We crave attention and if we got decent recognition we wouldn't be so destructive.
>
> (Female, 15 years old)

> Help schools that are trying their hardest to keep children from ending up in the streets or gutters. I know my school is trying their hardest to keep us away from the things that are happening in mainstream schools. I want the Government to help. I reckon if they help mainstream schools, they can help with Maori schools. And keep up our HISTORY.
>
> (Female, 14 years old).

This exercise illustrated that it is both possible and useful to engage children as key stakeholders in the development of policies and services that affect them. The submissions highlighted children's competence in taking part in consultation processes and in articulating what they would like to see the government do.

Importantly, the findings also indicated that while children shared some of the same views as child advocates and other adults, they also had a range of different ideas and different priorities. In responding to the same three questions, adult respondents were most commonly concerned about the impact of poverty on children, the need to reduce unemployment, the level of violence against children and health issues facing children and young people (MSD, 2001). Children also raised these issues, but their main concerns were a lack of autonomy over decisions in their daily lives and not being listened to by adults. These differences underline the importance of policy-makers engaging with children in the development of policies and services that affect them, and not just with adults acting on their behalf.

Children's concerns, views and suggestions played an important role in shaping the Agenda, particularly the whole child approach and the key action areas. A good example is children's request to be included in decisions that affect their lives. The Agenda includes a specific Action Area focused on increasing children's participation. Additionally, children's participation is incorporated in the whole child approach (Action Area 1), improving central government structures (Action Area 5), and improving local government and community planning for children (Action Area 6). A further example is the inclusion of a specific action area (4), which addresses bullying and violence. This was a direct response to children's concerns about violence and bullying; in particular, in their schools and communities.

Discussion

> The key to success will be the implementation of the strategy which will require a commitment of significant resources and change in the operational culture of agencies to put children at the forefront of their agenda.
>
> (Adult submission cited in MSD, 2002a).

Although it may be too soon to assess the Agenda's effectiveness in making New Zealand 'a great place for children', it is timely to reflect on the progress made in implementing its key action areas and its success in promoting children's interests, rights and needs.

Progress on action areas

Work on all seven Agenda action areas is well underway, including progress on some areas floated in the published Agenda as 'Possible future developments and directions'. Probably the most significant progress has been made on Action Area 3: 'An end to child poverty'. The government had already signaled, in the Agenda discussion document, an intention to give priority to addressing child poverty. The public responses to the discussion document, together with concerted calls from numerous child advocacy groups and research bodies for urgent action on child poverty, served to strengthen this commitment. The government initiated a major review of the whole family income assistance system in 2002. Budget 2003 included some improvements to the employment assistance system and, more recently, the Government has announced that the centrepiece of Budget 2004 will be a substantial investment package designed to increase the living standards of beneficiary and low-income working families with children, to ensure adequate incomes for all and to make work pay.[9]

There has also been significant progress on the other key action areas, both through the Agenda work programme and work in related strategies. For example, MSD has worked with a number of other agencies to develop the New Zealand local government toolkit for child and youth participation – a web-based toolkit giving local government staff practical information about involving children and young people in council planning and decision-making.[10] Work to address bullying has included research on different approaches taken in schools, while broader work to address family violence and child abuse is being progressed through *Te Rito: the New Zealand Family Violence Prevention Strategy* (MSD, 2002b), the *Care and Protection Blueprint 2003*[11] (MSD, 2003c: 11, 29) and through work to implement the recommendations of the 2003 first principles baseline review of the Department of Child, Youth and Family Services, the department responsible for statutory care and protection services to children at risk (New Zealand Treasury *et al.*, 2003).

Effectiveness of the Agenda in placing children on the political agenda

The Agenda received a high level of public attention, which can be largely attributed to the nationwide consultation process. An important element in making this consultation process a success was the involvement of government Ministers in launching the discussion documents and in consulting with groups of children across the country. The community reference group members were also instrumental in raising the public profile of the Agenda.

The many citations by child advocacy groups, academics and researchers of the Agenda's content and findings from the consultation with children further demonstrate the strong public engagement with the Agenda. Some authors have used material from the Agenda to lobby government to progress particular children's issues. For example, in October 2002, just four months after the release of the final report, a collective of 14 organisations working on children's issues published a report called *Making it Happen: Implementing New Zealand's Agenda for Children* (Institute of Public Policy at AUT *et al.*, 2002). This report supported the vision and principles set out in the Agenda but also urged government to consider a range of further actions under each of the Agenda's action areas and to commit to additional resourcing to better meet children's needs.

In 2003, the Children's Issues Centre hosted a conference on 'Joined Up Services: Linking Together Children and Families'. The explicit objective of the conference was to 'attempt to progress Action Area 1 of the government's Agenda for Children (AFC) – Promoting a whole child approach' (Smith, 2002). More recently, UNICEF New Zealand cited Agenda consultation responses to help support its proposals to eliminate child poverty (D'Souza and Wood, 2003: 26).

In the policy-making arena itself, the support of Government and government agencies for the Agenda and its action areas culminated in the 2002 Cabinet mandate that the whole child approach, along with the youth development approach outlined in the YDSA, was to be the basis for all child and youth policy and service development. In practice, this means that public service agencies are expected to apply these approaches to developing policies and services affecting children and young people.

As the department responsible for the Agenda, MSD has taken the lead in demonstrating its commitment to the strategy and to children by incorporating most of the key objectives of the Agenda into its *Statement of Intent 2003* (the publication which sets out the Ministry's strategic direction, priorities and goals for the next three years):

> Children and young people are respected and valued and have a say in the decisions that affect them. They are protected from the negative effects of poverty, violence, abuse or neglect, and they are able to reach their full potential. (MSD, 2003b: 39).

MSD has also undertaken work to build awareness of the Agenda (and, through this, children's issues) and an understanding of its role in policy-making across government. In early 2003, MSD commissioned a baseline survey of key government agencies in order to examine their knowledge and application of the whole child approach. The survey found that, while many core agencies have taken on board the importance of considering issues for children in their work, the actual knowledge and application of the Agenda and the whole child approach was variable. MSD has since published an information guide on engaging children in decision-making (MSD, 2003d) and a written guide for agencies on applying the whole child approach is in press. MSD and MYD have also hosted a series of training sessions for local and regional government staff and community agencies on child and youth participation.

Challenges to maintaining children's place on the political agenda

Each year in the government policy arena, new issues and priorities emerge and new initiatives develop. While a significant new achievement for government in 2002, the Agenda is no longer its 'flagship' strategy for children. Without doubt, though, the Agenda has helped forge a new path for child policy development in New Zealand and has informed the thinking behind more recent government initiatives in this area. Probably the most significant of these initiatives is the interagency 'Investing in Child and Youth Development' (ICYD) work programme. The ICYD programme is one of the four key work areas included in the Government's *Sustainable Development for New Zealand: Programme of Action*; released in January 2003, just six months after the Agenda. The overarching goal of ICYD is that 'All children and young people have the opportunity to participate, to succeed and to make contributions that benefit themselves and others, now and in the future' (Department of Prime Minister and Cabinet: 2003: 123).

The ICYD draws on both the Agenda and the YDSA in advocating a whole child and youth development approach for achieving better outcomes for children and young people. It aims to ensure the positive development of children and young people. A key difference between the initiatives is that whereas the Agenda was led by one agency (MSD) and sought the input and collaboration of other agencies to work on a few key priority areas, the ICYD strategy was explicitly developed as a more comprehensive cross-sectoral work programme, with lead responsibility for different actions shared across the education, health, justice and child and youth policy portfolios. Its monitoring framework *requires* agencies to report on progress against these action areas. The result is that the ICYD has had broader ministerial and cross-departmental buy-in than the Agenda work programme was able to achieve.

The ICYD work also includes the development of an 'indicators framework on child and youth well-being' (which takes forward a key action identified in the Agenda and will help New Zealand with its UNCRC reporting requirements) and development of an 'investment framework for child and youth development' to look strategically at investment decisions across agencies. The aim of the investment framework is to draw together evidence to guide decision-making across the social sector on investing in a way that promotes positive outcomes for children and young people.

The overall Sustainable Development framework, within which the ICYD work programme is placed, is probably also more likely to find wider political and public acceptance than the 'children's rights' framework which emphasises children's agency and voice. Is this a retrograde step? Earlier in this paper we discussed the limitations of a development-oriented approach to child policy and, in particular, the tendency of such an approach to lose sight of children's capacity, agency and status as citizens in their own right. However, as long as the ICYD continues to place emphasis on investing in children's well-being in the present as well as in the future (as articulated in its overarching goal), it has at least the potential to take forward the vision of the Agenda with the necessary political and cross-sectoral backing to enable real progress to be made.

As current actions on the Agenda work programme near completion, the future focus of the work programme will need to be reviewed. The programme could be widened to cover new and emerging child policy priorities, but this would risk duplicating the work being done in ICYD and sector-specific initiatives. Instead, a more useful focus for the programme could be to further develop MSD's leadership within government in promoting children's interests, rights and needs, and in ensuring that decision-makers consider the impacts of policies and services on children as a population group. This would build on work that MSD is already doing to increase government capability in this area by promoting the whole child approach, developing child wellbeing indicators and providing guidance on involving children in decisions that affect them.

This approach would complement the policy role that the Ministry of Youth Development has in respect of young people, as well as the independent monitoring and promotion work of the Office of the Commissioner for Children. In the longer term, central government structures for promoting children's and young people's interests could be further strengthened through the establishment of a Minister and a Ministry for Child and Youth Development.

Conclusion

Now that a number of nations have attempted to place children's interests, rights and needs more firmly at the centre of politics, an important opportunity exists to compare the different institutional mechanisms and approaches taken and their respective successes, limitations and lessons.

In New Zealand, the approach of developing an overarching strategy to guide child policy and service development has certainly been successful in raising awareness of issues for children in government and the wider community. By drawing the cultural shift occurring in academia into the policy arena, challenging policy-makers to think about children and child policy in a new way and by demonstrating the value of involving children in decision-making processes, the Agenda has helped inform the development of more recent child policy initiatives.

The Agenda has also been widely recognised by community and child advocacy groups, used as a teaching tool in various tertiary institutions and supported a range of community initiatives to advance the interests of children. One of the most important roles of the Agenda has been to encourage and support 'champions' at all levels to advance children's interests – in the community, in voluntary agencies, schools and all the other sites of children's day-to-day lives.

With the input of other agencies, MSD has made significant progress in implementing the Agenda work programme. However, it is unlikely that the scope of the Agenda work programme will be extended to deal with new cross-cutting priorities for children now that the ICYD project has effectively taken on this function. Instead, the next phase of the Agenda is likely to be one of consolidation – ensuring through a variety of means that children's interests, rights and needs remain at the centre of the policy-making process, and that new initiatives build on past achievements and are aligned with the overall vision of making New Zealand a great place for children.

Of course, the reality of a fast-changing political environment is that momentum on particular strategies can quickly dissipate and recent achievements be put to one side as new issues emerge. Fully realising the potential of the Agenda and keeping children's interests, rights and needs at the centre of policy development will require ongoing attention and effort.

Notes

1. Maree Brown and Jaleh McCormack both worked on the development and implementation of the Agenda for Children. By way of disclaimer the views in this paper are those of the authors and do not represent the views of the New Zealand Government nor the Ministry of Social Development.

2. The Labour Party also pledged to give the Commissioner for Children responsibility for monitoring New Zealand's implementation of UNCRC. In line with this, the Children's Commissioner Act 2003 gives the Commissioner for Children additional statutory functions and explicit statutory powers, in order to give better effect to UNCRC in New Zealand. The new functions include promoting the establishment of accessible and effective complaints mechanisms for children and monitoring complaints; raising awareness and understanding of children's interests, rights and welfare; raising awareness and understanding of UNCRC, and promoting children's participation, and an approach that gives weight to their views, in decisions affecting the lives of children.

3. The Children's Issues Centre is based at the University of Otago, Dunedin, New Zealand – www.otago.ac.nz/CIC/CIC.html.

4. See for example the Action for Children in Aotearoa 1996 NGO Report to the UN Committee on the Convention of the Rights of the Child, available at www.acya.org.nz. Numerous publications of the Child Poverty Action Group, including the second (2003) edition of its major report *Our Children: the Priority for Policy*, are available at www.cpag.org.nz.

5. Details on policy and principles of Children's Agenda are available at www.childrensagenda.org.nz.

6 . The meaning of whanau is similar to 'family' but it usually refers to a group which is broader than one household. For example, it usually includes extended family members, and sometimes kinship groups or other groups based on relationships of mutual commitment and support.

7. The most recent report was presented to the UN Committee in 2003 and the Committee's response can be found at URL: www.unhchr.ch/tbs/doc. nsf/898586b1dc7b4043c1256a450044f331/73f172e77b12c842c1256df2003 3829f/$FILE/G0344655.pdf.

8. See 'Every Child Matters' available at www.dfes.gov.uk/everychildmatters.'

9. For Budget 2003 information, see 15 May 2003 press release by the Minister for Social Services and Development, Hon Steve Maharey: '$153 million package to get people into work' , available at www.beehive.govt.nz. For announcements on Budget 2004, see 18 December 2003 press release by the Minister of Finance, Hon Michael Cullen: 'Budget numbers support family assistance package' and 12 February 2004 speech by Hon Steve Maharey: 'Building a great place for children', available at the same site.

10. Available at www.lgnz.co.nz.

11. The Blueprint explicitly references the Agenda and includes its own action plan for incorporating the views of children, young people and their families into planning and provision of care and protection services.

References

Agenda for Children team (2002) 'Listen to us and take us seriously': Young people's responses to the government's Agenda for Children consultation', *Childrenz Issues*, 6(2): 6–10.

Alderson, P. (2000) *Young Children's Rights: Exploring beliefs, principles and practices*, London: Jessica Kingsley Publishers.

Ball, D. and Wilson, M. (2002) 'The prevalence and persistence of low income among New Zealand children: Indicative measures from benefit dynamics data', *Social Policy Journal of New Zealand*, Issue 18: 92–117.

Bird, L. (2003) 'Seen and heard? Moving beyond discourses about children's needs and rights in educational policies', *New Zealand Journal of Educational Studies*, 38 (1): 37–49.

Blaiklock, A., Kiro, C., Belgrave, M., Low, W., Davenport, E. and Hassall, I. (2002) *When the invisible hand rocks the cradle: New Zealand children in a time of change*, Innocenti Working Paper No. 93. Florence: UNICEF Innocenti Research Centre.

Boston, J. (1999) 'New Zealand's Welfare State in Transition' in: Boston, J., Dalziel, P. and St John, S. (1999) *Redesigning the Welfare State in New Zealand: Problems, Policies, Prospects*, Auckland, Oxford University Press.

Bronfenbrenner, U. (1979) *The Ecology of Human Development: Experiments by nature and design*, Cambridge: Harvard University Press.

Corsaro, W. (1997) *The Sociology of Childhood*, London: Sage Publications Ltd.

D'Souza A., Wood, E. (2003) *Making New Zealand Fit for Children. Promoting a National Plan of Action for New Zealand Children (Healthy Lives Section)*, Wellington, UNICEF New Zealand.

Institute of Public Policy at AUT *et al.* (2002) *Making it Happen: Implementing New Zealand's Agenda for Children*, Institute of Public Policy at AUT, Children's Agenda and UNICEF New Zealand, Wellington.

James, A. and Prout, A. (1990) 'Introduction', in: James, A. and Prout, A. (eds), *Constructing and Reconstructing Childhood*. Hampshire: The Falmer Press: 1–6.

Jamison, A. and Gilbert, L. (2000) 'Facilitating children's voices in the community and government' in: Smith, A., Taylor, N. and Gollop, M. (eds), *Children's Voices: Research Policy and Practice*. Auckland: Pearson Education New Zealand Ltd: 181–201.

Lansdown, G. (1994) Children's Rights in: B. Mayall (ed.), *Children's Childhood's. Observed and Experienced*. London: Falmer Press: pp. 33–44.

Ludbrook, R. (2000) 'Victims of tokenism and hypocrisy: New Zealand's failure to implement the United Nations Convention on the Rights of the Child', in: Smith, A., Gollop, M., Marshall, K. and Nairn, K. (eds), *Advocating for Children: International perspectives on children's rights*. Dunedin: University of Otago Press: 109–125.

Matahaere-Atariki, D. (2000) *Maori Children in the Next Five Years*, Commentary to the Seminar on Children's Policy 19/20 July 2000, Parliament Buildings, Wellington. Available at www.msd.govt.nz/work-areas/children-and-young-people/agenda-for-children.

Ministry of Health (2003) *Fetal and Infant Deaths 1999*, Wellington: Ministry of Health. Available at: www.nzhis.govt.nz/publications/fetal99.pdf.

Ministry of Social Development (2001) *Submissions made by children and young people and by adults: A summary report*, Wellington: Ministry of Social

Development. Available at www.msd.govt.nz/work-areas/children-and-young-people/agenda-for-children.

Ministry of Social Development (2002a) *New Zealand's Agenda for Children: Making life better for children*. Wellington: Ministry of Social Development. Available at www.msd.govt.nz/work-areas/children-and-young-people/agenda-for-children.

Ministry of Social Development (2002b) *Te Rito: The New Zealand Family Violence Prevention Strategy*. Wellington: Ministry of Social Development.

Ministry of Social Development (2003a) *Social Report*. Wellington: Ministry of Social Development.

Ministry of Social Development (2003b) *Statement of Intent 2003*. Wellington: Ministry of Social Development.

Ministry of Social Development (2003c) *Care and Protection Blueprint 2003*. Wellington: Ministry of Social Development.

Ministry of Social Development (2003d) *Involving Children: A guide to involving children in decision-making*. Wellington: Ministry of Social Development.

Department of Prime Minister and Cabinet (2003) *Sustainable Development for New Zealand Programme of Action*, Wellington: Department of Prime Minister and Cabinet.

Ministry of Youth Affairs (2000) *Children in New Zealand: United Nations Convention on the Rights of the Child Second Periodic Report of New Zealand*. Wellington: Ministry of Youth Affairs.

Ministry of Youth Affairs (2002) *Youth Development Strategy Aotearoa*. Wellington: Ministry of Youth Affairs. Available at www.myd.govt.nz/sec.cfm?i=20.

New Zealand Alliance Party (1999) 1 January 1999 Policy Statement 'Children and Young People'. Available at www.alliance.org.nz/info.php3?Type=Policy&ID=988.

New Zealand Labour Party (1999) 'Labour on Welfare in the 21st Century' in *Labour New Zealand 2000; Security with Opportunity*. Wellington: New Zealand Labour Party.

New Zealand Treasury; Child, Youth and Family; Ministry of Social Development; State Services Commission (2003) *Report of the Department of Child, Youth and Family Services: First principles baseline review*, Wellington: Child, Youth and Family. Available at www.cyf.govt.nz/view.cfm?pid=204&t=single.

Prout, A. (2002) 'Researching Children as Social Actors: an Introduction to the Children 5–16 Programme', *Children and Society*, 16: 67–76.

Rayner, M. (2002) 'The state of children's rights in Australia' in: Franklin, B. (ed.), *The New Handbook of Children's Rights: Comparative Policy and Practice*. London: Routledge: 345–361.

Smith, A. and Taylor, N. (2000a) 'Introduction', in: Smith, A., Taylor, N. and Gollop, M. (eds) *Children's Voices: Research Policy and Practice*. Auckland: Pearson Education New Zealand Ltd: ix–xiii.

Smith, A. and Taylor, N. (2000b) 'The Sociocultural context of childhood: balancing dependency and agency', in: Smith, A., Taylor, N. and Gollop, M. (eds) *Children's Voices: Research Policy and Practice*. Auckland: Pearson Education New Zealand Ltd: 1–17.

Smith, A. (2003) in conference programme for 'Joined up Services: Linking Together for Children and Families' conference, Dunedin, Children's Issues Centre. Available at www.otago.ac.nz/CIC/downloads/ConfBook4.pdf.

Stephens, R. (1999) 'Poverty, Family Finances and Social Security' in: Boston, J., Dalziel, P. and St John, S. (1999) *Redesigning the Welfare State in New Zealand: Problems, Policies, Prospects,* Auckland, Oxford University Press.

Te Puni Kokiri (2000) 'Maori Children in the Next Five Years: Priorities for future policy and service development', Paper presented to the Seminar on Children's Policy 19/20 July 2000, Parliament Buildings, Wellington. Available at www.msd.govt.nz/work-areas/children-and-young-people/agenda-for-children/seminar.html.

12
The Representation of Children in the Media: Aspects of Agency and Literacy

Máire Messenger Davies & Nick Mosdell[1]

Introduction: Childhood and the media

In the spring of 2001, the issue of children's representation in the media and the role of adults in both promoting and safeguarding such representation made headlines in the British press. Tierney Gearon's photographs of her naked children, on show at the Saatchi Gallery in London, resulted in a police raid on the Gallery. A number of published comments on this case raised concerns about censorship and artistic freedom, but the less high-profile topic of children's consent was also raised in letters to a UK national daily newspaper, *The Guardian*: 'Children are beautiful but their beauty should be guarded until they are legally old enough to give consent to being so used', wrote one female correspondent (The Guardian, 12 March 2001).

The representation of children as themselves (not in acting roles) in adult non-fiction television programmes, takes place in a context – as with the above example – of a continuing public debate about the nature and security of childhood, a debate also conducted within the academic field of childhood studies. Sociologists and anthropologists of childhood say relatively little about the role of media and other cultural artefacts in constructing and disseminating representations of childhood (see, for instance, James and Prout's seminal 1990 collection, *Constructing and Reconstructing Childhood*). The media's role in the socialisation of children has been examined primarily by psychologists and educationists, who have been responsible for a somewhat negative paradigm of child/media relations. Albert Bandura's laboratory experiments with the notorious Bobo doll in 1963, purportedly demonstrating that film and television were a source of negative social modelling and aggression in young children, were, despite decades of criticism (see for instance Barker and Petley, 1997), repeated in a BBC documentary about childhood, *Child of Our Time,* in 2004. Patricia Holland's work (1992 and 2004) on the ways in which pictorial representations of childhood illustrate the underlying ideologies of western society towards children, or David Buckingham's (2000) discussion of the role of media in constructing children as potential citizens, provide a more relevant approach to the theorisation of childhood for the discussion of the study reported here. Holland's work points out the ways in which images of children – for instance, school-children sitting in orderly rows – can be used to demonstrate ideological positions towards the general role of children in society. Similarly, she draws attention to the ways in which art images, often recycled through advertising, can be used to illustrate facets of social constructions of childhood, of innocence or of sexualisation.

Such uses of child models raise questions about the consent of the children concerned – an even more serious issue now in the context of the increase in child pornography available on the internet. David Buckingham's work has long argued that debates about the relationship between media and children need to take place within a social, cultural and political context: this relationship should not be seen as a unidirectional one of simple modelling effects. In *The Making of Citizens* (2000: 221) he claims: 'media education is potentially a very significant site in defining future possibilities for citizenship.' Buckingham sees media education as a way of 'establishing the *relevance* [his emphasis] of politics and of *connecting* the "micro-politics" of personal experience with the "macro-politics" of the public sphere.'

This chapter, and the research on which it is based, is located within this broader tradition of media policy studies and audience research (see Davies, 1989, 2001; Buckingham, 2000a and b). This tradition, in common with the sociology of childhood, partly proceeds from concerns about ways in which children are constructed in public discourse and represented as inevitably vulnerable and dependent. Within media studies, much attention has been paid to negative effects – particularly the effects of violence and, more recently, the effects of commercialism and the induction of children as consumers. Media scholars have had to contend with a somewhat constricting model of 'normative' childhood and some scholars, like Buckingham, have demonstrated similar concerns to those of sociologists about the lack of agency and diversity attributed to children by such models.

The United Kingdom's Broadcasting Standards Commission commissioned the study on which this chapter is based in response to
public concern about the use, and claimed abuse, of children in television news, documentaries, game shows and chat shows. Media
items involving children raise issues of the extent to which children
themselves have any control over how they are represented and the
associated question of whose responsibility it is to ensure that children's consent is sought and acted upon. Where consent is not
'informed', because of children's presumed immaturity, or incapacity,
how can their wishes, needs and welfare be ascertained and safe-
guarded? The Broadcasting Standards Commission (BSC) wanted an
empirical study of these questions with TV viewers and we chose
families with children aged between seven and 14. Mass media,
particularly television, are now an inextricable ingredient of 'the
everyday' (see Scannell, 1996) and we believed that, to evaluate the
social and ethical impact of media representations, the family, with
all its potentially conflicting internal dynamics, was the most appropriate research setting. Moreover, as well as providing convenient
simultaneous access to both children and adults, the family setting is
the most naturalistic environment for the study of television reception. The study aimed to find out what adults and children thought
of the ways in which children are represented on television and to
establish whether parents could always be presumed to speak on
behalf of their children. We wanted to assess children's competence
in giving opinions in their own right.

Studying families

In childhood studies, the family is often the focus of research as a
source of potential social problems. This is illustrated by the dozen or
so reports produced between 1998 and 2003 by the Joseph Rowntree
Foundation on family breakdown, such as Rodgers and Pryor's (1998)
Divorce and separation; the outcomes for children. Clearly the funding of
such research proceeds from institutional policy concerns; the state
and its funding institutions must address the social, legal and economic problems arising from family dysfunction. Our work proceeded
from a different assumption about families, but still within a policy
agenda: a conception of the family (of whatever structure) as basically a well-functioning and dynamic site of inter-generational negotiation about what is, and is not, socially or ethically acceptable about
television.

The use of children on television

'Real' children (as distinct from professional child performers and models) are used increasingly in British television, not only in commercials and children's programmes but also to illustrate adult news items, such as the BSE food crisis, disaster stories such as floods and famines and, in both 2002 and in 2003, the impact of war in Afghanistan and Iraq. A content analysis of TV coverage of children before and during the war in Iraq in 2003 (Davies, in press) indicated that emotive images of children, denying them any agency or voice, is a routine technique in stories about war victims, refugees and disaster. Research with children about the ways in which they are represented in the news (Davies, in press) found strong objections to these passive representations, for instance: 'Children basically aren't seen in adult news – they don't care really. But I saw children carried off on stretchers in the Iraq war.' (Boy, 11, Glasgow). 'Children are shown as a responsibility in adult news ... something which commits teenage crimes and eats unhealthily. THIS IS NOT RIGHT.' (Girl, Glasgow, 12, capitals in original).

Young children are not only used for affective purposes in news coverage. They are also used as participants in non-fiction TV entertainment that is aimed at adults, such as the ITV (commercial channel) programme *Kids Say the Funniest Things,* in which children saying quite serious things are presented as comic. McCrum and Hughes (1998: 24–34), in a guidebook about the treatment of children in the media, list what children dislike about the ways in which the media represent them. These ways include being treated as a joke, being made to perform like circus animals or being 'shown up' as ignorant. The guide points out that, with all use of children in media, there must be written consent from their parents or guardians and adequate facilities for chaperones, first aid, rest, refreshments and transport.

The main stimulus for this study came from a sense that these safeguards might not be adequate in terms of ensuring children's own consent and were not always consistently applied by broadcasters. For example, there had been several complaints to the Broadcasting Standards Commission and to the Independent Television Commission in 1999–2000 from viewers who were disturbed by spectacles of suffering children on TV. One case showed a 10 year-old foster-child breaking down in tears in a *Panorama* programme about adoption. Another example was of two six-year-olds taking part in a 'staring competition' to win a speedboat for their families, in the Channel 4 pop magazine show, *TFI Friday,* after which the loser burst into tears. The Independent Television Commission (ITC) upheld the complaint about *TFI* and reprimanded Channel 4. The ITC Codes of Guidance explicitly state (section 6.4) that: [for] Performances by children under the upper limit of compulsory school age ... Parental consent alone is not enough.'

Children's agency and competence

In UK family law, increasing attempts have been made to give children consultation rights about what should happen to them; for instance, in divorce cases and to support their role as reliable witnesses in child abuse cases (see McNamee *et al.*, in this volume). Central to a recognition of the child's agency is a recognition of the child's competence to make decisions on his/her own behalf. 'Competence' is inevitably linked to age, sometimes in rather arbitrary ways, and James *et al.* (1998) rightly argue that age as a determinant of children's behaviour should be 'problematized'. However, legal definitions of children's competence, as in media regulation, are almost entirely reliant on age progression (for instance, the film classification system) and it seems unlikely that this will change. Families are aware of this. In designing our family study, we took account of the different ages of the children; not least because, as Goodnow and Collins (1990) argue, parents use 'age' as a working model for expectations about what the children sharing their households should, or should not, be doing. Age was an obvious factor in the family negotiations we observed – discussions about bedtimes, post-watershed television, whether children could complete our questionnaire by themselves, whether younger siblings felt overshadowed by older ones, and so on.

Hayes and Williams (1995), writing on UK family law, although asserting that, in general, parents are legally responsible for their children, point to cases where adults and children are in such serious conflict that 'the right to determine what should happen to the child' has to be established by legal action. In English family law, the central case precedent for decision-making by children against parents is the House of Lords' decision in Gillick v. East Norfolk and Wisbech Area Health Authority (1985). In this case, it was decided that a girl under the age of sexual consent (16) could be prescribed contraceptives without her parents' consent if she could be shown to be 'competent' to make the decision. The term 'Gillick competence' has entered legal language as a definition of the ability of children and young people to give informed consent if they have 'sufficient understanding and intelligence to make the decision and [this capacity] is not to be determined by reference to any judicially fixed age limit' (Hayes and Williams, 1995: 32).

Where media are concerned, professional child performers are protected by legislation safeguarding their health, safety and educational needs by means of the Employment of Children Act, 1933. This sets a lower age limit of 13 years for employment, requires licensing by Local Education Authorities, places restrictions on the number of hours they work and provides for mandatory educational provision and chaperones while children are working (see also Singleton Turner, 1999). The televised children in our study were appearing in non-drama productions and were not professional. Such 'real' children are not covered by all of the regulations relating to employment and their well-being depends on more general requirements. These requirements are the ITC Code, BSC codes on fairness and privacy and BBC producers' guidelines requiring children's consent and giving suggestions on how to ensure it. Such guidelines, while providing for children's consent and suggesting that expert advice should be sought to evaluate children's 'competence', appear to be interpreted flexibly by producers and to vary between different genres of programming and between different companies.

Public involvement in regulation: Research methodology

The research project focused on three stages of 'value formation' with regard to the ethics of 'real' children in television programmes; regulation, production and audience reception. This chapter focuses primarily on the third location of this value-forming process, the family at home. Although the family sphere can be characterised as 'private', as distinct from 'public' (Habermas, 1962), the family is a powerful construct in the public sphere of political discourse and 'family values' are invoked by vote-seeking politicians on both left and right. In traditional family models, children are seen primarily as adjuncts to, and dependents of, parents. However, the sociologist Jens Qvortrup (1995) has argued that children should be separately 'socially accounted' in social statistics and that they should be seen as contributing to the well-being of society through their productive role as students, rather than as an economic 'burden' on adults. Arising from this conception of socially-productive, rather than parasitic, children, the welfare and education of children becomes a general public concern, not just something to be primarily determined by their parents. Such a view is an integral part of the public service ideal of broadcasting, with its aim of providing children's services as a matter of right. It is a view which conflicts with current economic and social discourses championing 'choice', in which parents are seen as the sole arbiters of what cultural products are 'suitable' for children and the regulatory role of state institutions and regulators becomes unnecessary – an ethos illustrated by the replacement of the Broadcasting Standards Council (BSC) and Independent Television Commission (ITC) by the lighter-touch Office of Communications (OFCOM) in January 2004.

Our research suggests that a polarised view of regulation/public versus choice/private is not reflected in the ways in which actual families debate cultural issues. It also questions whether parents can always be taken to speak for their children, especially concerning the ethical and moral status of children themselves and the ways in which they are represented. At the level of reception of media products, it is in the home where any immediate impacts of media content and technique will occur. However, the home cannot be seen as a wholly private sphere. Since broadcasting has been able to convey public events and unfamiliar private behaviour into the living room, there has been concern about the dissolution of necessary barriers between public and private from media commentators such as Twitchell (1992) and Meyrowitz (1984). On the other hand, some anthropologists have argued that public codes and conventions have always been apparent within private family behaviours. Blum Kulka (1997), in her discourse-analytical study of family mealtimes in Israel and the USA, argues that dinnertime rituals occupy an 'interim' position between public and private. Like public festivals and celebrations, family meals are occasions where 'cultural codes – usually diffused, attenuated and submerged in the mundane order of things – lie closest to the behavioural surface' (Handelman, 1990: 9; in Blum-Kulka, 1997: 9).

Research questions

A central issue raised by our research was that of who speaks for the child when the child's and the parents' interests are seen to conflict in a broadcasting situation. In discussions with broadcasters after the research was published, producers did not have a clear answer to this question. They proposed professional integrity as the primary safeguard for children, whereas the regulators suggested that an independent third party should be available to speak on behalf of children and that producers should also provide written explanations of what was involved for all participants, including children, before those participants agreed to take part in a programme. This would, it was hoped, lead to consent being more truly informed.

Arising from these considerations, three central questions are addressed here:

1. To what extent do parents' and children's views about the representation of children on television concur, or diverge?
2. Are children competent to discuss issues of consent, particularly those issues involved in using children in controversial ways in adult programming?
3. Are children capable of asserting and maintaining their own views in discussion with adults, including parents?

Methodology of family research

It was decided to use a focus-group methodology, in which examples of children appearing on television would be shown to the family and they would be asked to discuss the resulting issues of consent, appropriateness, audience impact, and ethics after each clip. This would be a two-stage process; first, all the clips would be previewed by parents to get their permission for children to see them. Once parents had agreed on three examples to be shown to the whole family, including the children, the second stage involved an interviewer showing the selected clips to the family group and generating discussion around the issues raised. We also gave a questionnaire to each member of the family, so that views could be expressed privately.

Twenty-four families with children aged between 7 and 14 took part in the focus groups. They were based in five locations: London, Bristol, Reading, Bath and Cardiff. Tables 12.1 and 12.2 demonstrate the range of family types that was included: single parents; ethnic minorities; rural and urban; different numbers of children. An additional 14 families were recruited via these 24 families to fill in the questionnaire only. The sample thus comprised 53 adults and 78 children altogether. There were 27 boys and 24 girls in the 7–11 age group, and 12 boys and 15 girls in the 12–14 age group.

Family research: Viewing material

Five clips of children appearing in adult television, and three clips of a children's game show featuring children (*Mad for It*, ITV1), were

Table 12.1   Table of demographic data of the interviewed families

Location			Number of		
Location	London	5	**Number of**	One	9
	Reading	6	**Adults in the**	Two	15
	Bristol	5	**Household**		
	Gloucestershire	5			
	Cardiff	3			
Ethnicity*	White British	10	**Number of**	One	1
	British	4	**Children in**	Two	13
	White	2	**the Household**	Three	6
	Asian	2		Four	3
	White Other	1		Five	1
	Black African	1			
	Happy Go Lucky	1			
	Not Entered	3			
Religion	Church of England	9	**Household**	Less Than	5
	Catholic	6	**Income**	£10,000	
	Christian	3		£10–15,000	3
	None	3		£16–20,000	4
	Moslem	1		£21–25,000	4
	Sikh	1		£26–30,000	3
	Not Entered	1		£31–35,000	2
				More than	
				£35,000	1

* For the Religion and Ethnicity questions, respondents were asked how they would describe themselves (as is obvious from some of the answers!).

selected as a sample to show to the core 24 families. The clips from adult shows included the sequence from *Panorama* that has already been mentioned (BBC1), in which a boy seeking an adoptive family broke down in tears while being interviewed; the sequence from *TFI Friday* (Channel 4), in which two six-year-olds had a staring competition to win a speedboat for their parents; a sequence from *Good Morning with Richard and Judy* (ITV1), in which two five-year-olds, formerly conjoined twins, were present during a discussion with their parents about how they had nearly died as a result of an operation to separate them in the womb; and a sequence from *The Jenny Jones Show* (Channel 5) in which a six-year-old boy impersonated Michael Jackson to an adult studio audience. The sample also included one example of the 'fictional' use of a child – a sketch from the late night Channel 4 show, *Jam*, in which a six-year-old actress appeared to be slaughtering and cutting up a body, uttering obscenities as she did so. The *Panorama*, *TFI Friday* and *Jam* clips had all produced complaints to reg-

Table 12.2 Table of occupations of householders from the interviewed families

Male		Female	
Courier	2	Housewife	4
Security	1	Student	2
Carpenter	1	Secretary	1
Firefighter	1	Beautician	1
Director (careers)	1	Personal Assistant	1
Police Constable	1	Carer	1
Nursing	1	Playgroup Assistant	1
Farmer	1	Occupational Therapist	1
Financial Administrator	1	Child Care	1
		Learning Support	1
		Information Analyst	1
		Nursing	1
		Research Technician	1
		None	1
		Security	1
		Not Entered	3

ulators. These complaints were upheld in the *TFI* case but not in the *Jam* case, because in this latter case parental consent had been given and the child was an actress. This distinction was not accepted by the parents to whom we showed the clips; none of them would agree to let their children see the *Jam* sequence and all disapproved of the child's mother agreeing to let her perform in it.

Procedure

In getting parents to preview material, we were obviously carrying out a procedure which differed from the ways in which families usually watch television and the ways in which parents usually regulate their children's viewing. This was, however, a practical and ethical necessity in terms of gaining co-operation from the families concerned, within the overall context of 'informed consent'.

Many parents said to us that they would not normally vet the programmes their children saw, and even where they did not approve of us showing a particular clip to their children, they acknowledged that it was quite possible that their children would see such material in the normal course of their viewing, when parents were not monitoring them. However, in addition to the family interviews, we also gave each member of the family a questionnaire, which they filled in privately, and here some divergence between parents and children was able to emerge more openly.

In the event, we were able to make a virtue of the necessity of parental-previewing, since the preview session enabled parents to make explicit their values in judging what was, or was not, suitable viewing for their children and we were able to take note of these. The second session, the family viewing session with both parents and children, thus provided us with the opportunity to compare parental expectations about their children's reactions with the children's actual reactions – many inter-generational differences of perspective emerged here. In both sessions, the interviewers played an integral role in order to stimulate discussion – again, a procedure not found in everyday viewing situations but necessary with our focus group procedures.

One of Blum-Kulka's (1997) findings concerned the effect of the presence of children on the mealtime conversations that she studied. Having children present at the table created what she called 'formal criteria' for deciding what was, and was not, mentionable. She found that three topics were always taboo: money, sex and politics. This pattern was very different from the ways in which television was discussed in our family groups. All of the participants in the study, including the children, were uninhibited in talking about money, sex and politics, where these were relevant. Also, it was obvious from these conversations that these topics had not been introduced for the first time by the researcher but were related to on-going debates within the family. For instance, the G family of East London (two parents, a grandmother and four children) used the interview to re-open what was obviously a long-standing grievance between the 12-year-old daughter and the 11-year-old son about how she had been allowed to watch the homosexual drama, *Queer as Folk* (Channel 4), and he had not. Also, the mother, a practicing Roman Catholic, said that she did not mind her children seeing representations of consensual sex; what she objected to were recurring storylines involving rape and sexual brutality, for example in *The Bill* and *EastEnders*.

Some commentators (for instance Postman, 1982) might argue that this is yet more evidence of the corrupting effects of television in breaking down the barriers between public and private and introducing children to hitherto forbidden adult domains. However, this was not a view held by the families we interviewed, including, as in the case of Mrs. G, some with quite strong religious beliefs. Where parents wanted to protect their children, it was from scenes of children in distress (*Panorama*) or from very explicit violence and bad language (*Jam*).

These issues are discussed at greater length in the full report (Davies & Mosdell, 2001).

Results and discussion: differences between parents and children

Our first research question asked: To what extent do parents' and children's views about the representation of children on television concur, or diverge? Parents were asked whether they would allow their children to appear in programmes including the following: children's news (*Newsround*); 'survivor' type reality programmes (*Castaway*); children's drama (*Grange Hill; The Worst Witch*); children's game shows (*Mad for It*); children's magazine shows (*Live and Kicking*) and a radio phone-in. Also, children were asked whether they would like to appear in the same list of programmes. Table 12.3 gives an example of quantitative data from the questionnaire which illustrates a striking divergence of view between adults and children.

In every case, more adults than children agreed to the children appearing in the programmes – statistically highly significant (Sign test, x = 0; n = 8. Significance, p = 0.002). The greatest difference was between the large majority of adults (84 per cent) agreeing to their children appearing in the children's news programme, *Newsround*, with only 2 per cent disagreeing, and the small minority of 21 per cent of children agreeing to this, 49 per cent disagreeing and 31 per cent not sure. There was also a considerable contrast in adults' and

Table 12.3 Children's and adults' responses to prospective appearances in specific types of television programmes

Programme	Adults			Children		
	Agree %	*Not sure* %	*Disagree* %	*Agree* %	*Not sure* %	*Disagree* %
Castaway	27	43	31	23	45	32
Grange Hill	63	25	12	28	41	31
Live and Kicking	86	8	6	67	15	18
Mad for It	46	25	29	36	43	21
Newsround	84	14	2	21	31	49
'Phone-in	54	22	24	45	27	28
Worst Witch	60	27	13	40	19	41

Note: In answer to the question: 'I would like to appear/my children to appear in [name of programme]'

children's attitudes to children appearing in drama programmes. These findings were so unequivocal that a major recommendation to the study's sponsors was that children's consent to appearing in the media should always be sought independently of that of their parents where practically possible (i.e. in cases where participation is planned in advance). It was proposed that young children are quite capable of saying 'no' to appearing on television and their wishes should be respected.

Family discussions: children's competence

The second and third research questions were as follows:

- Are children competent to discuss issues of consent, particularly the issues involved in using children in controversial ways in adult programming?
- Are children capable of asserting and maintaining their own views in discussion with adults, including parents?

Here, the qualitative research provided a number of answers.

The following brief example of a response on these issues comes from the G family (mentioned above) talking about the clip from *Panorama*. In this clip, persistent questioning from an unseen interviewer to a young boy who wanted a family resulted in the boy beginning to cry – at which point, the director cut to a tight close-up of tears falling. The following exchange between the G father and son, (aged 11) illustrates the extent to which the boy was not prepared to accept his father's reading of the way the programme had 'exploited' the crying child:

> Interviewer: Can I ask the grown-ups, did you get that impression, ... about it being set up?
> Father: No.
> ...
> Son: Yes, but dad, look, the boy was half crying.
> F: Yes, he was, he was obviously upset about it, but there are some children that are in that situation.
> S: Yes, but [they don't have to go] on TV and tell everyone that his mum and dad are probably dead or can't properly look after him and he's getting moved from foster home to foster home. That's not the first thing you want to say on national TV, is it.

Later on in this conversation, the son (S) and the 12-year-old daughter (D1) demonstrated their awareness of the camera technique used to focus on the boy's distress:

> S: They zoomed in, so they could see the tears drop and stuff like that.
> D1: So that it's not fake, it really is happening, it shows that it is happening.
> ...
> I: Do you think that's a good thing to do with the camera?
> S: No
> I: Why not?
> S: Because that's just like, it's out of order. The boy's going to be on national TV crying like, it's not exactly like [?], people notice him crying on TV.
> D1: But then it might, oh look this is what happens, because there aren't enough people who are adopting and they might feel sorry for the boy.

Our analysis of the lengthy interview transcripts indicated a high degree of competence being exercised by the children. This was evident in the high proportion of their utterances in relation to those of adults, to the linguistic competence of their contributions and to their modality awareness of television techniques. For example, around 70 per cent of the utterances in the whole G family discussion came from the children. When the interviewer put a question to the whole family, it was often a child who answered first. There were many examples in all the family transcripts of conversational competence, such as the initiation of new topics. In the G family, the 8-year-old second daughter, mediating between the quarrelsome older siblings and the father, introduced a suggestion that actors could have been used instead of the distressed child. 'Modality awareness', sometimes described as 'media literacy' (Hodge and Tripp, 1986; Davies, 1997), was demonstrated in the son's comment about the camera movement: 'They zoomed in so they could see the tears drop ...' This attempt by the director to sensationalise the moment of the child's breakdown was noticed, and condemned, by all the families who saw this clip. There was an obvious rivalry between the son and the oldest daughter in the G family – an illustration of how discussions about television could map onto pre-existing family dynamics. The son was particularly combative – a characteristic of his discourse is the phrase

'Yes, but ...' in order to challenge both parents and older sister – and he did not back down.

Similar discussions occur in many of the transcripts from the other families, repeatedly showing children's views as distinct from those of their parents; thus the qualitative data supported the quantitative data. Children and parents differed in their opinions and they did so to each others' faces, as well as privately. There is also evidence of negotiation, with parents being willing to give way to their children and, in some cases during the parental preview, to each other.

We suggest that such negotiation is one way in which 'family values' are arrived at and, where necessary, altered within the home. Family values are not static, but have to be constantly negotiated between and within generations as children grow up and are exposed to external social and cultural experiences such as TV programmes. These qualities of flexibility and negotiability need to be recognised in public discussions about 'family values'. Such values, by their nature, are formed in a dynamic context, where people are constantly growing and changing, and hence cannot be viewed as fixed and rigid. Such negotiations, we suggest, are an indicator of functionality within the family and of developing competence on the part of the children.

We obviously recognise the contribution of the research situation to these outcomes. The families were being asked by an unknown interviewer to comment on short TV clips that had been especially selected for research purposes – not an everyday viewing situation for them. Nevertheless, the central research question of whether children and parents were in agreement, or not, about the ethical and production questions raised by the TV clips was not invalidated by the research setting. Both parents and children were in the same setting and they still diverged. The constructedness of the setting could be seen as inhibiting to children's performance, in ways that could be similar to children being asked for consent in television studios or other public settings. However, this, too, offers a possible measure of children's competence in such situations. The research procedure appeared to inspire most of the children in this study (except one or two of the very youngest) with what many of their parents acknowledged as surprising eloquence on complex ethical issues. Alternatively, one might argue that the focus of the research on the expressed views of children might have allowed the respondents to feel less inhibited, given that their views were actively sought. In either case, the capability of the children to give considered opinion that differs from that of their parents may lend support to the notion of some third party mediator.

Conclusion

This study was carried out as part of a policy agenda: The Broadcasting Standards Commission's statutory responsibility to investigate issues of public concern brought the subject of children's involvement in television programmes to their attention through the complaints of viewers. As we hope we have demonstrated, the issues raised by this study have relevance to the broader field of childhood studies. This is so, both theoretically, in terms of how models of childhood are constructed through broadcasting policy via, for instance, the watershed or producer guidelines, and more pragmatically, in terms of the kinds of social research which stress the need to provide 'a voice' for children and for them to be able to contribute to their general welfare (see McNamee *et al*. and Brown in this volume).

The focus group discussions indicated some sensitivity within these families to issues that are publicly debated by social policy commentators. These also provide a further argument for making sure that children (and parents) are consulted and give their fully-informed consent to any official procedures in which they are involved – whether it be custody cases or appearing in a BBC game show. The comments from our families exhibited protectionism – a desire to stop children from being exploited – but also a liberationist view of the child's rights. Liberationism was (perhaps obviously) strongest among children, but most parents respected their children's divergent views. There was also a recognition that the representation of children in distress on TV could have social and political advantages in drawing public attention to children's problems. Even among the youngest children, there was 'media literacy' – a pragmatic awareness of producers' motives, whether commercial, pro-social, or 'exploitative'. Television was not transparent to these families: they were aware of its constructedness and aware of institutional considerations determining production, scheduling and broadcasters' defensive responses to public debate.

As a result of the research, we recommended that whatever regulatory bodies exist (OFCOM is now the sole broadcasting regulator), they should continue to provide a forum for public debate of this kind, including providing a space for the voices, needs, rights and wishes of children to be heard independently of those of adults. This also involves respecting the place and importance of children's voices within the family, which remains an important site for the establishment and negotiation of public values.

Notes

1. The research described here was undertaken with the help of funding from the Broadcasting Standards Commission, UK, to whom grateful thanks are due. The full study is *'Consenting Children? The use of children in non-fiction television programmes'* (2001) by Máire Messenger Davies and Nick Mosdell, published by the BSC, London. Grateful thanks are also due to Gareth Andrewartha, George Bailey, Sunita Bhabra, Keri Facer, Fern Faux and Sofia Amarall Leitao who helped with preparation of material, interviewing and video analysis.

References

Bandura, A., Ross, D. & Ross, S. (1963) 'Imitation of film-mediated aggressive models', *Journal of Abnormal and Social Psychology:* 66, 3–11.

Barker, M. & Petley, J. (1997) (eds) *Ill Effects: The Media/Violence Debate.* London: Routledge.

Blumler, J. (1992) *The Future of Children's Television in Britain: An Enquiry for the Broadcasting Standards Council.* London: Broadcasting Standards Commission.

Blum-Kulka, S. (1997) *Dinner Talk: Cultural Patterns of Sociability and Socialisation in Family Discourse.* Mahwah NJ: Lawrence Erlbaum Associates.

Buckingham, D. (2000a) *The making of citizens: young people, news and politics,* London: Routledge.

Buckingham, D. (2000b) *After the Death of Childhood.* Cambridge: Polity Press.

Davies, M. M. (in press) 'Innocent victims/active agents: media coverage of children and war' in Biressi, A. and Nunn, H. (eds) *Media War* London: Lawrence and Wishart.

Davies, M. M. (2001) *'Dear BBC': Children, Television Storytelling and the Public Sphere.* Cambridge: Cambridge University Press.

Davies, M. M. (1997) *Fake, Fact and Fantasy: Children's Interpretations of Television Reality.* Mahwah NJ: Lawrence Erlbaum Associates.

Davies, M. M. (2001) *Television is Good for Your Kids* (2nd Edition), London: Hilary Shipman.

Davies, M. M. and Mosdell, N. (2001) *Consenting Children? The Use of Children in Television Reality Programmes.* London: Broadcasting Standards Commission.

Goodnow, J. J. & Collins, A. (1990) *Development According to Parents,* Hillsdale, NJ: Laurence Erlbaum Associates.

Habermas, J. (1989) *The Structural Transformation of the Public Sphere: An Inquiry into a Category of Bourgeois Society.* Cambridge, MA: MIT Press.

Hayes, M. & Williams, C. (1995) *Family Law: Principles, Policy and Practice.* London: Butterworth.

Hodge, B. and Tripp, D. (1986) *Children and Television.* Cambridge: Polity Press.

Holland, P. (1992) *What is a Child?: Popular Images of Childhood.* London; Virago.

Holland, P. (2004) *Picturing Childhood: the Myth of the Child in Popular Imagery.* London; I. B. Tauris.

Home, A. (1993) *Into the Box of Delights: A history of children's television.* London: BBC.

James, A., Jenks, C. & Prout, A. (1998) *Theorizing Childhood.* Cambridge: Polity Press.

Liebes, T. & Katz, E. (1990) *The export of meaning: cross-cultural readings of Dallas*. New York, Oxford: Oxford University Press.

McCrum, S. and Hughes, L. (1998) *Interviewing Children: A Guide for Journalists and Others*. London: Save the Children.

Meyrowitz, J. (1984) *No Sense of Place: The Impact of Electronic Media on Social Behaviour*. New York: Oxford University Press.

Morley, D. (1980) *The Nationwide Audience*. London: British Film Institute.

Palmer, E. (1988) *Television and America's Children: a Crisis of Neglect*. Oxford: Oxford University Press.

Postman, N. (1982) *The Disappearance of Childhood*. London: W. H. Allen.

Qvortrup, J. (1997) 'A voice for children in statistical and social accounting: a plea for children's right to be heard', in James, A. and Prout, A. (eds) *Constructing and Reconstructing Childhood: Contemporary Issues in the Sociological Study of Childhood*. London: Falmer Press: 78–98.

Rodgers, B. and Pryor, J. (1998) *Divorce and separation; the outcomes for children*. London & York: Joseph Rowntree Foundation.

Scannell, P. (1996) *Radio, television and modern life, a phenomenological approach*. Oxford: Blackwell.

Singleton Turner, R. (1999) *Children Acting on Television*. London: A. & C. Black.

Twitchell, J. B. (1992) *Carnival Culture*. New York: Columbia University Press.

13
Family Law and the Construction of Childhood in England and Wales

Sally McNamee, Adrian James and Allison James

Introduction

Listening to the voices of children has become somewhat of a mantra within the current politics of English childhood following the signing of the UN Convention on the Rights of the Child in 1990 and the implementation of the Children Act 1989. However, although the Convention establishes children's rights to be heard and the Act makes specific provisions for ensuring that children have a proper say in matters concerning their own welfare, it is clear that in England and Wales the courts still do not always listen to children's wishes and feelings (Lyon, 1995; Murch 1995; Parry, 1994). And in contexts outside of the family justice system, such as hospitals and schools, routine consultation with children about matters concerning their own welfare appears to be an even less well-established practice (Alderson, 1993, 2000; but see also Blair, this volume). Any firm commitment to listening to children's views would, therefore, still seem to be absent from the everyday practices of many professionals working directly with vulnerable children. As such, the contemporary day-to-day politics of childhood in Britain unfolds in ways which remain characterised by adultist concerns, rather than those of children, despite the Children Act 1989 being heralded as a 'children's charter'. How this happens and the implications this has for children is the subject of this chapter.

Rooted in recent theoretical developments in the social study of childhood, which have sought to identify some of the limitations of the developmental paradigm championed by writers such as Piaget (James and Prout, 1990; James, Jenks and Prout, 1998), the chapter also, therefore, addresses some of the broader politics of childhood by asking about its social construction in and through everyday life. Endeavouring to acknowledge, both through theoretical and empirical work, the agency and competence of children of *all* ages, such social constructionist perspectives represent a challenge to our thinking about children and childhood for, by removing the determinist strait-jacket of developmental 'age', emphasis has to be given to individual experiences. Thus, the universality of childhood and children's status can no longer be taken for granted and age can no longer be regarded as the overwhelming factor in determining what children can do and how we, as adults, think about children.

With respect to the operation of family law, and its realisation in a myriad of social policies concerning children and childhood that children themselves may encounter on a daily basis, this represents a considerable challenge since family law is based, overwhelmingly, on an assumption of the commonality that 'age' brings to children. It appears, for example, in assertions about what 'all ten-year-old children' are capable of or what might be expected of them. This view takes precedence, then, over any account being given to the diversities of social experience that might fragment the unity of those whom we regard as 'a group of ten-year-olds'. In addition, within different legal definitions, the age at which children may be held accountable or responsible for their actions, or up to which they need to be protected from various social evils, varies quite considerably. Thus, to challenge the idea that 'age' may not be the most important factor in making judgements about children's competence to express their wishes and feelings is to strike at some of the most fundamental aspects of the contemporary politics of British childhood (James and James, 2004). It is also, however, to expose those politics to a more public gaze by exploring the influence of law and social policy over the way in which childhood is constructed, and the impact of this for children in terms of their lived everyday experiences as children. Drawing on data from recently completed research[1] into the constructions of childhood held by two professional groups working with children, this chapter provides empirical illustration of the importance of such a theoretical perspective for understanding children's rights.

The research context

The two groups of professionals, whose ideas about childhood we sought to elicit, work within the family justice system in England and Wales and act, albeit in slightly different ways, as children's representatives within public and private law proceedings. Though they have recently been brought together under the organisational umbrella of the Children and Family Courts Advisory and Support Service (CAFCASS)[2] – Children's Guardians (hereafter CGs) work mainly in public law proceedings (i.e. child protection) and Child and Family Reporters (hereafter CFRs) operate in the sphere of private law proceedings (i.e. the breakdown of parental relationships and divorce). The research took place in one particular geographic area and involved a series of in-depth interviews with 19 professionals in each group spread over one year. The first interview focused on personal and professional biographies, while interviews 2 and 3 were discussions of vignettes designed as case studies. Through these, we aimed to analyse practitioners' accounts of how children's voices come to be heard within the contemporary family justice system and the obstacles that might work to prevent this happening. The main interviewees were self-selected volunteers who agreed to take part in the study following a presentation by the researchers. This means, therefore, that there are some limitations to the research in terms of, for example, exploring the potential influence of gender, ethnic or class background on the ideas of childhood that are our focus. Notwithstanding this caveat, as we explore below, there was a remarkable convergence of views amongst the practitioners about what childhood should be like and what children need.

Conceptions of childhood

Because CFRs and CGs are the only independent voices in the family justice system that can help children to be heard, it was important for us to establish, at the outset, the kinds of personal conceptions they held about children. Our first interview therefore sought to discover the ways in which our respondents viewed childhood by asking a series of questions relating to their own, their children's and other children's childhoods. Thus we asked what they thought an ideal childhood would look like and what they thought were the best and worst things about being a child.

There was much similarity between the two groups, with almost all of the professionals agreeing about children's need for security and stability, and the importance of having two parents. Both groups thought that an ideal childhood was about being loved and cared for by parents and about 'being' in a protected space devoid of conflict and tension. The 'best thing about being a child' was seen, in essence, as 'freedom from responsibility', which was identified in a variety of different ways; for example, having no decisions to make; experiencing security and trust; being loved and cared for; being carefree and innocent; having the ability to play; enjoying spontaneity and exploration. Implicit in these somewhat idyllic images of childhood was the notion of not knowing about, or having to care about, the realities of adult life. The following two excerpts are representative of this conception:

> The best thing about being a child? Have someone look after you, being allowed to sort of grow and develop really, you know there's nothing better I don't think than a child's playing; being in your own world, and being allowed to be in your own world without having to grow up too fast ... and not having the responsibility of, of sort of growing up ... worrying really. (CFR)

> The innocence, lack of responsibility ..., the fact that you can go out and play and not feel guilty. (CG)

The data concerning the 'worst thing about being a child' did not, however, reflect the exact opposite but was, instead, a cognate of this – 'the experience of powerlessness', i.e. the experience of *not being given* responsibility. This was also identified in a variety of different ways: lack of control; lack of information; not being listened to; dependence and vulnerability.

This absence of an exact opposite is interesting for it highlights an important tension in the conceptions of childhood held by these practitioners. The *best* thing about childhood – freedom from responsibility – is almost the *same* as the worst thing – feelings of powerlessness.

> [the worst thing about childhood is] Feeling powerless I think, feeling that you were not being listened to and not being accorded ... respect for your views and, you know, your thoughts if you feel that people are overlooking you. (CFR)

This suggests that those childish pleasures associated with the 'freedom from responsibility' can easily be transformed into darker feelings of 'powerlessness', which are, however, precisely those feelings, according to practitioners, that make childhood a less than happy experience! There is, it would seem, but a thin and delicate line between these rather different sets of childhood experiences.

Two points in particular are worth noting about this. First, *both* properties of childhood depend on children's interactions with adults, one being a more positive rendering of those interactions than the other. And second, following on from this observation, given that both sets of professionals are working with children undergoing difficult family and personal experiences, part of the challenge that these social work professionals have to face is that of turning children's negative feelings of powerlessness into more positive ones. One way to do this is to allow them to assert some power and control over their lives.

Indeed, this is arguably exactly what was intended by the Children Act 1989 when it gave welfare practitioners the responsibility to listen to children and to ascertain their wishes and feelings in family proceedings. However, if 'freedom from responsibility' is practitioners' personal ideal of the state of childhood, then assisting children also to exercise some kind of personal empowerment places practitioners in a rather ambiguous position – the opposite of being power*less* is being power*ful* and adults do not know how to deal with powerful children.

Analysis of the data also revealed two different status categories which children are seen to occupy and which position children rather differently in relation to adults: 'the child' as an age-based social status and 'the child' as kinship/generational status. While of course not mutually exclusive – any one child is always a member of both status categories – in practice, and at any one time, these are used as discrete and distinct attributions in the accounts of practitioners. It can be therefore argued that, in their everyday work with children, practitioners discriminate between, on the one hand, 'the child' as a social (kinship-based) status and, on the other, 'the child' as a legal (age-based) concept.

This means, therefore, that for certain purposes, the child has to be understood and located firmly within the context of kinship, as the practitioners explained:

> I think in a nutshell [...] an ideal childhood, well obviously you would want it to be a happy family unit, in an ideal situation with both parents, obviously on the scene, ideally together and playing as joint a role as possible in the upbringing of that child. (CFR)

> It is enormously important, the sort of family aspect [...] of your life, and you see it in the kids you work with [...] like that case I was telling you about, they still, they had this enormous family bond, even though there were [...] sort of glitches in it, and that to me is the most important. (CG)

In other practice contexts, however, the child has to be visualised as separate from the family and must, instead, be understood and dealt with in terms of their developmental age and position within the lifecourse:

> And I think grown-ups have an obligation, it's grown-ups' jobs to make decisions about children, and that's part of being an adult, to take that responsibility from children. (CG)

> I've always said to children, right from the beginning, even twelve-year-olds, er, thirteen-year-olds even, that you actually can't choose, because ..., you're not an adult, [you] haven't got the responsibility. Having said that, the older you are, the more your views will be taken into account, but I say to all, in fact, I explain 'til they're over sixteen they can't choose (CFR)

Such views comprise what we can call the 'double status' of children, and yet what is significant about this is that, through such conceptualisations, 'the child' is described, and thus thought about, primarily as an *object* rather than as a subject: 'the child' becomes seen as the object of legal rulings or the outcome of parenting practices. In both cases, then, the individual child, as a child with agency, as someone who might be listened to, becomes obscured by the use of these categorical terms.

> ... our job is to get involved with the children but also to acknowledge the fact that their parents are still parenting them. (CFR)

> I mean it is up to the parent to protect and to know about those things [...] so it comes back to, you know, parenting, to ... nurturing parenting. (CG)

> But you know ... it will depend on their age and understanding as to how much weight is put on these wishes and feelings by the court. (CG)

Although it is still possible, using these concepts, to see the child as some kind of *subject* – by for example, referring to the child in legal, age-based terms as *a minor* or to stress the social status of the child as *a family member* – neither of these new descriptions tells us much more about the child as an individual or as a person in their own right. In this sense, they are only ever visualised as *quasi-subjects*.

In addition, and as confirmed by the practitioners' own accounts presented above, 'childhood', whether as an age-based or kinship/ generationally-based construction of the life course, only derives its meaning through its relationship with adulthood and, primarily, from parenthood (c.f. Jenks 1996). So, even if we do conceptualise the child as *minor* or as *family member*, the meaning attributed to the concept of 'the child' is in terms of a status that is derived from the experience of being parented i.e. from being the *object* of parental love, care and protection. There appears, therefore, to be little conceptual space here for children to assume any agency of their own (Fig. 13.1).

Childhood- $\begin{cases} \text{age based} \\ \text{generational/kinship} \end{cases}$ 'the child' as *object* – product of parenting

Children- $\begin{cases} \text{a minor} \\ \text{a family member} \end{cases}$ 'the child' as *quasi-subject* – being parented

Figure 13.1   Childhood and children

Theorising the 'political' construction of childhood

Practitioners' accounts of childhood enable us to see, therefore, the ways in which the structural views of childhood and children's position in society are given everyday expression, for these conceptualisations of 'the child' are reinforced and made more robust by the different qualitative dimensions of 'childhood' described earlier. Thus, for example, that a child is both carefree *and* powerless is the direct result of their being either the object or quasi-subject of parenting practices; and, in occupying such a status, children's agency and personhood, and their potential as competent actors in the social world, is therefore further conceptually denied. Thus, when looked at in terms of their age-based status in law, a carefree childhood is ensured, for example, by children's lack of responsibilities; it is, however, experienced by children themselves in terms of having few rights. And when seen in terms of a kinship status, 'the child' who is carefree is so only as a result of being cared for, a form of social dependence that can also often be experienced as a form of powerlessness by children (c.f. Mayall, 2002).

	Age-based status	Generational/Kinship status
Being carefree =	not responsible	cared for/dependent
Being powerless =	no rights	controlled/dependent

Such theoretical and conceptual mapping is not, however, simply an exercise in logic. It has, we suggest, a number of potentially quite significant implications in the context of the Children Act 1989, in terms of the ways in which practitioners are, in practice, able to take account of 'the check list' of objective conditions against which they are obliged to determine a child's future welfare. For example, this analysis suggests that if, from the practitioner's point of view, 'the child' is nearly always conceived of as a product of *parenting*, and 'childhood' is generally assumed to be about the experience of *being parented*, then there is little conceptual space for practitioners to see 'the child' as having an identity in his/her own right – i.e. to be seen as possessing agency or as an individual in their own right. However – and here is the rub – unless the child *is* conceptualised as having an active agency, it may be hard for practitioners to give real credence to the importance of children's thoughts, wishes and feelings when making decisions on children's behalf. Similarly, it follows that the pervasive and much-used concept of 'the best interests of the child' is also at risk of being devalued and of becoming simply a generalised socio-legal concept, rather than an individualised human concept. It may well become a rhetorical device that is given meaning only by reference to the generalities of 'children' and 'childhood', from which is then derived what is, in effect, no more that an inferential understanding of any particular 'child'.

And the role of law in all of this is critical. Law defines both 'childhood' and 'the child' by defining and regulating the boundaries between adulthood and childhood, both through statute and case law, in various social spheres – for example, employment, health, education and the family. But, in performing this function, the law leans heavily on the apparent objectivity of judgements based on chronological age, derived from a generalised developmental model of childhood, rather than on more subjective, experiential definitions of competence. In this sense therefore, the law clearly reflects the widely held adult assumptions about 'childhood' and 'the child', noted above in the accounts of practitioners, which are firmly rooted in the developmental paradigm.

For example, 'childhood' is defined as an age-bounded part of the life course during which, until the appropriate legally-defined chronological threshold is passed, children are regarded, for many legal purposes, and especially in family law, as subjects requiring protection. Viewed in this way, the child simply cannot be seen as a competent actor, a person capable of independent thought and of exercising judgement (although there is, of course an important and anomalous exception to this in terms of the criminal law and the recent *de facto* change to the age of criminal responsibility).[3]

By defining 'childhood' in this way, therefore, the law (and therefore those adults such as welfare practitioners who work with the law) mediates between, and simultaneously helps to construct, the *child* as a minor, *vis à vis* the range of political and social rights associated with obtaining one's majority, and as a family member, *vis à vis* its parents upon whom it is deemed dependent. By the same token, and using exactly the same mechanisms, the law also therefore acts to reinforce the boundaries between adulthood and childhood.

The net effect of this is that those aspects of the individual child's existence and experience that each child uses to construct her or his own social identity, which reflect that child's agency and which define that child as a person, are effectively denied by law. This is precisely because the child, *by virtue of being a non-adult,* is deemed to be not competent, to be dependent and thus subject to the hegemony of adult views and judgements. In this sense the law, in itself, serves as a barrier towards seeing the child *as an individual.*

What this analysis suggests therefore is that a third status category would be needed to be able to make 'the child' real as an individual and to give childhood a meaning(s) that is to some extent separate, or at least separable, from adults and adulthood – the child as *actor.* It is only by introducing this third category that children can achieve agency, subjective meaning and social reality – i.e. personhood. The child as *actor* gains both meaning and context from his/her status as both object and subject, since these are important factors in terms of the social construction of personhood and social identity, but agency – arguably the key factor in personhood – comes from neither of these. It comes from within the child him or herself.

But because law works to regulate the achievement of adult status and the rights, responsibilities and competencies of adulthood, it is, therefore, only through the passage of time that adulthood, and thus citizenship and personhood, is achieved. And, as law controls this process, it both actively and passively *dis*ables children. Indeed, it is arguable that it *must* do so, for without the category of non-personhood and non-citizenship called 'child', the achievement of the status of adult would have no or many fewer meanings. It is therefore the non-personhood and non-citizenship of children that renders them powerless, since this is a necessary although not sufficient condition of being a child. And it is that very same lack of power that simultaneously makes childhood a time to be carefree because it also leaves children free from adult responsibility.

What, then, does all of this mean for those practitioners whose everyday work is supposed to help children express their wishes and feelings within the court system? In practical terms, family law in England and Wales (through the Family Proceedings Rules, 1991, Rule 9.1) defines a child as a 'person under disability', a status shared with anyone defined as a 'patient' under the Mental Health Act, 1983. This therefore denies all but the most limited scope for children as *actors* to exercise their agency. By the same token, CGs and CFRs, as employees of CAFCASS working within the framework of and with the constructs provided by the law in general and the Children Act 1989 in particular, also contribute to a praxis that circumscribes children's ability to participate fully and effectively, as Fig 13.2 reveals.

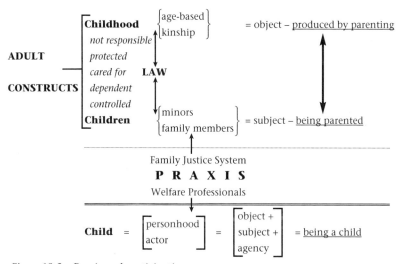

Figure 13.2   Praxis and participation

By making assessments and offering 'expert' advice that draw on the constructions of childhood and the child previously outlined, these welfare professionals are unable to acknowledge sufficiently, if at all, what being a child means in terms of that child's experience, agency and personhood. They cannot therefore enable the voice of the child to be heard in family proceedings. Rather, what is offered is an adult construction of what is in 'the best interests of the child', a construction that attempts to resolve the ambiguity inherent in the task of allowing the child's wishes and feelings to be heard in a system that struggles to acknowledge the child as an actor. Indeed, it could be argued that since the child is set apart from the adult world through its construction as either object or quasi-subject, the child can never be defined and addressed in law as an actor and that, therefore, none of the rhetoric or the devices used can ever ensure the effective participation of children in family proceedings. The resulting praxis creates significant tensions for practitioners, therefore, for it is they who have to reconcile this reality with their principled commitment to working for the best interests of the child.

This theoretical analysis, therefore, points to some important conceptual 'fault lines' in the way in which the concept of childhood is constructed in family proceedings and it is in the management of these disjunctions that significant tensions are created for welfare practitioners. Thus, although being strongly committed to child-centred practice in their work with children, practitioners have to work in the context of a legal system that, as we have shown, generates a praxis that has to work with adult constructs of the child and childhood.

Although one way out of this dilemma, for practitioners, would seem to be already provided by the Children Act – in that their role is precisely one of ascertaining children's wishes and feelings, and thus allowing their voices to be heard by the courts – in practice, empowering children in this way is not easy. It is therefore towards sustaining children's 'freedom from responsibility' and minimising any risk or harm, as part of the image of an ideal childhood, that practitioners often retreat – and they do this by effectively 'talking over' the voices of the children who are involved. Some of the different ways in which this occurs, in everyday practice, are described below.

The tensions of praxis

As argued above, practitioners' thinking about children is largely informed by a developmental and needs-based model of childhood that effectively militates against seeing children as social actors in their own right. This is despite the fact that, as described in detail elsewhere (James, James and McNamee, 2004), in their everyday practice individual practitioners' views may be tempered by such factors as their own biographical experiences and the gender and/or maturity of the individual child with whom they work. However, although such 'filters' might incline an individual practitioner towards acknowledging the agency of children and their role as social actors, especially in their face-to-face work with them, the family justice system nonetheless continues to exert a powerful constraint and inhibits practitioners in articulating an agency-centred perspective of the child.

Thus, for example, the concept of risk – risk to the carefree quality of childhood, its innocence and associated freedoms – works to reduce the extent to which practitioners might, in practice, feel able to allow children's voices full expression:

> Probably it's because of the nature of their work that there's so much emphasis on risk of harm, isn't there? By the time the Guardian's been appointed, the wishes [of the child] would have to come second ... yeah, I can see that. (CFR)

> One thing you don't take risks with is children. Now that's [...] the general standpoint that I have ... you can't take risks with children ... if there's any doubt, **any** doubt, you err on the side of protection. (CFR)

Thus the priority given to protection and children's welfare transcends children's wishes and feelings, children's lack of awareness of what constitutes 'risk', indeed, providing further evidence of their lack of competence and grounds for their wishes and feelings to be set aside.

There is a clear tension here, therefore, between on the one hand the idea of 'a common developmental trajectory' towards competence and, on the other, the specificity of individual children's circumstances, which might modify that trajectory. So, in everyday practice, practitioners must manage these tensions and disjunctions and in order to do this, they have to *interpret* what they hear. That is to say, they *make judgements* about the significance or weight to be given to children's voices – or to put it in the context of their views about childhood – they seek to balance the extent to which children should remain free from responsibilities against the possible risks of empowering them. Thus, for example, in relation to contact with parents, which is seen as being important developmentally, practitioners may be cautious about acting on children's wishes and feelings should they express the view that they do *not* wish for contact, because of the 'risk' this presents to their future development.

> a child needs to know who their dad is even if they don't get on with them. (CFR)

children are aided into adulthood by continuing contact with both their parents.(CG)

Alternatively, a child who might wish to have contact or live with a parent, who is considered by practitioners as *unsuitable*, may not be allowed contact.

> I suppose it would depend on whether these children were presenting with wanting to go home or not, that would be very significant wouldn't it? So [...] obviously it would all depend on assessment, but in ascertaining the children's wishes and feelings ... it's not simply a question of them saying we want to go home, and therefore that happens [...] because you put their welfare first. (CG)

Here, the risk element outweighs the views expressed by the child and the child's voice is silenced.

In such cases, then, the tension between empowering the child and freeing the child from responsibilities is managed through recourse to an overarching or higher order conception relating to childhood – i.e. the 'welfare principle'. For practitioners, a child's welfare (of which they are the judge) must override any consideration of the wishes and feelings of the child, even if this does produce feelings of powerlessness for children.

> children at seven, three, one ... are not going to be of an age and understanding to fully appreciate everything anyway and it may be that their wishes and feelings would have to be overridden anyway by questions of their protection . (CG)

> Okay, we listen to wishes and feelings but at the end of the day, we're adults and we've got to say, we have a child here, whatever age, but a child. Her wishes and feelings are this [...] but as an adult we can see those wishes and feelings don't key into what is their best interests, and we have to work it from the best interests point of view. (CFR)

> 'I'm a great advocate of listening to what children say, but essentially adults still need to make decisions for children. 'cos [...] they're children and we're adults. (CFR)

A commitment to listening to children does not therefore necessarily mean that children's views are acted on. Practitioners may ignore or attach little weight to these if they consider this to be 'in the child's best interests'. Additionally, however, even if children's views are heard by practitioners and even if children are judged by them to be competent, children's views may not be reported to the court if the practitioner feels that these may not be in child's best *future* interests:

> What I'm asking is [...] 'what is the experience of this child now?', and use what they say to relieve them of the responsibility of making the decision – but it's equipping us to make the best possible decision for what it will be like for them afterwards. (CFR)

Thus, though all the practitioners in our study subscribe to a developmentally-based view of childhood, and all adopted child-centred approaches to their work, it was evident that this generates a number of tensions for them in practice. Consequently, there are subtle differences in the ways in which the developmental model actually comes to inform practice and the extent to which 'child-centred' practices can in fact be sustained in different settings.

Over and above such everyday constraints and tensions, however, other factors contribute to the further silencing of children's voices when the 'private' encounters of practice have to become 'public' – that is, in the writing of court reports. Having ascertained a child's wishes and feelings, practitioners are faced with deciding how much of what a child has said can go in the court report, and in what form. While some practitioners will use direct quotes from the child, others produce a report that puts a gloss on what the child has said. This is often done to protect the child because parents see court reports and, if the child has said something about one or other of its parents which can be taken as negative, it may lead to trouble for that child. It is also done, however, to locate the individual child and their wishes and feelings in the context of what is seen to be 'normal', and therefore 'acceptable', for children, *in general*, at any given stage in the life course.

This can be illustrated by one particular case observed during the research, involving the preparation of a report concerning the welfare of three children whose parents were divorcing. While the report provides an accurate summary of what the children said overall, there is a great difference between what transpired in the interviews with the two older children and how their wishes and feelings were presented in the report. Both of the children were noticeably shaken during the interview, and both children were in tears at times. However, the younger of the two was obviously less able to keep his emotions on a tight rein. From the moment he came in to the room, his whole body shook and his voice trembled when he spoke. For the first few minutes he managed to answer the CFR's questions about what had happened before and since his parents' separation, until he was asked whether he thought things would stay as they were presently:

CFR   Does mum want to keep it like it is now?
Child No. She says she'll move us away
CFR   Has she said that to you or to someone else?
Child (begins to cry) that's what she said. When she was putting us to bed and I heard her say to [my big sister] she would be moving us away to where [her boyfriend's] army is.
CFR   That's upsetting you. It's a silly question but what makes you sad?
Child We won't see our family and friends as much
CFR   It's important for you to stay here then? (nods, still crying). Does that make you want to go and live with dad? (nods). Do you think mum knows how much it upsets you? (no). If she knew do you think she'd still do it or would she stop?
Child She'd do it anyway, don't know why she just would.

This entire exchange saw the child sobbing and barely able to speak. The report, however, simply states:

[he] has not adjusted to the fact of the separation as much as [his sister] has.

Throughout the meeting, the child kept repeating that he wanted to live with his father. Through play with toys, the CFR gave the child various scenarios and asked him what the best outcome would be. In reply to each one, the child said that the best thing would be to live with his dad. In response, the CFR would check in various ways that the child was saying this without having been prompted by his father.

The report, however, simply states:

If [the child] were given a completely free choice, he would want to live with his father ... but would want to spend very substantial contact time with his mother.

Again, this is an accurate description of the boy's wishes but the written text edits out the pain this child was obviously feeling. The section of the report dealing with the welfare checklist argues that the children's wishes and feelings are essentially for arrangements to remain as closely as possible to the way that they are now. In terms of their physical, emotional and educational needs, the report stated that:

> Obviously the children have suffered somewhat from the parental conflict ... and their sense of divided loyalties [...] if conflict does continue I am particularly worried how [the male child] will cope.

The view presented in the report – that of the children having 'suffered somewhat' – is at odds with our observations of the extent of that suffering during the children's interviews. This therefore raises a question about the accuracy or completeness of the representation of children's feelings in court reports, about the ways in which the emotional content may be toned down, and why. What are the risks of conveying these more completely and accurately?

One answer to this is that reports are not written for children, but for the *court* and for the *adults* in the case. Children's voices are therefore sometimes removed from the court report, or glossed over in order to protect children from their parents' reactions to any thing the child might have said or implied. Thus, although most court reports do include statements about the child's wishes and feelings, these are sometimes obscured by manipulating the report and by writing in code:

> I think when you write reports there is a certain amount of reading between the lines, you can say things that, that Judges and lawyers recognise, a sort of code really, which makes me feel very uncomfortable, I don't like doing it in code 'cos I think if the process has got to be transparent, the parents are entitled to know what's being said, [...] supposedly nothing in [our reports] is secret so if you start talking in code, then you're actually, misleading, deceiving – there's part of me that thinks that if that makes life easier for the child that's what I should be doing, so occasionally I do, and the effect I think is the same 'cos I think I can express a view for what the child wants and the Judge recognises that. (CFR)

There must, however, be a risk that the judge will not. Thus it is clear that children's voices are sometimes removed from the court report by practitioners in order to protect children from their parents' reactions to anything the child might have said or implied. On other occasions, what the child has said will only be represented to the court verbally:

> And, and also I'll save some stuff back to give when I'm a witness in the box. Depending on the case, if I think it's going to make this difficult for this child to, in the intervening months it can be before it's heard in court, then I will yeah, almost write it so that the judge reads between the lines. (CFR)

Children's voices are thus effectively filtered out at all stages of proceedings, although this is ostensibly not done to silence them, but in order to protect them from what they might have said.

Conclusion: giving the child a voice

James and James have argued that the law 'works to restrict children's agency through the reliance on adult interpretations of children's needs' (1999: 200). Children are only heard when they are older, when they have not 'been worked on' and when there are no over-riding protection issues. Although, under the 1989 Children Act, the welfare of the child is paramount, the praxis that is produced by the legal and social construction of childhood in the context of family proceedings is such that there can be no agency for children under the terms of the Act, and practitioners working in the Family Justice System *cannot* properly give effect to children's wishes and feelings where they conflict with their 'best interests' (as defined by adults). For example, if a child's wishes and feelings are that they do not want contact with a non-resident parent, the practitioner must use their professional judgement when making recommendations to the court:

> [...] I'm less interested in the child's wishes and the child's feelings, I'm much more interested in why they're saying 'I don't want to go and see Daddy' ... and I'd, I'd want to get the reasons and then I would want as, as an adult and an advisor to the court, to make an assessment of those reasons (CFR)

While both CGs and CFRs share the *same* model and commitment to children's best interests, in practice – when they work face to face with individual children – they have to construct reports, plans and recommendations that locate the childs' 'best interests' in the context of a universal model of childhood and 'the child', a model that is implicit within the Children Act. Key here is the developmental paradigm, which underpins the Act and western models of childhood and which frames the kinds of agency/rights which children are seen to have.

Similarly, the child protection provisions of the Act are couched *explicitly* in terms of the child's 'normal' development. This offers a 'standardized' model/sets of ideas of 'the child' and of how 'children', in general, best grow up and develop, both physically and emotionally. In Family Law, a child's needs (which are in effect culturally defined rights) and a child's 'best interests' – the right to be protected sufficiently to allow 'normal' development – are set within the parameters of scientifically-determined patterns of physical and psychological development. CFRs and CGs thus have a difficult and complex role in family proceedings, and we would not wish to indicate otherwise. Our data reveal, however, some of the tensions they encounter when working with children under the Children Act 1989. All of our respondents were extremely committed to their jobs and to the children they work with and for. However, the framework within which they have to work means that, in general, the child's right to be protected (*by* adults *from* adults) assumes greater importance than the child's right to be heard, a process which reveals the continuing dominance of adult paternalism over children's agency.

Notes

1. The research was funded by the ESRC, Award Ref: R000239102 and took place between 2001–3.
2. Previously Guardians ad Litem and Family Court Welfare Officers.
3. In England and Wales a child can now be held to be criminally responsible from the age of 10.

References

Alderson, P. (1993) *Children's Consent to Surgery*. Buckingham: Open University Press.

Alderson, P. (2000) 'School students' views on school councils and daily life at school', *Children and Society*, 14 (2): 121–135.

James, A. and Prout, A. (1990) (eds) *Constructing and Reconstructing Childhood*, London: Falmer.

James, A., Jenks, C. and Prout, A. (1998) *Theorising Childhood*. Cambridge: Polity Press.

James, A. L. and James, A. (1999) 'Pump Up the Volume: listening to children in separation and divorce', *Childhood* 6 (2): 189–206.

James, A. L. and James, A. (2004) *Constructing Childhood: Theory, Policy and Social Practice*. London: Palgrave.

James, A. L., James, A. and McNamee, S. (2004) 'Turn down the volume? – not hearing children in family proceedings', Child and Family Law Quarterly 16 (2).

Jenks, C. (1996) Childhood. London: Routledge.

Lyon, C. (1995) 'Representing Children – Towards 2000 and Beyond', Representing Children, 8(2): 8–18.

Mayall, B. (2002) Towards a Sociology for Childhood: thinking from children's lives. Buckingham: Open University Press.

Murch, M. (1995) 'Listening to the voice of the child – critical transitions, support and representation for children', *Representing Children* 8:2: 19–27.

Parry, M. (1994) 'Children's Welfare and The Law: The Children Act 1989 and Recent Developments', *Panel News* 7:3: 4–11.

14
Meeting the Challenge? Voicing Children and Young People in Mental Health Research

Vicki Coppock

Introduction

Over the last decade, there has been a growing interest within the United Kingdom in 'listening to children's voices'. A proliferation of research studies has emerged in which children and young people's views have been sought on various issues affecting their everyday lives (for example, the Economic and Social Research Council's *Children 5–16* Programme). This growth of interest is particularly evident at the level of policy-making, where a range of initiatives has been developed that are premised on improving consultation with, and the participation of, children and young people in the design, delivery and evaluation of services that affect them (Children and Young People's Unit, 2001; Department of Health, 1998; 2000; 2002). The sheer volume of such initiatives has invited the observation that listening to children's voices has now become part of the 'rhetorical orthodoxy' (Prout, 2003:11). In the context of the longstanding social, political and economic marginalisation of children and young people in the UK (see James and James, chapter 1 in this volume), these developments seem all the more remarkable.

Three specific developments are significant for understanding this process of change. The first of these is the continuing impact of national and international concern with the rights of children. The United Nations Convention on the Rights of the Child (UNCRC) (United Nations, 1989) was the culmination of almost 20 years of sustained pressure, from activists and non-governmental organisations around the world, to place children's rights in the public arena and onto the agendas of governments. In adopting the Convention, signatories agree to conform to its 54 Articles. Among the most significant of these is the requirement of Article 12 that States Parties:

> assure to the child who is capable of forming his or her own views the right to express those views freely in all matters affecting the child, the views of the child being given due weight in accordance with the age and maturity of the child (United Nations, 1989: Article 12.1).

While the UK did not ratify the Convention until 1991, changes to domestic child care legislation – namely the 1989 Children Act – anticipated some of its key principles; particularly Article 12. Notwithstanding the longstanding criticisms that have since been levelled at the UK government regarding its less-than-full implementation and compliance (United Nations Committee on the Rights of the Child, 1995; 2002), both the Convention and the 1989 Children Act have had a significant impact on the approach to children's services and to research and evaluation in the UK, in so far as they impose an *obligation* on government departments to ascertain the views of children and young people in a variety of contexts.

The second significant development underpinning change is the restructuring of welfare provision from the late 1980s onwards – a process that began during the long New Right Conservative administration and has intensified under New Labour's modernisation programme. The application of New Public Management principles to health and social care provision has challenged the traditional dominance of professionals in the design and delivery of services, theoretically making them more accountable to the consumers of those services. A new vocabulary has developed, reflecting the change in emphasis: 'patients charter', 'service user', 'clinical governance', 'clinical audit', 'best value', 'quality assurance', 'performance indicators'. An 'evidence-based practice' (EBP) approach to research and evaluation has emerged strongly in this context, driven by the increased pressure on professionals to demonstrate the effectiveness of their interventions. This can be seen in the work of The Centre For Evidence-based Social Services at the University of Exeter, and that of The Centre for Evidence-based Mental Health and The NHS Research and Development Centre for Evidence-based Medicine, both at the University of Oxford. Within this approach, children and young people are positioned as consumers of services and their participation and involvement in research and evaluation is premised on this basis.

The third driver of change is the emergence of a new paradigm for the sociology of childhood (James and Prout, 1997). Three central assumptions underpin this new approach. First, childhood is understood as a *social* rather than a biological construction. In this way, the traditional developmental model of childhood is problematised. So, too, is the notion of a 'universal' childhood. Second, children are seen as social actors and, as such, are considered worthy of study in their own right and from their own perspectives. Third, the ethnographic approach to social research is believed to be more compatible with a child-centred perspective than traditional positivistic research frameworks. These assumptions have informed the 'transition towards recognizing children as "knowers" – able to generate knowledge as well as being the recipients of knowledge, or being the objects of knowledge' (Foley, 2001: 99–100).

On face value, it is easy to assume that the approaches to children's research that are derived from this perspective are consistent, since each appears to be actively engaged with the process of 'listening to children's voices'. However, such an assumption is misleading. To conflate the various approaches used in this way obscures important tensions and contradictions between them. These differences need to be opened up for critical analysis, so that those processes that might serve to inhibit or colonise, rather than facilitate, children and young people's agency can be identified. Indeed, as the previous chapter demonstrates, while the rhetorical commitment to listening to children may be strong, the scope for 'voicing' children is all too often constrained in professional practice.

The following critical analysis of contemporary research and evaluation in child and adolescent mental health will reveal how the scope for 'voicing children' is compromised by the persistence of medicalising discourses in children and young people's lives. The continued prioritising of managerial agendas in research and evaluation includes a renewed enthusiasm for positivistic methodologies in the guise of evidence-based practice and marginalises emancipatory research with children and young people in mental distress.

Historical and theoretical contexts

Since the late nineteenth century, the lives of all children and young people have been constructed, interpreted and responded to within the hegemony of scientific discourse and professional practice. The positivistic tradition of child study – observing, weighing, measuring and classifying children – facilitated the translation of prevailing common-sense assumptions about 'childhood' into 'scientific truths' (Rose, 1985; 1990). Individual and developmental psychologists constructed the 'normal' child and the course that a normal childhood should take, informing judgements concerning what constitutes normal/appropriate and abnormal/inappropriate thoughts, feelings and behaviour in children and young people (Burman, 1994). Central to this approach is the notion of intrinsic childhood irrationality and incompetence. Rationality and competence are established as the hallmarks of adulthood – a status to which children and young people can only aspire, as they progress along their developmental journey through the life-course. Reduced to the status of human-becomings, the powerlessness of children and young people is confirmed and legitimated through the assertion of their incapacity (James and Prout, 1997). A range of competing explanatory models of human behaviour has emerged – neurological/biological, social, cognitive, behavioural, psychodynamic, systemic. However, all of these share a focus on individual, familial and/or social pathology within the overarching application of the medical model – identification, diagnosis, treatment and cure. These theoretical imperatives have been institutionalised in the state's response to children and young people and operationalised through professional practice.

The medical model and the scientific paradigm have long dominated child and adolescent mental health research, theory, policy and practice. The processes involved in defining, identifying, explaining and responding to mental distress in children and young people have been governed by a subscription to illness categories such as those found in the *Diagnostic and Statistical Manual of Mental Disorders* (DSM IV, American Psychiatric Association, 1994) or the *International Classification of Mental and Behavioural Disorders* (ICD 10, World Health Organisation, 1992). These formal diagnostic labels allow for a wide interpretation of 'disturbance', from lying and disobedience to attempted self-harm (Malek, 1991). Critical research has demonstrated significant discrepancies between the diagnostic criteria used and the assessment of individual cases, suggesting that the medical model of mental health is not always a reliable indicator of, or an appropriate response to, children and young people's mental distress (Coppock, 1997; 2002).

The medical model draws artificial boundaries around normality and abnormality, obscuring the influence of social and political processes in the conceptualisation of disorder. Indeed, the diagnosis of mental distress in children and young people has been found to rely heavily on the subjective impressions of parents and professionals as much as on any objective, 'scientific' evidence (Malek, 1991). Moreover, the therapeutic discourse of 'illness' and 'cure' can disguise the potency of the medical model as a means of social control. The power of adults to define the non-conforming behaviour of children and young people as problematic, and of the medical model to re-label that non-conformity as illness, has led to inappropriate and inconsistent institutional responses to children and young people in distress that have profound consequences for their lives and opportunities (Coppock, 1997).

The child's voice has rarely been sought, let alone heard, in this context. Indeed, much of the 'treatment' that children and young people receive is aimed at silencing them (Coppock, 2002). The majority of children and young people who use mental health services do so without having given their informed consent. It is their parents or other adults, acting *on their behalf*, who give permission for their treatment. Because children and young people are not afforded the status of valid subjects, their 'needs' are constructed by adults – whether parents or professionals – and things are done to them 'in their best interests' (see also Thomas, chapter 2 in this volume). It is an adult-led process, to which the child or young person is expected to submit and conform. Mentally distressed children and young people fall prey to the double burden of being judged as intrinsically suspect in terms of their mental competency by virtue of both their age and their 'illness' or 'disorder'. This concern lies at the heart of any critical analysis of contemporary mainstream research and evaluation in child and adolescent mental health:

> The central issue here is this group's experience of being disempowered and not listened to. Users of mental health services are still often not seen as appropriate people to consult, especially when their views diverge from those of professionals (Laws, 1999: 5).

The impact of the 1989 Children Act and the UN Convention

Rights critiques have been strongly articulated in the field of adult mental health research, policy and practice but are relatively underdeveloped in the child and adolescent mental health arena. Nevertheless, since the early 1990s concerns about rights and rights abuses have increasingly become the focus of critical researchers in child and adolescent mental health settings (Children's Legal Centre 1991; 1993; 2002; Hodgkin, 1993; 1994).

In principle, the UNCRC and the 1989 Children Act provide the apparatus for correcting the history of harms and abuses that have been inflicted on mentally distressed children and young people and provide a vehicle for their voices to be heard. However, a range of practice issues and legal anomalies have been exposed that cast doubt as to whether the language of rights and the mechanisms of convention and law provide a sufficient challenge to the oppressive structures of mainstream child and adolescent mental health research, policy and practice. Attention has focused on the failure of mainstream child and adolescent mental health services to respond to the needs of children and young people in mental distress (Community Care *et al.*, 2002; Mental Health Foundation, 1998; 1999). In particular, the issue of informed consent remains controversial.

In July 2001, the Department of Health published *Consent – what you have a right to expect: a guide for children and young people* (Department of Health, 2001). However, this guide fails to acknowledge the hidden processes of adult/professional power and authority bearing down on children and young people in mental distress. Indeed, the principle that parental rights must be exercised in line with the evolving capacities of the child (the *Gillick principle*) has been found wanting when applied to children and young people in mental distress, especially in situations where they wish to refuse consent to treatment. The cases of *Re R* and *Re W* (Bates, 1994; Children's Legal Centre, 1995; Freeman, 1993) involved consideration of the compulsory treatment of children and young people. In *Re R*, a 15-year-old girl diagnosed with bipolar affective disorder, resident in an adolescent unit, refused sedative drugs. The unit caring for her insisted that they needed a free hand to administer drugs to her, against her will if necessary. While the Court of Appeal conceded that, at the time of refusal, the girl was lucid and rational, it concluded that it would be dangerous to refuse to authorise medication on the grounds that a patient was lucid on a particular day. In *Re W*, a 16-year-old girl refused her consent to treatment for anorexia nervosa. The Court of Appeal authorised medical treatment against her wishes. Such a decision is alarming, given that self-determination and 'the urgent need to be in control of their own lives' (Bruch cited in Freeman, 1993:19) are central to the anorexic's experience of mental distress. In both cases, the right to refuse medical treatment was overridden in the child's 'best interests'. Moreover, their refusal to consent to treatment was considered indicative of their

Gillick incompetence. This action effectively removed autonomy and self-determination from young people at an age when *more* responsibility and self-direction was expected of them.

In such a hostile environment, it is difficult to conceive of any circumstance in which the voice of a mentally distressed child or young person could be both heard and *decisive.* As Masson, (1991: 529) states, it is the severity of the test for *Gillick competence* that 'provides the basis for decisions in individual cases which ignore the child's wishes', coupled with 'the belief that paternalism is better than self-determination where decisions relating to children are concerned'. Such an assumption is challenged by studies that demonstrate children's capacities for complex thought (see, for example, Messenger Davies and Mosdell in this volume; Glachan and Ney, 1992; Short, 1991, both cited in Thomas, 2002). The two crucial issues appear to be that, first, children need *more* experience of decision-making, since their competence improves with practice and, second, that adults must become more accomplished in communicating complex issues to children.

The rhetoric/reality divide between rights in discourse and rights in practice is indicative of the failure to acknowledge the persistence of those structures of power that lie at the heart of adult-child relations in child and adolescent mental health. Speaking of rights-based strategies in adult mental health, Rose (1986: 177) argues that, 'while rights strategies have won significant victories ... there are fundamental limitations to such rights strategies for mental health reform. They disguise problematic political objectives and depoliticise debate over the organization of psychiatry'. In other words, rather than empowering mental health service users, rights-based strategies may merely reorganise relations. That is, oppressive systems are capable of skilfully hijacking the language of rights to convey a powerful illusion of inclusivity, participation and empowerment. Rights-based strategies do not, of themselves, transform the relations of dominance between professionals and those subject to them. Power structures must be brought into the open.

Rose's critique can clearly be applied to the position of children and young people in mental distress. Notwithstanding the importance of an articulation of children's rights in convention and statute, critics have argued that while there are no meaningful penalties for breaches the value of such rights is merely symbolic. This is evidenced in the UK government's repeated failure to fully implement the UNCRC or to comply with the recommendations of the United Nations Committee

(1995; 2002). Although successive UK governments have produced a mountain of documentation and research initiatives that talk up the issues of inclusion and participation, the Committee has judged them guilty of paying little more than lip service to children and young people's rights. In this, the position of mentally-distressed children and young people remains unchanged. Despite the potential challenge of rights discourses to the dominance of medical authority, clinical research and practice still tends to exclude the views of mentally-distressed children and young people and treat them as passive objects.

Having considered the limitations of rights discourses within child and adolescent mental health research, policy and practice, it is now important to assess the impact of the challenge of consumerist discourse in this field.

The impact of the 'quality' agenda and the drive towards 'evidence-based practice'

Since the early 1990s, the rhetoric of quality assurance and service user involvement has dominated official discourse in UK government policy-making, research and evaluation. With regard to child and adolescent mental health, it has been acknowledged that, 'children, young people and families must all feel that a service has enabled them to present their own perspective on the problems that they bring and that they have been listened to ... Such communication is ... a potent test of a service's quality' (NHS Health Advisory Service, 1995: 82–83). This approach poses a significant challenge to practitioners used to adult-led, professionally-driven research agendas.

Partly in response to this challenge, the need to be seen to be making evidence-based decisions has permeated all areas of British public policy (see Black, 2001). At face value, it is entirely appropriate that practitioners should be accountable for their interventions and should be confident in the knowledge of what works best. Similarly, policy makers increasingly need to be reassured that scarce resources are being used to best effect. However, it is apparent that the dominant approach to researching effectiveness is heavily influenced by managerial priorities that privilege positivistic methodologies and quantitative methods. While these methods certainly have some value in terms of audit and accountancy, it must be recognised that overly-simplistic, reductionist approaches to research and evaluation fail to do justice to the inherently complex world of practice. This signifies a more fundamental problematic than a return to the well-rehearsed debate about the relative merits and demerits of quantitative versus qualitative methods. The managerialist drive towards quality assurance, performance indicators and evidence-based practice (EBP) reflects political and ideological priorities that could be considered antagonistic towards emancipatory goals, since the main focus of concern is the effective management of systems and organisations and not the life-worlds of individuals. Indeed, qualitative, child-centred approaches to research present a significant challenge to practitioners who are increasingly being expected to respond to goal- and outcomes-driven evaluation. Such approaches place a high value on aspects of mental health that are not easily measured in numerical terms.

EBP has gained a strong foothold in mainstream child and adolescent mental health research. For example, Joughin and Shaw, from the Royal College of Psychiatrists' child and adolescent mental health research department (FOCUS), have published an electronic book entitled *Finding the Evidence: A Gateway to the Literature in Child and Adolescent Mental Health* (2000) which claims to provide 'rapid access to some of the best available information on which to base clinical judgement and further learning' but includes no user research. The authors give credence only to 'high quality systematic reviews, meta-analyses and clinical guidelines', as they are 'scientifically, extremely valuable'. Similarly, the criteria for selection and review of articles for abstracting in the journal *Evidence Based Mental Health* states that 'to reduce unnecessary variations in clinical practice' any study of diagnosis must meet Diagnostic and Statistical Manual (DSM) criteria. Such publications are the powerful gatekeepers of what is to be considered legitimate knowledge. By them, readers are led only to research that is likely to confirm the status and authority of mainstream psychiatry and psychology. This is demonstrated clearly in Guevara and Stein's (2001) clinical review for the *British Medical Journal*, entitled 'Evidence based management of attention deficit hyperactivity disorder'. At the outset, the authors acknowledge the 'shakiness' of the 'evidence' for the existence of such a 'disorder':

> At present there is no biological marker that clearly identifies affected children. Furthermore it is unclear whether the disorder is unique or merely one end of the continuum of age appropriate behaviour (Guevara and Stein, 2001: 1232).

However, they go on to guide the clinician to 'high quality systematic reviews and evidence based guidelines' (from mainstream medical research databases, such as the Cochrane Library and the Centre for Evidence-Based Mental Health) that confirm a medical understanding and treatment of the child's presenting behaviour:

> You confirm the diagnosis of attention deficit hyperactivity disorder by using the DSM-IV diagnostic criteria and the Conners parent and teachers rating scales. You inform the parents of the potential risk of additional psychiatric disorders and persistence of symptoms into adolescence. You prescribe a stimulant drug and arrange review (ibid: 1235).

At no point is the clinician directed to consider critical research evidence on ADHD and its treatment (for example, Breggin, 1998). This process clearly demonstrates the intransigence of professionally-led, paternalistic responses to children and young people in mental distress and how this can 'contribute to stasis or inertia in (CAMHS) service development' (White, undated: 10).

The emergence and rapid growth of the EBP approach has been identified as an adaptive response to significant political issues and concerns of the late twentieth century; namely, the management of risk, critiques of science and professionalism and the emergence of managerialism and consumerism (Giddens, 1991; Reynolds and Trinder, 2000). Giddens has suggested that the promise of modernity, that risk can be assessed and controlled by expert knowledge, has been found wanting as the limitations of science and expert systems have become more evident. There has been an increased awareness of 'risky' systems – that is, iatrogenic risk. The Alder Hey Children's Hospital organ retention scandal and the conviction of Dr Harold Shipman for the multiple murders of his patients are just two recent examples of such risk.

Doubts have been raised concerning what constitutes legitimate 'knowledge' or 'truth' as a basis for professional practice. The emergence of EBP can be seen to fit with Giddens' notion of 'sustained optimism', in so far as it represents an adaptive reaction that re-asserts faith in rationality and science in the belief that perseverance will eventually produce solutions. This is particularly useful in understanding the growth of EBP in mental health research and evaluation, since the mental health system is replete with examples of iatrogenic risk (Pilgrim and Rogers, 1993). Embedded in the scientific tradition, mainstream psychiatry and psychology have nevertheless suffered from a 'loss of faith' in the medical model of mental health (Coppock and Hopton, 2000). EBP represents an opportunity to restore that faith.

This means that even though the limitations of professional knowledge and practice in mainstream child and adolescent mental health are conceded, there is a reassertion of the belief that perseverance with the scientific paradigm will eventually produce solutions. In this sense, EBP restores a sense of safety and control. As an adaptive response, EBP serves to reassert medical hegemony in the child and adolescent mental health field.

The new sociology of childhood and the scope for emancipatory research in child and adolescent mental health

A critical analysis of the EBP approach to child and adolescent mental health research exposes a number of questions that lie at the heart of an emancipatory research agenda. First, to what extent is it possible to acquire objective truth/knowledge about 'what works' in this field? This question is concerned with recognising that all research is inherently political, with practitioners/researchers attached to a particular/preferred theoretical and methodological approach. There is still considerable reluctance to acknowledge how the process of building evidence in child and adolescent psychiatry is shaped by values and interpretation. Although it can be argued that the EBP approach to research and evaluation has methodological rigour, conveying a sense of certainty and authority, this is often more illusory than is suggested by the evidence. The argument that such an approach is a neutral, contextless methodology that can simply be applied whenever and wherever required is unsustainable (see Black 2001; Reynolds and Trinder, 2000).

Second, to what extent can the EBP approach to research and evaluation in child and adolescent mental health do justice to other forms of knowledge, particularly user perspectives? This question is concerned with recognising that knowledge is inextricably linked to power, with some forms of knowledge being privileged over others (Foucault, 1977). By definition, its privileging devalues or excludes other forms of knowledge or values. By disputing it, we ask the question 'what counts as legitimate knowledge?' The evidence-based practice approach remains rooted in adult, professional definitions of what constitutes legitimate knowledge. Within this context, there is limited scope for the voice of the child to be heard, as it is the voice of the adult researcher or professional 'expert' that is privileged. The centrality of experience, narrative, the individual, qualitative evidence and analysis within user-led approaches to research are at odds with the rational, hierarchy-of-evidence approach of EBP. As Sophie Laws (1999: 3) argues, 'traditional research may enable young people to tell their experiences in response to questions from adults, but it does not allow young people to set the agenda'.

Finally, to what extent does the EBP approach facilitate a critical appraisal of the world of professional practice? The subtleties of the way in which adult-child power relationships are articulated and sustained in professional practice are usually overlooked in positivistic research and evaluation. Practitioners derive their understandings and approaches to practice from broad theoretical orientations and their professional training. They operate within a range of organisational and legal structures that define what children and childhood are, or should be, like and which determine the broader construction of child welfare policy, law and practice (James and Prout, 1990; James, Jenks and Prout, 1998; McNamee, James and James, in this volume). However, it is rarely acknowledged that these structures are not fixed but are continually contested and negotiated. They are informed by prevailing *social* constructions of 'childhood', 'youth' and 'family' that practitioners may find it difficult to recognise, thereby constituting a hidden agenda in the dynamic of practice. This suggests that there is a need for a research methodology that enables researchers to engage with this domain in order to expose and correct those elements of practice that militate against the realisation of a truly anti-oppressive, empowering practice with children and young people.

It is within the new sociology of childhood that discourses of empowerment can be identified that are consistent with the politics, principles and priorities of emancipatory research. In this context, the approach to research and evaluation with mentally distressed children and young people is derived within critical analysis of the complex dynamics of adult-child power relations and of oppressive professional discourse and practice where 'professionally delivered services are brought into question or are rendered problematic' (Pilgrim and Rogers, 1993: 175). It is an approach that is intrinsically committed to political action and substantive change in the life-worlds of children and young people.

An emancipatory model begins with recognising the validity of children and young people's voices and their right to define their own research agendas. In recent years, research studies have begun to emerge in the child and adolescent mental health field that are consistent with this approach (Laws, 1998; Laws *et al.*, 1999; Mental

Health Foundation, 1999; Smith and Leon, 2001; Youth Access, 2001; White, undated). These research studies have adopted sound method-ological protocols derived from the expanding literature on involving children and young people in research (see, for example, Alderson, 1995; Boyden and Ennew, 1998; Kirby, 2002). They are child and young person centred, placing a high value on both qualitative methods and dialogistic relationships between researchers and parti-cipants. They challenge the presumption of incompetence that charac-terises and dominates mainstream children's research in general and child and adolescent mental health research in particular. Children and young people are being recognised, here, as valid contributors to knowledge; their knowledge is being valued and disseminated with the intention of informing the development of policy and practice.

The disparities in status and power between adults and children in research are openly acknowledged in these studies and every effort is made to diminish them. The development of children and young people as peer researchers is an excellent example of this (Laws, 1998). There is recognition that, to be consistent with a philosophy of in-clusion and participation, the level and nature of participation of individuals/groups within the research has to be explored and negoti-ated. To this end, such studies have self-consciously paid close atten-tion to those typologies that clarify the level of commitment to children's and young people's participation (for example, Hart, 1992; Shier, 2000). Frameworks such as these demonstrate 'how processes which claim to be participatory might involve minimal or no change in power relations' (Laws, 1999: 4).

The messages from children and young people in these studies pose a fundamental challenge to mainstream CAMHS research, policy and practice. They reveal that:

- Children and young people want accessible, informal, 'ordinary', flexible sources of help
- They want a greater range of options in services
- They want services to be responsive to their definitions of mental distress, not just professional, medical definitions
- They don't want access to help and services to be contingent upon the application of a pathologising, stigmatising formal diagnosis
- They want more say about their own treatment
- They want less reliance on drug treatments
- They would value more peer support mechanisms – befriending, advising, supporting

- They want to be listened to
- They want to have their competence recognised, particularly their ability to articulate their needs/views and to create solutions to their own distress
- They want to be understood, respected, acknowledged and supported (see Laws, 1998; Laws *et al.*, 1999; Mental Health Foundation, 1999; Smith and Leon, 2001; Youth Access, 2001; White, undated).

Nevertheless, research such as this is overwhelmingly funded and commissioned through NGOs and so tends to remain outside of the mainstream. Moreover, because the hierarchy of evidence approach persists in child and adolescent mental health research and evaluation, as research *evidence* these studies remain 'subordinate' to mainstream CAMHS research and are therefore marginalised. This is exemplified in the constitution and activities of the *Mental Health and Psychological Well Being of Children and Young People* External Working Group, one of six groups set up to develop the *Children's National Service Framework* (Department of Health, 2003). The main group membership consists of twenty-one senior professionals from psychiatry, psychology, health and education. Seven of the nine sub-groups consist of up to nine adults of similar senior professional status. The 'user participation' subgroup consists of just two individuals, both experts at the Department of Health. There is no direct representation of children and young people themselves. While some user consultation research has been commissioned (Baruch and James, 2003), the messages from which are consistent with those outlined above, it is the adult voice that is dominating the activities of this group. While such imbalances persist it is unlikely that anything will change and the Audit Commission's observation that, 'what had been learnt from consultation with users and carers had not actually been used to inform service development' (cited in National Children's Bureau, 1999: 2), will continue to hold true.

Summary and conclusion

A critical analysis of research and evaluation in child and adolescent mental health has revealed that while there is much rhetoric around listening to the voices of mentally distressed children and young people, there is little evidence of substantive change in their lifeworlds. It is still rarely the case that children and young people's voices are *decisive* in the planning, development and delivery of mental health services. This suggests the persistence of adult/professional power structures that militate against children and young people's agency.

Adult, professionally-driven approaches have dominated the field of child and adolescent mental health research and evaluation. These have been based on medicalising discourses about children and young people's lives and misplaced assumptions regarding children and young people's limited capacity for making meaningful contributions to the knowledge base, thereby marginalising them from the sites of power in policy and practice. Similarly, notwithstanding the emergence of critical research and campaigns revealing rights abuses in child and adolescent mental health, a critical examination of the impact of the 1989 Children Act and the UN Convention on the Rights of the Child has revealed the limitations of law and convention in facilitating the voices of children and young people in mental health research, policy and practice.

'Voicing' mentally distressed children and young people is fundamentally a project of emancipation. Emancipatory research in child and adolescent mental health, derived within the theoretical and methodological approach of the new sociology of childhood, has the potential to bring about substantive changes to child and adolescent mental health service provision. However, the empowerment of children in mental distress will only be achieved if the adult professionals charged with their care listen to their voices and act upon their views. Unless this happens, children and young people in mental distress will remain powerless.

References

Alderson, P. (1995) *Listening to Children: Ethics and Social Research*, Barkingside: Barnardo's.

Baruch, G. and James, K. (2003) *The National Framework for Children, Young People and Maternity Services: The Mental Health and Psychological Wellbeing of Children and Young People. Report from Consultation with Users of Child and Adolescent Mental Health Services*, London: Department of Health.

Bates, P. (1994) 'Children in secure psychiatric units: Re K, W and H – 'out of sight, out of mind'?', *Journal of Child Law*, 6, 3: 131–137.

Black, N. (2001) 'Evidence based policy: proceed with care', *British Medical Journal*, 323: 275–278.

Boyden, J. and Ennew, J. (1998) *Children in Focus: A Manual for Participatory Research with Children*, Stockholm: Radda Barnen.

Burman, E. (1994) *Deconstructing Developmental Psychology*, London: Routledge.

Children and Young People's Unit (2001) *Learning to Listen – Core Principles for the Involvement of Children and Young People*, London: DfEE.

Children's Legal Centre (1991) 'Young People, Mental Health and the Law', *Childright*, 78: 23–25.

Children's Legal Centre (1993) 'Mental Health Code Revised', *Childright*, 101: 7–8.

Children's Legal Centre (1995) 'Consent to medical treatment – young people's legal rights', *Childright*, 115: 11–14.

Children's Legal Centre (2002) 'Children and Mental Health', *Childright*, 189: 16–19.

Community Care Magazine, Mental Health Foundation and Young Minds (2002) 'Changing Minds: Better Mental Health Care for Children', *Community Care*, July 2002.

Coppock, V. (1997) 'Mad, Bad or Misunderstood?' in Scraton, P. (ed.) *'Childhood' in 'Crisis'?*, London: UCL Press.

Coppock, V. (2002) 'Medicalising children's behaviour' in Franklin, B. (ed.) *The New Handbook of Children's Rights: comparative policy and practice*, London: Routledge.

Coppock, V. and Hopton, J. (2000) *Critical Perspectives on Mental Health*, London: Routledge.

Department of Health (1998) *Quality Protects*, London: Department of Health.

Department of Health (2000) *Children's National Service Framework* and *Children's Taskforce*, London: Department of Health.

Department of Health (2001) *Consent – what you have a right to expect: a guide for children and young people*, London: Department of Health.

Department of Health (2002) *Listening, Hearing and Responding: Department of Health Action Plan: core principles for the involvement of children and young people*, London: Department of Health.

Foley, P. (2001) 'Our Bodies, Ourselves'?: Mothers, Children and Health Care at Home', in Foley, P., Roche, J. and Tucker, S. (eds) *Children in Society*, Basingstoke: Palgrave.

Foucault, M. (1977) *Discipline and Punish: The Birth of the Prison*, London: Allen and Unwin.

Freeman, M. (1993) 'Removing Rights from Adolescents', *Adoption and Fostering*, 17, 1: 14–21.

Giddens, A. (1991) *The Consequences of Modernity*, Cambridge: Polity Press.

Guevara, J. P. and Stein, M. T. (2001) 'Evidence based management of attention deficit hyperactivity disorder', *British Medical Journal*, 323: 1232–1235.

Hart, R. (1992) *Children's Participation: From Tokenism to Citizenship*, Florence: UNICEF.

Hodgkin, R. (1993) 'Measures of Control in Psychiatric Units', *Childright*, 99: 3–6.

Hodgkin, R. (1994) 'The Right to Consent to Treatment', *Children UK*, Winter 4–5.

James, A., Jenks, C. and Prout, A. (1998) *Theorizing Childhood*, Cambridge: Polity Press.

James, A. and Prout, A. (eds) (1997) *Constructing and Reconstructing Childhood*, London: Falmer Press.

Joughin, C. and Shaw, M. (2000) *Finding the Evidence: A Gateway to the Literature in Child and Adolescent Mental Health*, London: Gaskell.

Kirby, P. (2002) 'Involving young people in research' in Franklin, B. (ed.) *The New Handbook of Children's Rights: comparative policy and practice*, London: Routledge.

Kurtz, Z., Thornes, R. and Wolkind, S. (1994) *Services for the mental health of children and young people in England: a national review*, London: Maudsley Hospital and South Thames (West) Regional Health Authority.

Laws, S. (1998) *Hear Me! Consulting with young people on mental health services*, London: Mental Health Foundation.

Laws, S. (1999) 'Involving children and young people in the monitoring and evaluation of mental health services', *Healthy Minds*, London: National Children's Bureau.

Laws, S., Armitt, D., Metzendor, W., Percival, P. and Reisel, J. (1999) *Time to Listen: young people's experiences of mental health services*, London: Save the Children.

Malek, M. (1991) *Psychiatric Admissions*, London: The Children's Society.

Masson, J. (1991) 'Adolescent Crisis and Parental Power', *Family Law*, December, 528–531.

Mental Health Foundation (1998) *The Big Picture: promoting children and young people's mental health*, London: Mental Health Foundation.

Mental Health Foundation (1999) *Bright Futures: promoting children and young people's mental health*, London: Mental Health Foundation.

National Children's Bureau (1999) *Healthy Minds, The Newsletter of the Young People's Mental Health and Well-Being Project*, Issue no. 6, November.

NHS Health Advisory Service (1995) *Together We Stand: The Commissioning, Role and Management of Child and Adolescent Mental Health Services*, London: HMSO.

Pilgrim, D. and Rogers, A. (1993) *A Sociology of Mental Health and Illness*, Buckingham: Open University Press.

Prout, A. (2003) 'Participation, policy and the changing conditions of childhood' in Hallett, C. and Prout, A. (eds) *Hearing the Voices of Children: Social Policy for a New Century*, London: Routledge Falmer.

Reynolds, S. and Trinder, L. (2000) *Evidence-Based Practice: A Critical Approach*, London: Blackwell.

Rose, N. (1985) *The Psychology Complex: Psychology, Politics and Society in England 1869–1939*, London: RKP.

Rose, N. (1986) 'Law, rights and psychiatry', in Miller, P. and Rose, N. (eds) *The Power of Psychiatry*, Cambridge: Cambridge University Press.

Rose, N. (1990) *Governing the Soul*, London: Routledge.

Shier, H. (2000) 'Pathways to participation: openings, opportunities and obligations, *Children and Society*, 14: 111–117.

Smith, K. and Leon, L. (2001) *Turned Upside Down: Developing community-based crisis services for 16–25 year olds experiencing a mental health crisis*, London: Mental Health Foundation.

Thomas, N. (2002) *Children, Family and the State*, Bristol: The Policy Press.

United Nations (1989) *Convention on the Rights of the Child*, Geneva: United Nations.

United Nations Committee on the Rights of the Child (1995) *Eighth session. Consideration of Reports Submitted by States Parties Under Article 44 of the Convention, United Kingdom of Great Britain and Northern Ireland*, Geneva: United Nations.

United Nations Committee on the Rights of the Child (2002) *Thirty-first session. Consideration of Reports Submitted by States Parties Under Article 44 of the Convention, United Kingdom of Great Britain and Northern Ireland*, Geneva: United Nations.

Youth Access (2001) *Breaking down the barriers: Key evaluation findings on young people's mental health needs*, London: Youth Access.

White, S. (undated) *In Their Own Words: Young People's Accounts of Their Experiences as Users of Child and Adolescent Mental Health Services in Stockport*, The University of Manchester/Mental Health Foundation.

15
Future Directions for the Study of Childhood

Jim Goddard¹

Introduction

This final chapter draws upon the earlier contributions within this volume in order to offer some thoughts about issues that may be particularly important, or remain so, in future work in the field of childhood studies. Such a task is inevitably qualified by uncertainties and the difficulties of making predictions, but there are certainly some points from the chapters in this volume that are worth highlighting. When we, as editors, set out to produce this book, we were aware that there are a large number of scholars across the world doing interesting work on historical and contemporary childhoods. We could not hope to adequately represent the diversity of this work in a volume such as ours. However, the chapters that we have brought together in this volume, as well as being worthwhile and interesting in themselves, give some significant insights into the range of possible avenues for future research on childhood.

Fortunately, when planning the book, we were able to identify some common themes and issues in the papers that we read. We grouped these into some key themes and enabled our authors to conduct some dialogue with each other within those themes. Such themes reflected some of the major issues in the lives of children, including education, work and power. In addressing those themes, our authors considered a range of voices that affect the lives of children. Whilst these include the voices of children themselves, they also include the voices of parents, professionals, policy-makers and other adults. The tensions between these latter voices and those of children clearly differ according to particular global and other environments and this chapter considers some of the wider contexts within which many of the developments reported in these chapters take place.

The politics of childhood: history, work, education and power

Although this is very much a book about the contemporary world, it does contain helpful reminders that there is much to learn from historical analysis and perspectives about the condition of contemporary childhoods. Jim Block's chapter, for example, shows that there are strong parallels between nineteenth-century attempts to guide childhood in conditions of novelty and uncertainty in the formative years of the United States and the heightened concerns of contemporary policy-makers in many countries with the importance of child welfare and education during a period of social and cultural flux. The post-revolutionary focus of the new United States of America on producing self-reliant, self-motivated individuals who were nevertheless committed to the social good has strong echoes in the contemporary UK policy agenda of producing flexible, well-educated individuals who are fitted to play a full part in the increasingly fluid 'knowledge' and service economies of the early years of the early 21st century.

Following on from this consideration of how children are prepared for the adult world of work, one of the themes by which we organised our chapters was the actual work undertaken by large numbers of them. Some of the issues surrounding such work concern visible and 'problematic' behaviour, while others concern less visible activities. The work of 'street children' falls into the former category. Heesterman notes that such work is not necessarily exploitative and damaging to the child (see also Bar-on, 1997). Such a perspective, based on research that draws on children's own voices, is a useful corrective to the blanket perception, of some activists in the child labour field, of all child labourers as victims. When we begin to ask children about their own experiences, such a picture inevitably becomes more complex. This is particularly clear from Julie Seymour's chapter, which stresses the ambiguities surrounding emotional labour by children in the service and hospitality sectors. This and other chapters show that, as new avenues for research on the voices of children are opened, the capacity of such voices for challenging adult characterisations of the 'best interests' of children will widen.

With respect to another of our themes, education, the chapters of Blasco and Tremlett remind us of strong global differences in both educational practice and experience. In advanced industrialised countries, the prospect of parents using entitlement to education as a bargaining tool is largely redundant because of the role of the state, whereas in Mexico it clearly remains very much a live issue for large numbers of poor children. Paradoxically, this gives children a certain level of decision-making power about school attendance that children in more economically advanced countries lack. However, it is a power exercised within a context of strong family pressures and obligations – a reminder of the overwhelming importance of context when we judge the merits of children's participation and decision-making. Tremlett's vivid account of discrimination against Roma children in Hungary provides a rather different lesson. This is that children are often the most direct victims of more general discrimination against minority ethnic groups. Moreover, such victimhood, sharp as it often is, then allows them to be further used by opponents of discrimination. This comes across strongly in De Schweinitz's chapter, which illustrates how the battles of social reform are often fought over the experiences of children, even where the dominant voices are those of adults. How different all this is to the concerns of Ann Blair with the involvement and participation rights of children in the UK education system. It is telling that in Blasco's and Tremlett's chapters the issues are not about rights within education – to participation in decision-making, for example – but are about rights to education itself, on an equal basis, irrespective of socio-economic, cultural or ethnic background. The concern with the right to participation becomes much more of a live issue once the right to education itself becomes accepted. However, once this has happened there is clearly no guarantee that participation, in any form, will follow. Not only Blair, but others have also pointed out the singular lack of progress on educational participation in the UK in particular (Hendrick, 2003: 216–224). Indeed, to such authors the key focus of contemporary UK policy is perceived to be towards treating children as 'human capital', as objects rather than as subjects.

On the subject of power and decision-making more generally, we have had a number of contributions that illustrate both the subtlety and the complexity of power relations between children and adults once the voices of children are allowed to enter the debate. That of Maree Brown and Jaleh McCormack is particularly useful in focussing on the dilemmas and opportunities presented by putting a children's rights perspective into practice within government. For our purposes, one of the most interesting features of New Zealand's Agenda for Children is that it started from the premise that developing a government strategy for improving outcomes for children should begin by asking children about their central concerns. An obvious strategy, one might have thought, but a relatively rare one. There is a clear logic, in a context in which the experience of childhood is changing rapidly, in basing policy responses at least partly on the views of children rather than on the potentially misleading perspectives and out-of-date memories and experiences of adults. Some of the language of the Agenda for Children suggests that the concerns of the sociology of childhood with the subjectivity of children is moving beyond academia and into the deci-sion-making realm of policy-makers. Indeed, the influence of such per-spectives is explicitly acknowledged by the authors. It is fortunate that in this context the authors have both academic and policy interests; in most such studies, the links between ideas and policy are insufficiently acknowledged and analysed.

As well as those of policy-makers, the voices of professionals have also featured in our chapters. This particularly applies to those chapters by, firstly, McNamee, James and James and, secondly, by Coppock. The former, in considering the voices of some child welfare professionals, explores how the effects of their views of childhood impact on their professional task of helping children. They found that, since these adults act as intermediaries in the expression of the views of children in some important proceedings (such as divorce), their views act as significant filtering mechanisms on the views of children, mechanisms which can have major impacts on the child's future life. Such filtering can take place in the context of seeking the child's 'best interests' – for example, in relation to contact disputes between parents – but it is an adult interpretation of 'best interests' that effectively denies children their true voice and, judging by the findings of McNamee, James and James, it does so systematically, albeit not necessarily self-consciously.

Adding to this concern with professional views, Coppock shows how professional perspectives operating in a wider, ideological, sense affect the voice of children at least as systematically in the field of mental health. Children in mental distress, of course, suffer the double bind of being judged incapable of making judgements by virtue of both their childhood and their mental health status. Here, it is not just profes-sional views of childhood that lead to such judgements, but also a whole medical research agenda.

Like Coppock, Nigel Thomas calls for the greater recognition of the capacity of children to voice their own needs and perspectives. On most occasions when this happens, both in studies in this volume but also elsewhere, it throws up results that are surprising – to adults – and worthwhile. One of the most important and intriguing findings from the approach adopted in New Zealand, for example, is the different priorities for a child-centred public policy (such as a focus on tackling bullying and giving children responsibility) that emerge when one asks both children and adults about what this should focus on. This provides the best possible argument for why it is inadequate to have child-centred policy approaches constructed without the involvement of children. This same lesson appears from the Messenger-Davies and Mosdell chapter, with reference to more intimate, family-level decision-making. In a finding which strongly challenges prevailing reliance on parental consent before children appear in television programmes, they noted that parents were much more willing than children to endorse such appearances. This finding, as the authors point out, has direct policy relevance for broadcasters.

Globalisation and childhood

One of the features of childhood studies that is reflected in the origins and content of these papers is that the subject is highly global in scope. This globalisation is partly a response to the fact that developments in childhood policy now increasingly cross international borders and are recognised as doing so. This, in turn, both reflects and is reflected in the tendency of social policy as an academic discipline to move beyond its traditional focus on the nation state. It is noticeable from Blasco's chapter and others that many governments are having to take more interest in children in response to global factors. In Blasco's case, a key influence is the competitive pressures on Mexico that were attendant on membership of the North American Free Trade Agreement. In the case of Tremlett's paper, developments in the education of Roma children were shaped by Hungary's need to respond to the anti-discrimination requirements of prospective European Union membership (which was achieved in May 2004). The relevance of such cross-national factors suggests the importance of studies which focus on the international context within which children now operate (and not just in relation to the UNCRC), as well as the national.

Some subjects combine both global and national dimensions. For example, with regards to 'street children', discussed in Heesterman's chapter, recent years have seen increasing recognition that this phenomenon is not just an issue for South Asia, Africa and Latin America but also applies within more affluent regions of the globe, such as Europe and the USA (see Altanis and Goddard, 2004). Also, in relation to policy on child welfare, Brown and McCormack note the parallels between developments in New Zealand and those in both Ireland and the UK. In the latter two countries, such developments have reflected another under-researched global phenomenon of recent decades: the uncovering of widespread child abuse within state and private sector child care institutions in previous decades (Wolmar, 2000: 206–216). It was partly for this reason that UNCRC Article 12 participation rights featured strongly in new policy strategies in both Ireland and the UK, even if rather selectively in the case of the latter (Fawcett, Featherstone and Goddard, 2004; Pinkerton, 2004). Indeed, some of the policy parallels between the Irish and New Zealand cases are striking – especially those concerned with consulting children during the development of policy (Pinkerton, 2004). Such parallels have, in general, been insufficiently explored and although the phenomenon of 'policy transfer' has gained increasing recognition within the academic study of public policy (e.g. Dolowitz *et al.*, 2000) the parallels and influences revealed here suggest further areas of application.

The control and visibility of childhood

This leads on to a key issue highlighted by a number of our chapters. Academics and governments are taking more interest in child welfare – a good thing – but this also means that children themselves are becoming increasingly prey to extra supervision by parents and other adults. As James and James have noted elsewhere:

> In spite of the UN Convention ... and all of the political rhetoric about children and their rights to be heard, it can be argued that this may, in effect, amount to little more than an artifice which conceals the real nature of the way in which mechanisms for retaining and increasing the control over children are being sustained and even extended. It would appear that the net of social control has an increasingly fine mesh and is permeating more areas of more children's lives than ever before. (James and James, 2001: 225–6).

Although this applies at a policy level, it also applies at the family level. Seymour, for example, noted in her chapter the extent to which the demands of being a good parent in the modern context, which includes closer supervision of children and greater involvement in shared activities, could cause conflict for her boarding house and hotel parents when set against wider notions of an ideal western childhood which specifically rejects work in favour of play and education. Other authors have also noted that 'children are one of the most governed groups by both the state and civic society' (Hill *et al.*, 2004: 76).

Children have become more important, some argue, because adult ties have become more fragile (Jenks, 1996). For example, Hutchinson and Charlesworth (2000: 577) have noted, with respect to the United States, that 'there has been a recent sharp rise in the sentimental and emotional value of children, as marital ties have weakened and become less significant in the lives of many adults'. As Block reminded us at the start of this chapter, it is insecurity in a context of uncertainty that often drives an increased interest in children. If we look at the UK case, we can see that the post-1997 Labour Governments have been much more interventionist on child welfare policy than their predecessors (Little, Axford and Morpeth, 2003; Fawcett, Featherstone and Goddard, 2004).

How do we make sense of such a development in a context in which the voices of children are relatively silent in some significant policy areas? This increased interest can be seen within the context of a growing focus, within a number of countries, on the development of a 'social investment state' (Giddens, 1998; Jenson and St Martin, 2001; Esping-Andersen, 2002; Lister, 2002). Such a state supports greater interventionism with children, but it does so with particular reference to specific groups of children and to particular stages of development (e.g. early years). Therefore, whilst rendering certain groups of children more visible it also ignores the commonalities amongst children and does not necessarily have much to say about basic power differentials between children and adults. Such an emphasis is evident in the New Zealand case, as well, where the Agenda for Children was partly prompted by a relative lack of success in New Zealand on some important child welfare outcome measures (such as on poverty, educational performance and infant mortality). Hence the focus, similarly to the UK, on early intervention and prevention and on joined-up policy-making and policy-implementation.

Such a social investment approach also tends to rely on the centrality of parents in supporting child welfare. Indeed, one of the key issues in relation to policy towards children in any country is the extent to which it genuinely focuses on children rather than being merely another name for policy towards parents. Moss (2000) has argued that the UK approach over-emphasises the role of parents in children's lives and underplays the role that children play in each other's lives.

However, it is not only cultural and social insecurity that is at work here. This increased emphasis on investing in children is also linked to a need to develop adequate national responses to economic globalisation. In the UK context, this is linked to the emphasis on the needs of the 'knowledge economy' and for flexible labour markets that demand literate and multi-skilled individuals. Such perceived needs demand a high level of state intervention in the lives of children. According to Esping-Andersen (2002), this should be accepted as the only sustainable and socially desirable way forward for the enhancement of poor children's welfare and for fostering their future life chances. This is because the basic requisites for a good life increasingly depend upon skills and professional qualifications which increase the likelihood of employment: 'Remedial policies for adults are a poor (and costly) substitute for interventions in childhood... since a person's job and career prospects depend increasingly on his or her cognitive abilities, this is where it all begins' (Esping-Andersen, 2002: 49). For this reason, there have been significant developments in the UK in the context of education in recent years, with a corresponding increase in pressure on children through the use of Standard Assessment Tests and other ways of testing performance. As we have seen in Blair's chapter, increasing state attention and central control of the education system in the UK has proven inimical to meaningful participation and involvement (see also Jeffs, 2002; 45–59; Lansdown, 2001; 96). In short, a variety of global pressures have led to increased interest in children in recent years but this has not necessarily led to an increased interest in their own voices and priorities.

In this context, it is worth noting that, whilst only one of a number of global factors, the UNCRC has a particularly important role to play because it provides a genuinely international focus on children and their rights (see James and James, 2004). The emergence of a rights discourse, rooted in the provisions of the UNCRC, is a significant counterbalance to the emerging trend for greater state interventionism. This makes the Convention a liberal touchstone for potentially illiberal states. For example, UNCRC signatory states have to provide a report on progress with respect to Convention implementation to the United Nations Committee on the Rights of the Child every five years. Through the associated mass media publicity, this provides the potential for regular political embarrassment to governments who are dilatory or reckless with respect to Convention rights (e.g. Featherstone, Fawcett and Goddard, 2002). Indeed, one of the key future strands for the development of childhood studies may be the study of the emerging tensions between the requirements of the UNCRC and the interventionist ambitions of individual states.

Notes

1. The author would like to thank Adrian James, Allison James and Sally McNamee for their comments on this chapter.

References

Altanis, P. and Goddard, J., 'Street Children in Contemporary Greece', *Children and Society*, 18 (4).

Barnes, M. (2003) Presentation to the Social Policy Association Annual Conference 17 July 2003, University of Middlesbrough.

Bar-on, A. (1997) 'Criminalising Survival: Images and Reality of Street Children'. *Journal of Social Policy* 26: 63–78.

Dolowitz, P., with Hume, R., Nellis, M. and O'Neill, F. (2000) *Policy Transfer and British Social Policy: Learning from the USA?* Buckingham: Open University Press.

Esping-Andersen, G. (2002) 'A Child-centred Social Investment Strategy', in: Esping-Andersen, G., with Gallie, G. Hemerijck, A. and Myles, J., *Why We Need A New Welfare State*. Oxford: Oxford University Press.

Fawcett, B., Featherstone, B. and Goddard, J., *Contemporary Childcare Policy and Practice*. London: Palgrave Macmillan.

Featherstone, B., Fawcett, B. and Goddard, J. (2002) 'New Labour, Children's Rights and the United Nations: 'Could Do Better'', *Journal of Social Welfare and Family Law*, 24 (4): 475–484.

Giddens, A. (1998) *The Third Way: The Renewal of Social Democracy*. Cambridge: Polity Press.

Hendrick, H. (2003) *Child Welfare: Historical Dimensions, Contemporary Debates*. Bristol: Policy Press.

Hill, M., Davis, J., Prout, A., and Tisdall, K. (2004) 'Moving the Participation Agenda Forward', *Children and Society*, 18: 77–96.

Hutchinson, E. D. and Charlesworth, L. W. (2000) 'Securing the Welfare of Children: Policies Past, Present and Future', *Families in Society*, 81(6), pp. 576–585.

James, A. L. and James, A. (2001) 'Tightening the net: children, community and control', *British Journal of Sociology* 52 (2): 211–228.

James, A. and James, A. L. (2004) *Constructing Childhood: theory, policy and social practice*. Palgrave: London and New York.

Jeffs, T. (2002) 'Schooling, Education and Children's Rights', in Franklin, B. (ed.), *The New Handbook of Children's Rights: Comparative Policy and Practice*. London: Routledge, pp. 45–59.

Lansdown, G. (2001) 'Children's Welfare and Children's Rights', in Foley, P., Roche, J. and Tucker, S. (eds) *Children in Society: Contemporary Theory, Policy and Practice*. Basingstoke: Palgrave, pp. 87–97.

Lister, R. (2002) 'Investing in citizen-workers of the future: New Labour's "third way" in welfare reform', Paper for Panel 10555–8FB: Redesigning Welfare Regimes: The Building Blocks of a New Architecture, Annual Meeting of the American Political Association.

Pinkerton, J. (2004) 'Children's Participation in the Policy Process: Some Thoughts on Policy Evaluation Based on the Irish National Children's Strategy', *Children and Society* 18: 119–130.

Wolmar, C. (2000) *Forgotten Children: The Secret Abuse Scandal in Children's Homes*. London: Vision Paperbacks.

Index